BODY
CONNECTION

BODY
CONNECTION

T. L. FRASER

Library of Congress Control Number:		2011902299
ISBN:	Hardcover	978-1-4568-6882-6
	Softcover	978-1-4568-6881-9
	Ebook	978-1-4568-6883-3

Cover Art Work - Enrique Simmons

Cover Concept - T.L. Fraser

This book was printed in the United States of America.

Rev. date: 05/07/2014

To order additional copies of this book, contact:
Xlibris LLC
1-888-795-4274
www.Xlibris.com
Orders@Xlibris.com
547883

CONTENTS

PREFACE

If you believe you play no role in the determination of self, then perhaps this book is not for you. In fact, *stop* right where you are because all your actions are really meaningless. It matters not what you do or do not do; your course is unchangeably set, predetermined, and predestined. *You have stopped living a long time ago.*

For those who believe otherwise, that is, that we are responsible for ourselves and the lives we choose to live, *continue* reading because you have taken responsibility for your actions and understand that you are not a victim of fate but a master of your own destiny.

As you read, you'll learn about yourself, self-mastery, and self-mastery techniques you can apply to your daily living.

You are on a journey to find your connection to everything around you, and there is a connection to everything and everyone you encounter by chance, deliberately or otherwise.

Be guided as I did; read then reexamine. The concepts have been simplified, and the techniques are practical. Always keep in mind that we are related to everything in the universe and everything in the universe is related to us.

My hope and desire is that as you read the various chapters, you would then take that which you have digested and immediately apply it to your daily lives. Even if you don't immediately, keep searching for your connection. *Keep discovering who you are.* Stay connected.

ACKNOWLEDGMENTS

To my family, both immediate and extended—and this includes friends and acquaintances—who all have touched my life in some way and knowingly or unknowingly helped to shape who I am today and hence have contributed to what I have imparted in these pages, thank you.

To all the students I have taught, I have learned as much from you as you have from me. Thank you for your contribution.

I have purposefully omitted names from these acknowledgments. You are too numerous to mention; thus, I am being all-inclusive by omittance.

My inspiration comes from one source, GOD; thus, I acknowledge his presence in this endeavor and in everything I do.

CHAPTER 1

DISCOVERING SELF (4-4-4)

The elevation and the improvement of your life, while to a lesser extent, is dependent on others, your *self-mastery* is primarily your responsibility. For while we are inextricably linked to each other and will find it quite difficult to exist in a vacuum, we must make choices and live with the consequences of those choices. Therefore, improving our lot becomes a task for each of us, and the quality of our lives is our responsibility once we become independent adults.

Discovering our purposes or the purpose for our existence enables us to make the necessary choices that would inevitably enrich our lives, and the earlier that purpose is discovered, the more purposeful individuals can set about the task of *self-mastery*. Choices in career, education, social life, material wealth, and spiritual growth are decisions we all will make sooner or later once we make it to adulthood or become independent thinkers, and inevitably, if we live long enough, we will all discover that our existence all leads to one universal purpose, that is, making our way back to the perfection from which we came—the "I AM THAT I AM" spiritual oneness with the universal Father who resides at the core of our being.

The link between each and every human being allows us to fulfill our common basic earthly purpose, which is service to humanity and meeting each other's emotional, social, physical, and psychological needs, and parallel to this goal is to achieve our highest spiritual self or higher consciousness. For the sake of clarity, while we sometimes interchangeably use the terms religion and spirituality, they are not synonymous, for religion is based on the teachings of a principle or certain principles that are intended for individuals to adhere to or follow as the rules or the teachings of that religious doctrine dictate.

Spirituality, on the other hand, is a state of being; it follows no set doctrine and it follows all doctrines of human relationships, based on moral foundations to do what is in the best interest of humanity, cohesively within the principles of righteousness, godliness, self-discipline, self-control, and all those principles that would allow us to function in harmony with natural and spiritual laws and with each other in perfection.

We were created in his image (that is, in the image of God), and he is perfect, and so then by inference, we are perfect. We still marvel at creation and yet doubt the existence of a God (Creator).

We claim imperfection and then declare we cannot live in perfection. In our search for perfection—the perfect job, the perfect mate, the perfect home, and the perfect everything, including perfect life's fulfillments—we fall short in our pursuit of human gratification. The self-discovery of life's imperfection (our imperfections) creates within us frustration. We then blame others for these imperfections, without fully realizing that the changes we desire are within us, and so we follow paths of selfishness, envy, greed, jealousy, intolerance, and total disregard for the well-being of each other, subverting our perfection with imperfection, finding exactly what we seek, reaping exactly what we sow.

We must begin our self-mastery by believing that there is goodness in all of us, that we are, as human beings, intrinsically good and perfect but sometimes do things that are considered immoral, unjust and imperfect.

Our laws subscribe that crimes against humanity be met with certain types of punishment befitting the crime. These punishments are meant to be self-improvements, oftentimes referred to as deterrents, but are all meant to harmonize and bring us into perfection with each other.

Prisons were constructed with the forethought that individuals who commit crimes needed to be separated from the rest of society so as not to pollute or endanger the rest of that society—be reinstitutionalized so to speak—until the realization by the Industrial Complex Establishmentarians (ICE) that as an institutionalized business, these establishments provide tremendous economic wealth to the complex and to individuals. Consequently, establishments quickly lost sight of their real purposes, which was to bring the imperfect closer to his and her perfection.

Separating major offenders and the recalcitrant from the rest of society was thought to be a way of rehabilitating them, allowing them to improve their behaviors through a combination of separation, isolation, and rehabilitative programming, but time and time again, we witness how easy it is to lose sight of our initial vision and purpose when profit becomes the dominant factor. We must therefore look to self to do what others invariably cannot do for us.

This approach to rehabilitation to a large extent has not worked and will not work as we examine some facts. According to the Bureau of Justice Statistics,

September 30, 2006, "Fifty-six percent of the violent felons convicted in the 75 most populous countries from 1990 through 2002 had a prior conviction . . . 38 percent had a prior felony conviction and 15 percent had been previously convicted for a violent felony," and in another finding, "youths under the age of 21 commit 30 percent of all homicides."[1] Why?, Because the economic viability of the process has taken precedent over the more nobler aim of socializing, rehabilitating, reinstituting, reforming, and indeed self-improving the psyche, ideas, philosophy, and physical and emotional conditions of these offenders.

Once we believe in the God-ness within us all (from the premise that we are all intrinsically good), we suspend labels. Thus, understanding that, it is not the person who is bad but rather the deed, we can then commence to change the thinking process beginning with the changes in self. For improvement to take root in the process of self-mastery, we must be able to separate the messenger from the message, listen first, and judge last—not a simple task, yet it is one that must be undertaken.

We must change the collective mindset, break down old habits, and replace our anemic ideas and ideologies with improved versions of the same. Believe first and then see the goodness of self in everyone and everything—a subtle yet almost radical programming change in the way we think, which is the essence of *self-mastery*. And while changes may sometimes appear to be radical, when examined closely, we realize it's merely synthesis at work.

Since all changes result from the interplay of three elements—thesis, antithesis, and synthesis—where every thesis generates an antithesis, which is its opposite, and the interaction of the two produces a synthesis, which then transcends both, the emerging synthesis, in turn, becomes a new thesis, and the entire process repeats itself again and again. This is in theory how we improve from one dimension to a higher dimension on the same plain—from a higher self to a higher self—measurably called self-mastery, the complete acceptance of self.

As in the alchemist principle of changing base metal to gold, it is simply producing a new and improved version of the old; so too should be our transition. Once information is allowed pass our filters and once we listen with open minds, not ignoring the message because we're at odds with the messenger, change cannot help but occur—sometimes radical and yet oftentimes in minuscule increments.

Therefore, as you read these pages, approach each chapter, technique, and thought unfiltered. Begin to understand that as you seek the truth and as you seek to create a new and improved version of self, you may also find many contradictions of self along the way. That simply means you must keep searching because you are on the verge of self-discovery, and what you may discover about self along the way may simply amaze you.

As we explore self-mastery in these pages, we will discuss and dissect self-improvement/self mastery through the *4-4-4 connection method*: *the four selves*—self-concept, self-esteem, self-awareness, and self-disclosure; *the four lower bodies*—the mental, the physical, the emotional, and the etheric; and *the four elements or planes of matter*—air, earth, water, and fire. Being governed by natural and spiritual laws, we must examine how these affect our lives as well.

The term "4-4-4 connection (method)" was coined to help describe these principles and how they interrelate to achieve individual self-mastery. Thus, while the title of the book is 'Body Connection", the term 4-4-4 connection is used alternatively in various passages as a means of describing methodology. While the term may have originated with me, may I quickly add that many of its principles, ideas, and theories are but inspirations through lessons passed on to me by the masters of this knowledge whose readings and works I have studied, reread, and labored over to fully understand and then impart.

The direct and indirect testimonials of the many students who have consciously and subconsciously taken on the task of mastering self through the various lessons, teachings, and courses I have taught are an inspiration and an important part of these writings, for they document the experiences of ordinary individuals who have taken the extraordinary task and first step toward self-discovery and self-mastery, first acknowledging that there is a need for change and self-improvement in their lives and then doing something about it. Their experiences speak volumes; so will yours.

Let me begin by asking you to indulge in an exercise that will help you as you begin the process of discovering self. Try this exercise and witness what happens.

Walk up to someone you don't know very well, and ask this question: "Who are you?" The answer would most likely be "I am," followed by their name. Does this response surprise you? Perhaps not and then let's take this exercise one step further.

In a room of people (I have done this as a classroom exercise), after inquiring as to the names of the individuals within the room, select one person. Let's say his name is Mike. Pull four or five individuals aside, males and/or females, and quietly whisper to them that their names are now Mike.

Now you're ready to ask that individual his name again: "Who are you?" His answer will most likely be "Mike" (his name). You then say, "Thank you. Mike, would you stand up please." The four or five individuals whom you have whispered to will also stand simultaneously, along with Mike. Mike will look around the room somewhat bemused and a little surprised. However, Mike will realize that he's not the only Mike in the room. Suddenly he realizes that Mike can be anyone, and it's just a name. Most importantly, Mike and the other Mikes will immediately become aware that our names are not who we are, for who we are goes beyond simply how we choose to address ourselves or how others address us.

Some of us are engaged, fascinated, enthralled, and even mortified by titles—professor, president, CEO, secretary, mother, father, and so on—all quite meaningless really, for while these titles might suggest what we do, it does not indicate who we are.

This simple exercise exposes two interesting points: One is in discovering self and determining who we really are; the second is paying attention to what others say and how we interpret self.

The first point, self-discovery and determining who we are, begins with being able to correctly answer the most basic but important question of ourselves, "Who am I really?"

While names and titles might be identifiers and quickly allow us to acknowledge others, it neither helps us or others to become familiar with who we are. So what should the answer be when asked, "Who are you?" First of all, we need to listen to the question that is not "What is your name?" but rather "Who are you?"

It is quite simple to explicitly address "What is your name?" with a straightforward answer: "My name is," followed by your name. On the other hand, "Who are you?" allows for copious answers, even though it may not have been the intent of the inquirer. We therefore must seek clarity, both in the question and in this discursive about self.

"Who are you?" requires a clarifier, such as "What do you mean?" or "Do you mean what is my name?" In turn, this would allow for a more meaningful exchange.

In the journey to discovering self, we must first ask, seek answers, and receive clarification, and then and only then could we correctly address who we are. This is the simplified process to discovering self and subsequently mastering self.

To explore, who you are, here's an exercise: Write down five to ten self attributes, both negative and positive, for example, kind, friendly, determined, impatient, prudent, and intense. Then next to each attribute, write a brief statement of why you've used these adjectives to describe yourself; for example, it might be that others have described you this way or, through some circumstance, you have come to the realization that this attribute fits you. Be honest in your acceptance of the attributes, especially the unflattering ones.

The second interesting point is ask an acquaintance, a close friend, and/or a family member to help you determine which of the attributes you've used to describe yourself best describes you, and as you add and subtract adjectives, over the course of time of indulging in this exercise, you will develop an immutable idea of who you are, and if you've been paying attention, before long, you will have embarked on your journey to self-mastery and self-improvement, in fact, complete self-awareness.

CHAPTER 2

THE BODY DISCONNECTION
MY JOURNEY

I set about to write this book because I felt a necessity to do so, although the initial challenge came from one of my communication students, who, one day during a discussion on this subject, asked, "So why haven't *you* written a book about this?" I did not answer immediately but thought about it for a moment and then responded by saying, "I haven't gotten around to it as yet," but knew that in the scholastic world, somehow, you're not legitimized as an educator unless and until you have penned your thoughts and experiences tangibly and be published.

My reasoning goes beyond just these facts, but it was the next logical step that I had to take. I needed to write (a book) for those with a desire to know. I supine the reason books are written and the reason for this one.

This effort to me is about identifying given clues to help develop the talents that all mankind possess and then defining as clearly as I could what others have already defined in their unique way—that the universe is one with us and we are one with the universe.

There is nothing new in any of these pages. I may have stated the facts differently in my style; however, in the end, I hope that the language I have selected helps to further clarify what many know and have also documented.

Self-mastery, among other things, is also about *belief*, first, in yourself and then in the impossible. Then watch what happens when you add a pinch of desire and a dash of expectation, and once armed with *expectation, desire, hope, faith, honesty,* and *emotion*, you begin to find in the smallest gifts intricate treasures.

As a child, I consumed books—any type of book—the comics and mystery novels. I also did some serious reading. Curiosity is perhaps what led me to metaphysical books at the age of ten or eleven. I read books on clairvoyance, psychic phenomenon, astral projection, and the likes, even before my teens. I particularly enjoyed books by T. Lobsang Rampa, a clairvoyant and meditationalist.

Rampa would painfully explain how some of the meditational and astral projection techniques worked, and after reading some of his books, I would then test out some of these techniques to see if they really worked. I was always surprised and excited when some of them did work like the astral projection.

I hardly understood what I was embarking on. In fact, I was clueless but somehow knew this was exciting stuff. My astral projection worked surprisingly well, perhaps too well for my liking, I was now compelled to find out how it all worked. This would be the beginning of my journey to self-mastery. Needless to say, my journey is far from its completion. I am still as we all are—a work in progress.

Self-mastery is a life-long journey, for every time you believe you have made an incredible discovery, another one lies just ahead of it, which you must examine. Be continually curious. Stay connected.

The journey oftentimes exacts a price and tests our character. I have, however, come to realize that everything we need is within our reach and accessible. We should always begin our search with self and then afterward, work in harmony with the universe, following spiritual and cosmic laws, with the knowledge and the understanding that life is continuous and as immortal as energy and the only person to be afraid of is ourselves.

We must be prepared to immerse the self in the sea of universal wisdom, light, and purpose so that the soul can be saturated. Be continually curious. Stay connected.

On this afternoon, feeling rather adventurous, I read about astral projection and then decided that I would perform it just as the book explained. I knew nothing about what the astral plane was or, in fact, what astral projection in fact really was.

The astral plane is the repository of the total or collective conscious and unconscious thoughts and feeling patterns of mankind.[1] It is a frequency higher than the earth's frequency or the physical; that is, its frequency of time and space is beyond the physical but below the mental.

The real purpose of this frequency is for the manifestation or amplification of God's purity in thoughts and feelings as made manifest in man. Unfortunately, because man's thoughts and feelings are not always pure, the astral plane or frequency has become polluted with streams of impure thoughts and feelings, and I have often said this to my students, if you play in mud, you will become muddy. Therefore, in deep meditation, where the meditator astrally projects his or her spirit far away from the physical body, one must always pray for the protection of the spirit and the body prior to these types of projections.

The astral body can thus be explained as the desire or feeling body, corresponding to the frequency of the emotional body and embodying the characteristics of the astral plane.[2] Astral projection is thus projecting the spirit/emotional body to this frequency for the general purpose of helping others as well as one's self positively.

Astral projection can also be used as a nonphysical way of gathering intelligence,[3] and all mankind have the ability and the capability of gathering information through the psyche. *Psyche* refers to the soul, the spirit, or the mind, and the term *psychic* comes from *psyche* and simply means operating outside of the physical world, that is, using either the soul, the spirit, or the mind to gain intelligence, which is experiencing beyond the physical intelligence of seeing, hearing, touching, tasting, and smelling.

When faced with very traumatic or stressful situations, some of us may experience some form of psychic or astral experience. Some people suddenly acquire super human strength due to the adrenaline surge in that stressful situation, and again, there are times when it may seem as if everything has slowed down and there is absolute clarity.

The out-of-body experience undergone in a drug-induced state, while somewhat similar in the sense of the ethereal feeling, is quite different. In astral travel, the personality is unaltered and the thoughts and the feelings are deliberate.

Those who have described having out-of-body experiences after heavy drug usage (whether it was alcohol or other drugs) would sometimes hallucinate and experience the sensation of being detached from the physical body, as if watching a movie of themselves from a distance. While the experience might seem to be euphoric, there is a lack of control over self in these states.

During sleep, while most of us do not associate dreaming with astral travel, we are indeed experiencing astral trips, mostly subconsciously. During meditation, practitioners can enter what we refer to as the alpha region of the brain[4] (the sleep region) consciously and with full awareness and perform astral projections usually to further the betterment of loved ones, to solve problems, or even to obtain clarity on issues within relationships.

So after I grasped the theory of what I had read in Ramps's book, I was now ready for the practical application, so I followed the directions outlined.

It was described that it would be like a dream and that I must tell myself before I sleep exactly what I'll do and how I'll get there. So I decided that for the fun of it, I would visit a friend (a childhood playmate).

It was a sunny afternoon somewhere between 4:00 p.m. and 5:00 p.m. I did my astral projection, lying in bed on my back. I told myself I'll go to my friend's house just to say hello. I repeated silently to myself exactly how I'll get there: Go through the window, down the street (this friend lived about five blocks away), and I'll be there.

I had no expectations and full expectations, meaning I believed that it could be done, hence the reason for attempting it. I exercised the first lesson in self-mastery without even realizing it—faith. Even though my faith took the form of curiosity and childlike innocence, it was full of expectation. Not having ever done this type of exercise before, I knew not what to expect.

I fell asleep, and to my surprise, I found myself there. I say to my surprise because this was my first projection, and I was not quite sure if and how this thing worked. Again, I didn't really know what to expect, but there I was quite unexpectedly.

I don't remember entering the house. I just found myself in his room, observing him as he combed his hair in the mirror. I could see the mirror but did not see myself in the mirror. I remembered speaking to him as though I was standing behind him over his shoulder, but I could also see his face.

I said words to the effect, "Hey, what's up?" My lips did not move. I realized that I was communicating with him telepathically. I asked him either what he was doing or where he was going telepathically. He responded that he was going to his brother's house. It then dawned on me that this was happening just as I had planned before I embarked on this astral trip.

I became anxious, apprehensive . . . okay, *scared,* and as fear crept in, I knew I wanted out of there fast, and the moment I thought to myself I had to leave, I was back in my bedroom, and so glad was I to be back. But there was one slight problem—I must have returned too quickly.

I opened my eyes before my spirit had reentered my body. So there I was as I saw myself hovering over me. I was lying on the bed, conscious of the fact that my spirit was hovering over me.

This was my first experience of conscious awareness or the alpha level of consciousness. I was lying on the bed on my back. My left leg extended flat against the bed, and my right leg cocked at a 90-degree angle, bent in a relaxed position with the sole of that foot in contact with the bed, and this was the same position in which I also saw myself. This shimmering spiritual form that I knew was me, hovering over my body, and in that moment, I was also conscious of the other occupants of the house (my mother and my aunt). I could hear their conversations indistinctly and their movements in the adjoining room that happened to be the kitchen.

In that moment in which I opened my eyes and saw my spirit hovering over my body, I also had the sudden insight (the insight came later) that the physical body (my outer shell) lying on the bed was meaningless, and I say shell deliberately, for that's all the body is, just a shell. Its only connection is to earth. This connection will be discussed in the third phase of body connection 4-4-4—the four elements *earth, fire, air,* and *water.*

I make the analogy of my body lying on the bed to that of the shell casing of a bullet. As the gun is fired, the casing gets ejected and is left behind. The bullet travels on to its target. But I also knew one thing: At that moment, I wanted to get back into this shell.

Another insight I was able to put into perspective through this experience later on was that the physical body was not really who we were, but I was a bit too young and much too scared at the time to fully comprehend these wonderful insights.

I instinctively closed my eyes and began to try to call for help. I tried to open my mouth. I knew I was making every effort to do so because I felt myself trying, but it was like a bad dream. I could hear them; they could not hear me, but I was determined.

I attempted to call out to my mom or whoever would answer, for I could hear the voices in the next room but soon realized that there was no sound emanating from my lips. For a brief moment, I wondered why, and then I heard (in my mind) myself call out again, "Mommy, help!" but again, there was no sound. I wondered how I could hear their voices but they could not hear mine. I had to figure this out fast.

I knew now that I was on my own. I had to figure this out myself. I did not panic, but I knew I was scared. My subconscious mind became active, and suddenly, I began to read the book again. I remembered passages I had read and allowed the information to flow through my mind. It was almost as if I had begun to reread that chapter and the exercise.

I remembered reading that I needed to remind myself to relax and that the only person to be afraid of was myself. It came back to me and repeated itself over and over: "Relax, relax, the only person to be afraid of is yourself." I repeated this over and over, and I began to relax, and slowly, as I found myself repeating those lines, a gentle wave enveloped me.

I describe it to be like a wave because of the undulating, smooth, side-to-side rocking motion, like a silent glider landing gently. My spirit was slowly reentering my body as if being gently lowered from a cliff or a mountaintop to float gently back to earth.

It must have taken no more than a few seconds, but for a brief moment, as if I had crossed a bridge, I lapsed momentarily into unawareness or perhaps darkness. I cannot describe it as unconsciousness, for somehow I felt there was always conscious awareness. Then suddenly, I was awake, fully conscious or in *Beta,* (the outer consciousness state).

My mom and aunt were exactly where I had heard them—in the kitchen. I climbed down from the top bunk of the bed a bit shakily, definitely shaken but happy to be back in my room. I could feel my heart pounding. A few days later, I verified the facts of my trip with my friend as they had occurred, even though I knew I really did not have to.

I was amazed at how accurate the information I gathered on this projection was. Of course, my friend did try to pressure me into telling him how I had obtained the information and what had happened. I never told him. In fact, I never shared this experience with anyone for many years, not even with family members, in spite of the fact that for several weeks after this incident, I was afraid to go to sleep for fear I would dream.

I associated dreaming with astral projection or with the spirit leaving the body. Therefore, to sleep would be to dream, and I did not want to dream because I knew now that my spirit could travel to places.

My greatest fear was that I would wake up each night and would have to negotiate with my spirit to return to its shell. So each night, as I began to drift off to sleep, I became aware of my spirit lifting off in astral flight, leaving my body and drifting upward, as was in my astral experience. I would immediately awaken, and this would be repeated several times during the night until I would fall off to sleep only after having thoroughly convinced myself not to dream.

I'm not sure how many nights or weeks this continued, but I'm quite sure I was somewhat sleep deprived, and so it would continue each night. I would try to sleep while reminding myself that I must not dream, and each night I would begin to dream and wake myself up.

After a while, I either did not have dreams that I'd remember or I did not dream, and that was perfectly fine with me for the time being because I no longer had astral journeys, or so I thought.

I was not knowledgeable enough at that time to understand the important lessons of this experience. However, I knew I had stumbled onto something that was truly amazing, and as time went on, I began to realize how that moment in my journey has helped me in this present journey and in my quest to obtain self-mastery, and although the experience did slow my immediate experimentation down a bit, it by no means stopped me from investigating, for the portal had been opened.

My lessons then were vital to my journey today. I understand the importance of the words "Relax, relax," as well as the phrase "the only person to be afraid of is yourself." These are key phrases in my journey to self-mastery that helps me.

As a student of life, as you begin your steps in the process, being able to relax is soothing and comforting. It calmed my spirit at that instant. I am always in control. We are always in control of our destiny, of our lives, of our power, and of everything we are, want to be, and will become.

No one is more in control than we are, and *no one* can take anything away from us, not unless we give it to them. These phrases more than any others are what I continuously repeat to myself, use diligently, and encourage students on their journey to use continuously.

Once I understood that control and belief were two key stations in the journey to self-mastery and that I had full control over these and no one else, I knew how I needed to travel, but I also knew there was so much more to learn. I was just getting started.

CHAPTER 3

SPIRITUAL GROWTH AND WEALTH

Seek first the Kingdom of God and his righteousness, and all these things shall be added to you.

—Matthew 6:33[1]

There were many and there will be many more who had and will have the opportunity to experience improved lives but, through fear, timidity, lack of understanding, and ignorance, have chosen and will continue to choose not to, believing falsely that what measures their contentment and happiness and hence their progress and improvement are economic gain, power, material wealth and social status, all things without.

This is the equivalent to chasing shadows or maybe rainbows, travelling down paths that lead to infinite dissatisfaction. Real self-mastery, as you will come to understand, is spiritual growth and spiritual wealth, which then enables you to discover your true purpose and relationship to the universe, and once you follow the path, what you will discover will surely be for the betterment of self and humanity.

Wherever your focus is, there will your energies be spent. So then, important is to know where to concentrate your energies. If you focus your energies on spiritual wealth, concerns for material wealth and other concerns tend to dissipate and become secondary.

The Bible, as an instrument of spiritual teachings and knowledge, in Matthew 6:33, says, "Seek first the kingdom of God and his righteousness, and all these things shall be added to you." That is, if you focus on your righteousness and spiritual growth and on developing a relationship with your God-ness and God-self and the Creator first, then whatever else you need in your life is easily attained. All that we are and strive to be is embodied in what we concern ourselves about, and our lives become an outgrowth of this.

Rather than being concerned about the things of tomorrow, concentrate on developing a relationship with your creator, who is within. Let go and let God.

As you seek righteousness, you attain the wisdom and the understanding that everything and anything is possible and what you accumulate is an outgrowth and by-product of where your energies are.

Just as corruption cannot produce incorruption, even so God-ness produces G(o)od-ness. Thus, material wealth becomes an outgrowth and by-product of your spiritual wealth (your goodness), made manifest through the beneficial services you provide.

The greater the need or demand is for that service, it stands to reason that the greater the wealth. However, material wealth is wholly external; therefore, the wise and prudent man first chooses love, wisdom, and richness in spirit, that is, high ideals, power that does not impose itself on others but seeks harmony, and a true understanding of life and of one's destiny as heir of God—things that can neither be pilfered nor wasted. By choosing thus, the choice is happiness, for the wise and prudent knows that happiness exists as a derivative of spiritual richness, born out of inner satisfaction and peace of mind, referred to as contentment, and spiritual growth is the destination of self.

Spiritual growth is hastened through spiritual alliance, and spiritual alliance hastens self-mastery.

When viewed abstractly, mastering one's self appears to be a somewhat selfish, self-serving, and nonbenevolent act, which primarily benefits only he that is improved. However, this is only true if used selfishly, and some do acquire their gifts at the expense of stifling the growth and the advancement of others. In this instance, the improvement of self is not for the collective good but mainly for self-aggrandizement.

Because our mastery also requires external applications for the measurement of its value, our alliances enables us to measure up to our growth potential, and since it derives its value from others, self-mastery should be a constant in every facet of our lives, where each and every facet mastered enriches the lives of those with whom we make contact. Diversely, failure to engage in the process of mastering self also signals a reluctance to act according to the collective good.

In the process of mastering self, it is important to yoke oneself with those of like minds on similar paths of spiritual growth and wealth, just as it is important to understand how we begin to grow spiritually and how that spiritual growth and wealth manifests itself in a life that is improving.

First, let's examine who we are. We are spirit. The spirit can never die, even though the soul can be lost. Our center of energy is our spirit. God is a spirit, and the souls of men are the living potential of God.

However, the soul demands free will, and because of its demand for free will, the soul separated itself from God with its descent into the flesh, referred to as re-embodiment. Our spirit and soul must once again become reunited again in honor and to the fullness of that God-ness, God state, or God estate—the I AM THAT I AM,[2] which is the one Spirit of all life. And so we seek spiritual growth so that our souls, the fallen potential, can once again be imbued with the reality of spirit and return to the glory from which it descended, creating once more the full unity of soul and spirit.

This marriage determines the destiny of self, as this unification is realized in each of us, the potential of God is then realized in each of us. Sometimes we interchangeably refer to the spirit as the soul and the soul as the spirit, and sometimes refer to spirit or "spirits" as discarnates or astral entities who are not of the earthly realm, but we always think of these energies as having higher powers or greater potential than us of the earthly realm.

Therefore, as we consider spiritual growth, we ought to view this growth as the development of the higher self, the true aspect of self-mastery, and the best self-mastery plan is the one you have begun—the positive one that moves you forward and toward your desired goal—and once you're honest about it, there will be results, albeit sometimes in very small unnoticeable increments. Use time as a measurement of self-mastery, understanding that it is only on this earthly realm that time is measured, understanding therefore that the process of self-mastery is one that is continuous until such time that there is self-mastery, and as we take from it, we give to it.

Self-mastery then is indeed moment to moment, with small, seemingly nebulous increments.

The techniques you will read about in these pages will allow you to think, prepare, and perform outside of your comfort zones. They will enable you to see the world and your lives from at least three different perspectives: science, reality, and imagination, each one being as real as the other, enabling you to reach your genius, already prepared for you to take hold of. Remember: The only person to be afraid of is yourself.

Be prepared for pleasant surprises and astonishing moments, for with your growth and improvement, you'll help those around you grow and improve spiritually and in all facets of their lives, truly recognizing that finding yourself means realizing all the possibilities you've been hiding from yourself. Let your self-mastery begin by seeking what's hidden within.

The following was taken from Saint Germain on alchemy,[3] recorded by Mark L. Prophet and Elizabeth Clare Prophet, Summit University Press. I wish to share it here because it fits so perfectly any explanation I can offer as to the importance of listening and seeking what's hidden within.

> Let us then reiterate for all
> That life is not so simple as men have dreamed,
> But it is a scheme so vast and tall
> As to literally enfolded us all,
> Men and gods and Masters, too,
> Parts of life you do not view
> Right now, but one day will,
> If you will only learn to listen and be still,
> Knowing I AM God Within

Saint Germain on Alchemy for the Adept in the Aquarian Age

Recorded by: Mark L. Prophet
Elizabeth Clare Prophet

CHAPTER 4

IMPEDANCE TO SELF-MASTERY

Keep your heart with all diligence, for out of it spring the issues of life.
—Proverbs 4:23[1]

Being human is a most precious gift but can sometimes be our greatest shortcoming, for we can become the greatest detractors to our successes in life and therefore, potentially, our greatest enemy. We must therefore be mindful of ourselves, the greatest impeder to the mastering of self.

Man's nature is threefold: the body, the mind or soul (psyche), and the spirit. Of the three, the spirit is the greatest revealer of the truth. Nothing is revealed to man except through the spirit, as summated in 1 Corinthians 2:10-12, spiritual truths are not of human wisdom but revealed by God. See (1Corinthians 2:8-12).[2]

The body is the first tier of man's nature. The soul is the second tier, residing in the psyche or mind of man, and the third tier is the spirit, the core of man, within the heart-house of man. Each nature is the gatekeeper of the other. Thus, the body is the gatekeeper of the soul, and the soul is the gatekeeper of the spirit.

The body is the lowest of man's nature. It is of the physical world and receives its information from the physical world through the five gateways or senses[3]: *sight*, which the eye-gateway brings into the body, stimulating imagination within the soul; *smell*, which the nose-gateway brings into the body, stimulating the conscience within the soul. Man's conscience houses the moral sense of right and wrong, and in the study of olfactory as a science, we learn of its power to therapeutically stimulate patients with amnesia, triggering memory recall. *Sound* or *hearing*, which the ear-gateway brings into the body, stimulates memory within the soul. *Taste*, which the mouth-gateway brings into the body, stimulates reason within the soul.

While all the senses work in concert with each other, scientifically there is seemingly a heightened connection between the smell and taste gateways, where one directly and instantaneously affects the function of the other. Taste stimulates reason within the soul. Touch, the feel-gateway, brings its sensation into the body through the physical sense of feeling, stimulating affections within the soul.

In these five senses herein lies the earthly or worldly wisdom of man—wisdom not of the spirit.

Man in his carnal state will behave as mere men, for in that carnal state, spiritual growth is devoid (I Corinthians 3:1-3).[4] Thus, as the information from man's base nature enters the gateways of the body to be processed within the soul, how that information is processed and understood is dependent on that man's current nature or natural state.

In a completely carnal (worldly) state, spiritual information cannot be processed since mere human wisdom would be the application to the processing of that which is spiritually perceived; thus, improvement is impeded at this level since understanding is dependent on the wisdom or knowledge of that individual making the decision. If that is lacking or limited, then the decision would be limited. Hence, the importance of spiritual growth to further the mastery of self is crucial if we are to enjoy full and lasting self-growth.

Once the information reaches the soul, which is the mind or psyche of man, again, anything spiritual to the natural man would seem like foolishness since these things can only be spiritually understood. The individual decides at the level of the soul whether the information received is conducive to his or her lifestyle. If it is not acceptable, it is discarded or disregarded by the will. If acceptable, the information is then transferred to the spirit and gets processed for manifestation.

Here is where we must be especially mindful, so allow me to divert for a minute and jump ahead to revelations that I intend to provide later on but that warrants some comment at this juncture, for the acceptance or discarding of information being processed at the level of the soul is exercised through choice, and these choices are determined and affected by tendencies, impulses, urges, and other seemingly logical factors and temptations, and the choice to do one or the other are more often than not equally attractive.

Therefore, the question is "How does the individual make the correct choice that would invariably lead to self-mastery if chosen correctly or is utterly disastrous if chosen incorrectly?" The answer lies in our understanding of spiritual and natural laws and its role in self-mastery. This we will examine in more detail further on.

Man's imagination, conscience, memory, reasoning, and affections are constantly being bombarded with carnal or worldly stimuli, affecting our actions and choices, with the will being the buffer to the spirit, transferring to the spirit the data received from the body and processed by the soul.

In its growth and strife for improvement, through the gift of choice, man's soul may choose the plane of relativity[5] based on that man's perspective of good or evil, or man may choose the plane of absolute,[6] the acceptance of the divine plan, where good is real and evil is unreal and God is living truth and there is the opportunity to live in the consciousness of love. Information is not only received from the physical world but from the Creator (God) as well. This information from the Creator is received directly into the spirit of man.

Where's the spirit? In the heart-house of man, and in the heart is where man's intelligence resides. God's spirit, which is holy, communicates with the spirit of man, and when in tune to the teachings, the higher self and sense faculties are developed.

As we decide on a career or a path to take in life, we determine our fates and establish our destinies through our choices, and because man's reasoning cannot rise higher than the premises upon which his actions are based, oftentimes unreasonable and incorrect choices are made.

Let me further explain. The premises of knowledge forming the foundation of man's analytical reasoning (which in effect determines those actions) do not often consider or include factors or knowledge of the teachings of the spirit or spiritual laws, knowledge of external influences, and knowledge of natural or cosmic laws but merely man's wisdom. Therefore, yielding to an urge or inspiration or submitting to impulses and temptations under these conditions can often lead to a life of turmoil and degradation.

Free will is a gift, but it is not infinite. It has a life span, and the soul is limited to a certain number of life cycles or opportunities for self-mastery, and at the end of these opportunities to improve, the use that the soul has made of the gift of free will determines its fate. It would have chosen either to glorify the divine ego[7]—reality—or the human ego—unreality. And unreality points in one direction, the permanent loss of the soul and spirit.

All final decisions are made in the heart, and someone with a highly developed spiritual intelligence—that is, one having the ability to learn the truth, to learn facts about self and events, and then to seek spiritual wisdom, knowledge, and understanding and one who, having gained spiritual insight, apply it judiciously to all facets of his or her life—will, in accord, indeed keep his or her heart with all diligence.

In the heart lies a threefold spiritual flame[8]: a blue plume, a yellow plume, and a pink plume of God-charged electronic radian light. Each plume is representative of God's qualities manifested.

The blue plume is spiritual *power* and relates to faith, goodwill, and divine intent. The yellow plume is divine *wisdom* and relates to knowledge, which is the expansion of intelligence as it relates to godliness, and the pink plume is divine *love*. It is the life crown, housing qualities of mercy, compassion, justice, and creativity, as well as God's happiness.

When we allow the yellow plumes' fires of wisdom to illuminate by calling on God's spiritual radiating power, the flow of light through our human consciousness, which are the gateways, burns off the erroneous thoughts and feelings previously assembled in the human psyche or mind, thus allowing the flow of light to radiate unimpeded, bringing forth wisdom, knowledge, and understanding and thus spiritual progress and improvement of the entire self and thereby self-mastery.

So man's actions arise out of many intricate interactions in concert at the innermost parts of the being, and oftentimes, even the doer knows not what his or her actions would be. Oftentimes some are only aware of the requirement to act or react in accord to certain activities, and those actions we call behavior, which is the attitude with which each person carry out their actions, whether it is a reaction or a creative act. Regardless, the decision is made in the heart; thus, the heart must be kept diligent. We must be vigilant and always mindful as to who and what enters therein.

CHAPTER 5

PERCEPTION AND SELF-MASTERY

Perception plays a role in self-mastery in two major ways—as the great hinderer or the wonderful benefactor—and this largely depends on how we utilize our perceptions, which in turn is dependent on our experiences and its psychological and emotional effect on us.

The perceptual process involves three primary factors: The first is our focus (selective attention); the second, our organization of the data we perceive; and the third factor, our interpretation or analysis of the information focused on and organized.

For our perceptual process to be effective, we must first fine-tune our focus. As we attend to specific data, we must be aware of psychological and physiological barriers ever present that can create false perceptions. Therefore, creating the best conditions for the receptivity of that which we choose to focus on is paramount to accurate analysis of the information. Secondly, we must resist the urge to filter that which we object to. These filters can result from a wide range of factors—from simply a tone of delivery to any information that does not fit comfortably with our way of thinking. Thirdly, we need to utilize all receptive channels available to us, including and not limited to our senses.

In the process of selectively attending to sensory information or focusing attention, there are certain unavoidable limitations, and we are all faced with these limitations simply because we make choices as humans. Our needs, interests, and expectations will determine what takes precedent in our lives at any given moment in time, and these are further limited by what we can see and hear at that time. We therefore cannot and should not concern ourselves with factors over which we have no control (though easier said than done).

However, we must understand how we are applying the rules governing our actions, as well as how they might influence us and thus our perceptions.

Psychologists discuss seven influences on perception[1]: *implicit personality theory, self-fulfilling prophecy, perceptual accentuation, consistency, stereotyping, and primacy-recency.* To understand perception in perspective to self-mastery warrants an examination of each of these characteristics.

Implicit Personality Theory

This theory follows a set of subconscious rules that associate characteristics of individuals to help determine the personality. Therefore, if you believe that someone has certain positive qualities—for example, an individual is a church-going, religious person—then you will make the assertion that the person is also charitable, loving and giving, and adheres to certain religious and moral principles. Therefore, the belief in certain positive qualities in an individual infers other associated positive qualities.

The downside to this is that we may ignore inconsistencies or negative qualities in an individual's personality and consequently have a distorted or false perception of that individual, believing they are good or bad based on our associated inferences. Therefore, in order to perceive correctly, we must be careful to suspend judgment and resist the urge to jump to conclusions.

Self-Fulfilling Prophecy

This perceptual influence is based on predictions being fulfilled mainly because the individual who predicted it or on whom it was predicted acted it out as if it were true. This tendency in our perceptions has a direct influence on how we approach self-mastery. Viewed from a positive perspective, you can influence other people's behavior, especially their belief in you based on your tendency to fulfill your own prophecy. On the other hand, you can create distortions in your perceptions by being influenced by what you predicted rather than by the reality, again, because of the tendency to fulfill your own predictions. Honest appraisal of self and developing true self-awareness is of great influence to our self-fulfilling prophecy and drives self-mastery.

Perceptual Accentuation

You see what you expect or want to see, accentuating what will satisfy your needs and desires.

A potential barrier to self-mastery with accentuation is a tendency to perceive what we want or need, which can lead to the distortion of reality, meaning we can believe we have mastered self because we have a burning desire to do so, whereas we may not have mastered self at all. We therefore, in this instant, have filtered or distorted information that might damage or threaten our self-image.

Secondly, there is a tendency to perceive and remember positive qualities more strongly than negative ones. This may not be such a bad thing if there is honest appraisal of self (improved self-awareness) since the greater there is an awareness of self, the better able we are to control our thoughts, feelings, and emotions without judging them.

For accuracy in perception to occur without perceptual accentuation being a hindrance or distraction, we must first accept who we are (with all our limitations and shortcomings) and accept what we see and hear after analyzing the facts regardless of how we may feel about it. There needs to be honest self-appraisal and self-acceptance through self-discovery.

In phase 1 of the 4-4-4 method to self-mastery, the above is explored in the discussion of effectively balancing the four selves: self-concept, self-esteem, self-awareness, and self-disclosure.

Finally, perceptual awareness in perceptual accentuation requires us to become as little children—innocent, humble, and faithful (Matthew 18:3 and 4)[2].

Primacy-Recency

Depending on what comes first or last, it will exert the most influence. If what comes first exerts more influence, the result is a primacy effect, and if what comes last exerts the most influence, the result is a recency effect. An obstacle of this perceptual effect to self-mastery is the tendency to form a total picture of an individual on the basis of initial impressions that may be inaccurate. Later on, so as not to contradict those initial impressions, we may discount or distort later perceptions.

Mastery of our perceptions helps to sharpen our decision-making process, enabling us to rely with greater confidence on our instincts and spiritual insights, sometimes referred to as vibe or intuition. Remember: There is an inner voice that speaks to each of us. It is seldom wrong, but we must learn to listen.

Consistency

This perceptual characteristic of consistency allows for balance maintenance in our attitudes based on our expectations. The problems with consistency as we attempt to master perception is our tendency to see consistency in inconsistencies; that is, we can ignore or distort perceptions of inconsistent behaviors that are real. Additionally, our desire for consistency might lead us to perceive mostly negative in those people we dislike and mostly positive in those we like.

In our meditation classes for reprogramming attitudes, students are encouraged to practice behavioral techniques in the same manner each and every time, thus creating consistency. The brain learns and retains through habit. The purpose of reprogramming attitudes is to rid ourselves of ill-formed habits through behavioral programming.

In training sessions, individuals are taught to function at deeper levels of consciousness to solve problems and find solutions. These mastering sessions teach and reinforce trust and faith on the subconscious to provide answers not always attainable on the conscious level, thereby creating a high level of consistent faith on our higher selves for answers and solutions to the most difficult questions and problems we may face. Therefore, we begin to change our inconsistencies through positive, consistent reinforcement at levels where we are least resistant.

Stereotyping

To hold simplified and standardized concepts of others is to ignore the greatest characteristic central to us as being human, that is, our uniqueness. In stereotyping, we judge based on assumptions, and we greatly endanger our relationship with others when we do so. We also retard self-mastery. The hypocritical often fails to examine self acutely.

Grouping individuals into classes and responding to them as a member of that class or group, whether it is based on religion, ethnicity, race, or nationality, is a dangerous practice that has led to catastrophic results in countries and among nations who were at one time or another engaged in race, ethnic, religious, and other forms of "cleansing." The wholesale slaughter of other human beings because of their groupings or class, wherever it has been practiced, has always had the same *tragic* results.

The very survival of us as a race (human race) rests on our ability to be different and unique and to express these qualities, for borne out of these diverse expressions are our abilities to seek wisdom, knowledge, power, and love; create; advance; self-discover; and be human. To make scientific advances and, in essence, to find individual happiness and improve our lot regardless of how temporary it may seem, this characteristic still has that abiding quality that makes us, like our DNAs, unique.

> Hypocrite! First remove the plank from your own eye, and then you will see clearly to remove the speck from your brother's eye. (Matthew 7:5)[3]

Attribution

Through this perceptual process, we attempt to understand the reasons behind someone's behavior and even behind our behavior. In attribution, we attempt to analyze individuals and the situations through *consensus*; for example, if the general consensus on someone's behavior is in accord with the behavior, then we look no further than to the individual, but if the general consensus says this is not how that individual would behave, we would then examine the situation or the circumstance to determine what caused that type of behavior.

Analysis of attribution is also examined through *consistency*. We first examine whether there is consistency in behavior in similar situations. If there is high consistency, then the behavior would be attributed to some type of internal motivation on the person's part and not the circumstance. *Distinctiveness* and *controllability* are also used in the analysis of attribution.

In distinctiveness, we would conclude that a person's behavior has an internal cause (unique to that individual) if that person acted in similar ways in different situations. Whereas with controllability, if we believe or think a person was or is in control of their behavior, our reaction to them would be negative. Understanding there is so much to overcome in efforts to master self must certainly give us pause as we examine these characteristics.

The potential barriers to improvement in attribution are the tendencies to make hasty conclusions without attempting to gather and analyze all the facts, to make assumptions, and more critically, to attribute positive behavior to our efforts and negative behavior to others.

Increasing the accuracy of our perceptions is paramount to self-mastery and to the improvement in the way we see the world, others, and ourselves. We must become more aware of our perceptions and become active perceivers—ask more questions for confirmation, don't label, and describe accurately what we see and hear. We must reduce uncertainty by reducing ambiguity. This translates to seeking more information for verification.

Be sensitive to the differences in others, especially cultural differences; recognize our individuality and uniqueness; and see the world through the eyes of children. Distinguish facts from inferences by checking sources and contexts.

In perception, as in self-mastery, we must be open-minded and allow new ideas and changes to be introduced into our subconscious but be vigilant in checking our perceptions to determine that those ideas producing the incremental changes that serve as stepping stones on the ladder to greater changes in us contain the positive attributes required for mastery of self.

Science gives us a perspective that is verifiable though not in all instances tangible. For example, based on scientific research, we know of atoms and molecules. We also know that placing one end of an iron or metal rod in fire while holding the other end will eventually cause us to be burned because the heat is conducted along the rod by the molecules within the rod, and although we cannot see these tiny particles, we know they exist. We also know there is matter all around us, even though we cannot see it. This is one dimension of reality that provides us with a certain perception.

Our senses provide us with a verifiable perspective. We sense, see, hear, and experience an event; therefore, it exists, and unfortunately, we have relied too much on this one-dimensional aspect of reality for verification of perception and meaning of our world; hence, we are more often and quite easily deceived by distorted perceptions.

Consider this example for those of us who must see it to believe it. Our ability to see is based on reflected light or light rays being reflected off of an object. White light is made up of seven colors referred to as the colors of the spectrum. They are red, orange, yellow, green, blue, indigo, and violet. We see an object—let's say a blue chair. Our ability to see the chair as blue is simply because when light strikes the chair and is then reflected, our eyes see the reflected light or the light rays the object (in this case the chair) rejects. The chair rejects the blue light rays; however, all objects that reflect light also absorb light, and while we cannot see the light rays the chair absorbs, we know that it does.

Hence, we can surmise that the chair is really all the colors except that color which it rejects, in this instant, the color blue. Now where does that leave our perception? Is the chair really blue? Yes, but based only on one aspect of reality—our physical senses. Does that chair possess other colors? Yes, quite so, and simply because we cannot see them does not mean they don't exist. Begin to see the world from all perspectives, and you will become more perceptive in your journey to mastering self.

Imagination is the third dimension we must use for a more accurate perceptive perspective.

Can you say to an inventor of a device while that device is still an imagination that what that inventor has envisioned is not real? It would be incorrect to do so for this reason: All things tangible were first created in the mind of its inventor, and while to us that device may not be real simply because there is no tangibility, to its inventor, the device is real. It has already been perceived and now requires the creativity for its applicable usage.

The airplane, for example, the Wright Brothers, made numerous attempts at the flying machine before its perfection. The examples are numerous—the computer, the cell phone, the camera, and the millions of technological devices created within the past one hundred years. For the creators of these devices, they are real while still invisible.

Therefore, it stands to reason that our imaginations are real since we must first imagine it before it can be created, and once we are able to create it, it is no longer just an imagination but a tangible device. When we are able to find practical applications for that device, at this juncture, that device is now tangible. At the moment its creator finds a way to have its usefulness made available for consumption by others, we recognize its usefulness and use. Even if it's merely created for self use, it has moved beyond imagination.

We create from that which is not seen (imagination), and so, that which is invisible—is it there even if we cannot physically see it? Yes, it has to be, for if it were totally nonexistent, it could never be made manifest or be constructed.

We therefore create the visible (the tangible) from the invisible (the imagination). Whatever we can imagine, we can find a way to create.

Therefore, we should not and cannot dismiss or discard science, the senses, or the imagination but must utilize all three in concert, for each gives a separate and distinct perspective of reality and, collectively, a much more reliable view and broader vista of perception. Do not be impeded; stay connected.

CHAPTER 6

THE FOUR LOWER BODIES (PHYSICAL BODY: VEHICLE FOR THE EARTH'S SOJOURN)

To everything there is a season, a time for every purpose under heaven.
—Ecclesiastes 3:1[1]

To begin self-mastery, the questions that must be answered are "Who am I really?" "Am I happy with who I am?" "Do I need to change anything about myself, and why should I?" "Who am I changing for, myself or someone else?" and finally, "If I change and no one else does, how does this affect me?"

Growth is change and change is natural to our existence. All positive change is referred to as improvement, and all individualized changes that transform us in some way we can refer to as self-transformation. If we recognize these transformations as good or positive in our lives, we can then say that these are growths or improvements. Once we have complete control over our lives and once we have positive and full control over our impulses and behavior in ways that manifests these positive changes, regardless of circumstances and especially in adverse situations, we are well on our way to self-mastery, but alas, there is still work to be done.

Life is a constant vortex of existence and of motion, and whether we accept it or not, change is inevitable; that is, we either choose to change or change will choose us. It is difficult to remain constant or steadfast in the face of change, but is your change harmonious with the surrounding vibrations?

If all movement is in harmony with the surrounding vibrations, we are moving in perfect rhythm. We feel and experience life because there is motion. We see because there is motion. If the earth were to stop revolving and if motion were to cease, then we would feel nothing, see nothing, and hear nothing.

It is this motion (and motion is change) that gives us a sense of being alive, and so even if we chose to remain as we are, constant in our circumstance and in our aspect of being, there would still be change—natural changes that will occur—that we can neither control nor prevent but simply must adjust to or suffer the consequences.

If the adjustment adds comfort or provides us with positive advantages we did not have prior, even if the change causes some discomfort, it is still an opportunity to grow and improve.

Changes, physical and otherwise, are governed by natural and spiritual laws, and no change is more obvious than physical changes. How we change is determined by how we adhere to spiritual and natural laws. The effects of these changes on the lower bodies will be indicators to us on how we have lived our lives and mastered self.

The four lower bodies[2] represent the first phase of the 4-4-4 connection method to self-mastery. They are four distinct frequencies (see figure 1A, page 54) that surround the soul. These four bodies—physical, emotional, mental, and etheric—are vehicles for the soul's journey in the physical world or through time/space travel.

The highest frequency or vibration is the etheric body (which shall be discussed in more detail in its own chapter). This body is the gateway to the higher selves or the three higher bodies[3]: the *Christ self*, the *I AM presence*, and the *causal body*.

The Christ self, the level to which the soul must rise, is our real self—our mediator between us and God. It is our anointment or walk in godliness, our Christ consciousness, or higher consciousness, which is the true identity of the soul.

The I AM presence is the God identity of each one of us or the individualized presence of God. We get to the I AM presence when we get to the personification of God and the God flame for each of us or for each individual. In other words, we have achieved the I AM THAT I AM when we have achieved perfection—perfect everything: thoughts, words, feelings, and so on.

The causal body is the habitation or mansion of the spirit of perfection. It is the consciousness that surrounds the I AM presence in the planes of spirit. This consciousness is the good works done in all past lives. The Lord's word and works that is.

While each lower body is examined as a separate entity, understand that it is interlocking *spiritual garment or energy*, each body being a unit of the whole and cannot function harmoniously without the other. If one is developed at the expense of the others, imbalance and dysfunction within that individual will most definitely manifest itself.

The four lower bodies—the physical, the mental, the emotional, and the etheric—must work together in complete harmony to effect positive changes, where changes in one affects the others. And paramount to self-mastery is the understanding of the function of each body in the soul's development and how the system relates to itself as a whole, to cosmic/natural and spiritual laws, and under the influence of the four elements or quadrants of matter. For the student of metaphysics and the sciences, to understand cosmic and spiritual laws is to understand the flow of electrical pulsations (electromagnetic energy) and how these currents of energy affect our balance and development.

Physical Body

The physical body is one-fourth of the *I* or ego or consciousness of the human being but the lowest aspect—the outer garment and the power supply to the system (the entire body). Here power relates to conscious energy, and when the power begins to be depleted, the body begins to die. However, because energy cannot be destroyed but simply changes form, there is constant renewed energy, albeit in different forms.

It is important to understand that each lower body possesses its own source of power and, in turn, infuses or recharges each unit of the lower body with energy. Each unit therefore is plugged into the other. For example, to carry out an act or action, while the power source may have originated in the emotional body, the act still requires the physical body to complete its arc, for without the physical capability, the emotional body would seem powerless and would subsequently have to find other means for the manifestation of its urgings.

The physical body therefore is the storehouse of energy for the system in its physical sojourn. When the energy within the storehouse becomes spent, it becomes necessary to reinfuse the body cells with energy in order for power to be restored.

Power to the physical body is generated in numerous ways, but the three primary ways are through physical exercise, the correct intake of nutrients, and rest.

Physical Exercise

Athletes, for example, understand the importance of both exercise and nourishment for the sustenance and maintenance of top-level performance. Hundreds of hours are spent in the gym, on the field, and in training rooms, working on technique and power through weight training and other forms of strengthening and speed exercises. Various exercises strengthen and build muscles, provide endurance or stamina, as well as add energy to the physical body once applied correctly, and once the regiment of exercise is maintained, the power to the physical body is maintained and constantly renewed.

As a track athlete, I understood not only the importance of training but also the importance of applying techniques in the same manner repetitively until it becomes second nature. The hardest part of competing was the training and the discipline to maintain it.

Those who exercise regularly know the feeling of renewed energy after a good workout. The energy you feel is the recharging of the unit's cells—the reinfusion of energy to the cells of the physical body, transmitted in the form of adrenaline.

The physical body can endure a tremendous amount of stress without breaking down. Unfortunately, however, it eventually does, but a well-maintained physical body, one having a correct balance of nutrients, exercise, and rest, recuperates rapidly.

Food/fuel

We were instructed centuries ago as to the foods[4] most beneficial for our physical bodies so that we may maintain an existence truly in service to the divine legislation, to God, and to our purpose (Leviticus 11:1-47). Unfortunately, today, many of us have drifted away from the teachings of spiritual and cosmic laws, and we are all paying a dreadful price for it. Our health relates directly to how we treat the physical body and that includes what we eat.

Eating correctly is vital, not only as a source of energy, but for maintaining balance in health, ease rather than dis-ease (disease). Food is the fuel and a vital source of power, and you truly get out what you put into your system. Incidentally, that goes for the health of our planet as well.

Remember, self-mastery is not only having the knowledge but also the wisdom and the understanding of how to apply these principles to your life. You will fail to master self if you know yet follow not, and as in physical training, it requires discipline.

We as a culture and society have drifted further and further away from nature and what it provides us for victuals. As a result, diseases are rampant, and more frightening are the series of new diseases with no apparent cures.

Nature gave us fruits, vegetables, and seeds, along with the most natural beverage on earth, water. And the Bible instructed us on which animals and birds were good for our consumption. Years ago, we lived longer and healthier, and in spite of our modern medicines and so-called miracle cures, we're still dying at a faster rate and living shorter lives that are unhealthier. We must ask ourselves why when the universe has given us everything we need. Perhaps we need to reexamine our relationship to nature and the natural law.

Foods rich in particular nutritional contents are generally recommended as good for consumption for maintaining internal balance, especially when a physical body is dis-eased, although we need not wait until this has happened.

The internal in all aspects of our lives must parallel the external; therefore, as we think about what we intake internally, we should also think of how we wish it to manifest itself externally, for it always does in one way or the other manifests itself externally on the physical.

Athletes, for example, when in training, are oftentimes advised by nutritionists to consume certain types of foods, perhaps foods rich in protein or other nutritional values to build and maintain power and energy. Energy, in turn, manifests itself within our cells in the form of light, and light equates to life. We are energy and that energy is light—spiritual light—and that spiritual light is the energy of God or the potential of the Christ in us.

In the books of John 1:4 and 8 as well as Matthew, Revelation, and Isaiah, " . . .life . . .light of men"[5], *light* and *life* are used synonymously as explanations of us being enlightened, energized, or renewed, not necessarily through exercise in those examples but by understanding how to use the spiritual law as a guide in all that we do, including the guidance as to what should be our rightful diet.

There are seven light centers located within the spiritual body that are the energy centers called the chakras (see also the etheric body). These centers radiate energy, and each center radiates a specific energy ray identified by its color. These colors serve as a guide in determining the types of natural foods (fruits and vegetables) nature or the natural law has given us as nourishment for a particular area of the body.

Fruits and vegetables are not colored by accident. Nature has color coded them for us—purple, green, yellow, and so on—for each serves a purpose to provide nourishment, which in turn, radiates energy within each cell of the body and helps to maintain balance within the physical body.

Some practitioners have slight variations as to the chakras colors at some of the light/energy centers, which are the seven centers I will identify.

According to numerous studies done of the human aura and based on meditation and Buddhist practices, the following colors are identified for the selected light centers. These centers are also referred to as the chakras[6] (see figure 2D, page 193). (1) *The throat*—blue, accordingly blue and purple fruits and vegetables; (2) the *crown of the head*—violet & white, accordingly blue and purple for fruits and vegetables; (3) the *heart*—pink, also green (the chest area), accordingly green fruits and vegetables;(4) root or *base of spine*—red, accordingly red fruits and vegetables; (5) *third eye*, between brows—purple/indigo, accordingly blue/purple fruits and vegetables; (6) *solar plexus*—yellow and gold, accordingly yellow fruits and vegetables; (7) *seat of the soul*, the navel area—orange, accordingly, orange fruits and vegetables. More on this later on.

While some are of the belief that superior strength gives the edge in competitive sports and bigger is better in our culture and way of thinking, athletes and others are now discovering that the edge is not as much in the physical at all, as it is in the mental. I'm only using athletes here as an example, but this could be applied across the board in any arena and capacity. All else being equal, the difference oftentimes between success and failure or winning and losing resides in who has the mental edge, who is more focused, and who is able to concentrate a little harder and remain calm and poised under pressure.

The biggest fear, for example, for most of my public speaking students is to stand in front of the class and deliver a three-minute speech. I've had students who withdrew from public speaking rather than face a room full of their peers for three to four minutes. Why? Because they just could not overcome that fear and caved in to the mental pressure.

Athletes and others have undergone meditation and relaxation techniques that help to provide a balance between the physical and mental bodies.

Rest/Relaxation

Relaxation allows the physical body to recuperate, heal, and recharge. Without rest, the cells of the physical body would eventually die. Our physical body, through its interconnection and intercommunication with the mental body, signals the physical when it's time to rest.

In my relaxation classes, I use techniques quite similar to the techniques employed by The Silva Mind Control School.[7] Relaxation techniques take place at the *alpha* level of the brain, where these techniques are reinforced by simply using the power of visualization, counting from 3 to 1 three times for each number as these numbers are visualized.

Once at the relaxed level, problem solving and breaking negative habits are then programmed. At relaxed levels, our minds are more open to the acceptance of information. However, it is important that thoughts and feelings remain positive and constructive while at a deep level of meditation.

Relaxation works best when it begins from the feet to the crown of the head, thus counting backward from twenty or twenty-five to one helps your body to relax, and then in returning to an outer consciousness state, counting forward from one to five allows for the return to that beta state of outer consciousness.

Applying the technique in the same way each time allows the mind to reach that state of relaxation faster and faster and, with constant practice allows the mind to remain at this relaxed state in spite of minor disturbances, but with complete awareness of where you are and what you would need to do should you have to react if danger arises. Performing the techniques the same way each time reinforces automated patterns and eventually automated behavior.

The physical body will relax when the mental body does. In meditation exercises, we are actually inducing the mental body to relax by first relaxing the physical body.

Vigilance must be exercised in the pursuit of the development of the physical body. Care must be exercised to remain selfless and to avoid excesses.

Hastening the physical development, especially if there's the belief that physical superiority (more bulk and/or more power) will provide an edge competitively, can invariably lead to abuse, vanity, and subsequent neglect of the development of the system in concert.

This, in turn, may lead to overindulgence brought on by vanity, misguided and misused power, and neglect of the higher ideals of self, which invariably can lead to other abuses on the physical body, such as the intake of substances (like drugs), to further advance selfish appetites. The system subsequently becomes unbalanced, and the body will eventually deteriorate and die from dis-ease and other malfunctions.

Finally, in being vigilant, care must also be exercised so that the body's cells do not become clogged with other forms of misused power, such as negative thoughts and feelings. This prevents the flow of energy in the body since the body cells would become negatively charged, ultimately causing loss of power in the form of fatigue and, if it remains unchecked, eventually death. Always remember that we die from the inside out.

CHAPTER 7

MENTAL BODY
VEHICLE OR VESSEL FOR
THE MIND OF GOD

Mental Body

It is the immortal spirit and storehouse of the system. The mental body regulates and maintains the activities of the spirit within the astral body (the desire or feeling body or emotional body). The mental body has its own power source. It interpenetrates the physical body, and while it seemingly operates independent of the physical body's power, it needs the physical body as a focal point of power distribution and flow, just as the emotional body does.

Because of the close relationship between the physical body and the mental body, where the mental interpenetrates the physical, there is the appearance of a constant power struggle between the two. Physical urges seem to dominate and control the mental ability to resist these urges.

For example, an addict might have a physical dependency on nicotine or on some other drug, and to satisfy the physical craving would take these drugs that may eventually lead to the abuse of the physical body. The addiction in this instant is both physiological and psychological since the craving that may appear to be totally physical is mental as well.

The power to resist the urge is overwhelmed by the power to indulge, thus satisfying the powerful urges of the physical body.

A similar occurrence takes place in the act of quitting, whether it is temporarily or permanently. Once the physical body is satisfied, there is no longer a yearning until the urge is again triggered. When the decision is made (through the power of the mental body) to reform a negative habit or change a course of action, for example, to quit smoking, the battle lines are drawn and a struggle ensues between the power of the physical body and the power of the mental body within that individual. It is a battle of wills (an internal/external power struggle).

There are withdrawal effects on the physical body, as it reacts to the cessation of a formed habit and dependency. If that individual is mentally strong, then the battle would be won by the mental body.

The densities from drugs and other impurities in the system can clog the brain cells, impeding light and thus energy from the mental power source. Once this occurs and if the blockages cannot be effectively purged, then the mental faculties may become impaired.

The most powerful and complex of the bodies is the mental body, using more energy than the others but capable of accomplishing just about anything. However, for the mental body to operate at optimum efficiency, the physical, emotional, and spiritual body alignments must be in perfection since the mental body receives its cues from the effects, both positive and negative, on the other three.

For the sake of simplification, it being much more complex than being described here, once data are accumulated from experiences and after analysis by the mental body, they are then dispersed to the emotional, physical, and spiritual bodies.

The mental body, the storehouse, compartmentalizes the information it receives into various so-called data bases or storehouses, lower mental and higher mental, old and new, past and present, positive and negative, short term and long term, effective and noneffective storehouses. The information then awaits retrieval. The results and the effects of these results determine actions and future actions. Patterns become wired to form habits. Repetition allows the brain to easily and instantaneously recognize these patterns and act according to experience and desired results.

Based on the power of the mind, the amount of light source within the cells bring about understanding. Spiritual light infuses the mind to receive truth, and truth opens up the mind to receive wisdom. Understanding through wisdom brings about clarity, and the amount of clarity is equivalent to the amount of illumination within the mind.

Therefore, it is imperative that we illuminate the mind with truth, the truth of our existence, of who we really are and of our purposes and then accept ourselves truthfully and noncritically, for that light is the energy of God.

The intention of the mind body or *mental body*[1] is as a vehicle for the Christ mind or mind of God. The Christ or God within us is manifested through the power of our minds or mental body. Thoughts centered on carnal or worldly matters leads to the accumulation of carnal knowledge.

The mental body comprises of a higher mental body and a lower mental body. The higher mental body is the universal mind or the mind of Christ or the Christ consciousness, the mind that adheres to spiritual law. The lower mental body is the carnal mind, the worldly mind, or the mind that adheres to the concerns of the world. We can possess worldly intelligence, with high IQs, yet be ignorant. That is because we may not have been enlightened to the Christ consciousness within us or the spiritual law. "For we know that the law is spiritual, but I am carnal sold under sin" (Romans 7:14)[2].

It is difficult for the carnal mind to comprehend spiritual language, even though a spiritual mind can comprehend carnal thoughts and language, because the spiritual mind is of the higher mental body.

Similarly, there are those who are book smart, yet commonsense foolish. The power of the mental body, which is wisdom, therefore does not necessarily relate to how worldly intelligent you are, but rather it speaks to the Christ consciousness you possess, that is, the higher mental body and how that body functions under spiritual law.

Recall Matthew 6:33 paraphrased once you seek God first (God-ness), then everything else becomes as gifts to us. How so? Because to truly understand the power of the mental body is to understand the real power we possess, and to access this power source, we must understand how spiritual and cosmic law governs our lives.

We must understand our relationship to the universe and recognize that the universe belongs to us, understanding that the one universal truth to our existence is what we all seek, and once we have discovered that truth, we have mastered self, for that truth we find is the self truth.

Scientists who have been studying the brain for years deduced that to be able to function at higher levels of the mind or self-awareness (another aspect of the 4-4-4 method toward self-mastery), we must be able to control our thoughts in ways that would provide us with other avenues or channels of information not often easily or readily available in a fully conscious state due to blockages such as negativity, self-doubt, or fear.

These scientists divided the brain into four dimensions[3]: the *beta*, outer conscious state, fully conscious, or wide awake; the *alpha*, inner conscious state, semi-conscious or dream state; the *theta*, another inner conscious state or dimension but deeper than the alpha, an unconscious or unaware state; and the *delta*, another inner consciousness state or dimension, referred to as death.

Alpha-beta translates to alphabet, the code for the beginning of our conscious learning of a language. Each language spoken comprises of alpha-beta or an alphabet.

With the use of techniques of relaxation and focus, the power of the mental body could then be used to acquire information not readily available. There are proven examples of how the power of the mental body can be accessed and used for the acquisition of data to help and benefit others positively. These lessons I have imparted to the students who have studied the theoretical and practical applications of self-mastery with me.

Some practitioners are able to perform astral projections, that is, tap into frequencies of time and space that are beyond the physical but below the mental on the astral plane. The astral plane was meant to be a frequency to be used for the betterment of the collective unconsciousness of mankind, but it has been usurped by practitioners who transmit impure thoughts and feelings, thus making the very word itself, "astral," a negative connotation and context.

Vigilance must be exercised that the power of the mental body is not used to manipulate, oppress, and suppress others and that its power is used wisely, for with the infusion of power/light/energy to the cells of the mental body comes an increase in wisdom.

Misuse of this power can be detrimental to the victim as well as for the so-called victor. This new power can easily be abused and misused if not focused correctly.

Wisdom must be balanced with the universal gift and power of love. Avoid at all costs impure thoughts. All hateful and negative thoughts are impure thoughts. Avoid toxic people. Toxicity recognizes itself; that is, negative, impure thoughts are generally dispensed from toxic, negative people.

In my self-mastery classes, all students are programmed that there will be mental blocks if any information is attempted to be used for any other purpose other than what it is intended, which is to positively benefit humanity and self. The functions of the mental faculties must therefore remain unclogged and unimpaired from the densities that would cause its power to be misused.

CHAPTER 8

EMOTIONAL BODY
VEHICLE FOR THE DESIRES AND
FEELINGS OF GOD

Emotional Body

The emotional body houses the power of desire and feelings. It is the feeling body of the system, also referred to as the astral body. The greatest misuse of power often occurs at this lower body, and in its misuse, the emotional body may become very volatile and violent.

The emotional body requires the most discipline to come in line with the other lower bodies and in the mastery of self.

Remember, each body has its own power or energy, and the energies of the emotional body has a tendency to lead individuals down paths of self-destruction since its power when discharged can override the mental and physical bodies, causing any power of logic or reasoning to be negated. The physical body is then almost instantaneously infused with this power and charge, and actions in accordance with the desires and the feelings, regardless of its negative intent, may manifest itself within the physical body. Power flow to the mental body is subjected to the etheric body's power for the most part; however, flow of power to the physical body is subjected to the power of the emotional body.

This is the most important reason why we *must* master each of the lower bodies. Equilibrium must be created and power distributed across the board for balance to be maintained and energy and power to remain in check.

We cannot speak of emotion and not speak of power. They are synonymous, for as the lack of power creates certain tensions, so does the acquisition of power. Most, if not all men strive for recognition or indirectly, power, because power offers us the ability to do or act. Lack of recognition signifies to most limited power, lack of power, or no power at all, and none of the three is desirable.

In the tension created by the lack of power, children, for example, act out or become emotional because they want attention or recognition. They do recognize that in general, they have little or no power and, in efforts to acquire power, will do things that will direct attention to themselves. It is their way of saying, "Don't ignore me. Here I am. Pay some attention to me. recognize me, for I'm important too."

If we understand that a child would rather be praised than punished but rather be punished than ignored, then we begin to recognize how power is often used and frequently misused when in the hands of those ignorant of the laws governing the flow and use of emotional energy.

Adults act out as well when their deeds, but especially when their emotional needs, are not given proper attention or recognition. The difference between an adult and a child exercising the power of the emotional body is the power each possesses to create negative charges. While both may have the ability to misuse the emotional power in their thinking and doing, because of expectations, adults wield greater power and thus greater responsibility to use that power judiciously.

Empathy, the cognitive process of being able to identify with someone else's feelings, thoughts, or attitudes, speaks to the tension created by the acquisition of power. How we show empathy or demonstrate our ability to empathize really speaks to our use of the emotional power we possess.

Empathy is shown in general through the ways we respond to others, the way we respond to others who respond to us, or just in the ways we respond period, and we show these responses via. *empathic responsiveness*,[1] when we can sense the sadness or happiness of another person and parallel that response with our own emotional response to that person's happiness or sadness; via *perspective taking*,[2] when we can imagine ourselves in another person's place, experiencing as if it were really our experience what they have experienced or are experiencing (in other words, we have taken that person's perspective of the situation); and finally, via *sympathetic responsiveness*, being able to feel sorry for, concern for, or compassion for another person, a basic emotional concern, because that person is like us, human.

Being able to respond to the concerns of others places an awful amount of emotional power in our hands, and we can choose to use this power wisely by measuring the type of response we provide, either emotional support, making the person feel better about themselves or about the way they may have behaved with a hug or a touch, or a supportive response, saying something comforting or offering a statement that helps to soothe or cheer up that individual.

We must, however, attempt to create an environment that would lend itself to meeting that person's immediate needs or concerns, and that's the positive power of the emotional body, which can also be summed up as in the use of passion and com-passion.

The volatility of the *emotional body* incidentally also resides in its use of passion. Psychologists who have defined passion describe it as strong, intense emotion, highly charged emotional feelings, transcending urges and impulses, and when confined to interpersonal relationships, a complete identification and/or absorption with the person you feel passionate about. The power of the emotional body in this instance is virtually unfettered, undisciplined, and out of control, for passion is often characterized by possession and obsession.

An emotionally charged individual may not always recognize that an individual with whom they may be having an interpersonal relationship have freedom of choice and the right to exercise those choices; therefore, the rights of that individual to exercise those choices becomes negated because of the intensity of passion the other person feels.

While empathy is cognitive or thoughtful, using the head, passion is mostly emotional, using the heart. Therefore, the response is condemnation or some other form of inappropriate behavior instead of supportive, constructive behavior, with high emotional power and charge attached to it, which in effect makes it highly combustible, volatile, and disastrous.

The discipline of the emotional body is vital, even though it may seem difficult to control. In the self-mastery classes, in setting the stage for change, students must decide what needs changing and what habits require reformation, and in this effort of change or graduation to self-mastery, among others, *belief*, *expectancy*, and *desire* are the key mechanisms.

Belief places what we imagine or wish for on parallel paths with what we have experienced. There's no difference; therefore, there's no doubt, and as long as there's strong emotional power behind the belief, then the unification of the impressions is even stronger. Expectancy goes beyond belief, for its character is totally unquestioning or doubtless. Desire makes the effort work for us, for we cannot do nor accomplish anything unless we first desire to do so. Emotion provides the correct attitude, force, and clarity to do and be self-masters, but passion must be tempered with compassion, warmth, tolerance, and trust.

Care must be exercised to discipline one's self in the right use of power, particularly in the use of the emotional power of anger, for the presence of anger denotes the absence of compassion, and in anger, actions are hasty, deliberate, and oftentimes thoughtless. Temper yourself with compassion, even as you offer correction and discipline.

Vigilance must be exercised in choosing our friends and others we keep company with, as well as how much we allow those around us to influence our behavior and our way of thinking. Therefore, we must choose carefully with whom we yoke ourselves. Silent and careful observation of ourselves must be considered.

We must diligently work on our self-concept and self-esteem (which shall be discussed later on) and avoid boredom, dissatisfaction, doubt, and especially jealousy, one of the most destructive forces of the emotional body and the most threatening to relationships. All of these are volatile emotions with great power.

All in all, we must exercise better control over the emotional body's undisciplined tendencies through the identification and reformation of our habits and tendencies. This will invariably lead to discipline of the emotional body and eventually mastery of it, thus self-mastery.

CHAPTER 9

ETHERIC BODY (THE MEMORY BODY) HOLDS THE BLUEPRINT OF THE DIVINE PLAN

Etheric Body

The etheric body is the memory body, blueprint, and energy power house of the divine plan of Christ's perfection in us and for us—the highest self of the four lower bodies. The etheric body is the wedding or connection between the higher consciousness or Christ consciousness and the lower body. It is the higher of the two mental planes, and in the mastery of self, learning to walk in the light or in the understanding of the spiritual law infuses the etheric body with the light/energy required for its transcendence to higher consciousness power.

The etheric body (the body between energy and matter), which relates to the first quadrant of matter, radiates energy in the form of vortices of light that surround the physical body. A clairvoyant sees this as a bluish white light that pulsates along energy lines that surrounds the entire physical body and moves in a wavelike manner throughout the entire body of the individual. Movement is constant and in quick rhythm.

According to the Kheper[1] Web site at http://www.kheper.net, the color of the etheric body varies from gray to blue, with the entire body appearing like a weblike structure of light. All the organs of the physical body can be seen, but appears as if formed of this bluish light.

If you visualize the dense human body being surrounded by sheets, sort of like the same way a computer document page would have layer upon layer that you can continuously close or peel away until you get to the first page opened, it's the same concept.

The physical body is layered by the energy vortex of the emotional body's energy field, and then layered by the mental body's energy field and then finally by the etheric body's energy field, each extending about one-quarter to two inches from the next and each having its corresponding color that pulsates and often changes color depending on the mood (emotional disposition) as well as the spiritual and healthful conditions of the individual.

Etheric Body (The Memory Body)

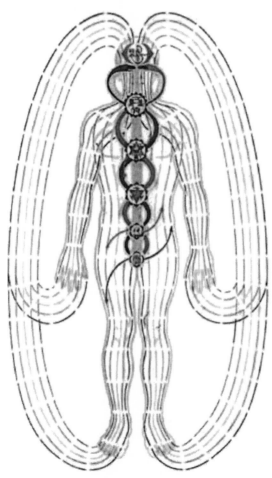

Representation of the etheric body (figure 1A).
Photo credit: http://www. crystalinks.com

All of us have a determined amount of time to learn, develop, and master certain skills. The most important of these is the divine plan,[2] which is our purpose. So long as we have not fulfilled the plan, we must keep on working on it until it is done. However, even in this, we are allotted a prescribed amount of tries for its accomplishment, and then we're done, meaning our souls are forever lost after the prescribed amount of embodiments is exhausted.

Think of it in this way: As you begin your journey on this earth, you immediately begin acquiring the knowledge you need for this life's journey. You obtain both carnal and spiritual knowledge, and at particular stages in your life, through this knowledge, you begin to develop the basic skills needed to function as a social human being to fit in.

Part of that process involves formal education, and no matter the methodology, you must first learn to master the basics like your ABCs (if you speak English) to acquire the necessary skills of that language.

If your study is music, you must first learn the rudiments of music, the lines and the spaces, and the notes that make up those lines and spaces in both the G clef and F clef, or the treble and the bass. These are the basic skills you must acquire if you are to eventually succeed at this art.

Eventually, once you have been diligent, you will find that you have mastered the fundamentals to the point where you can now graduate to a higher level of study. The journey is a constant, upward and forward, to higher and higher levels of understanding and higher pinnacles in the acquisition of knowledge.

Many things can happen along the way. You can become distracted and find yourself following a completely different path than the one you had originally embarked upon, and you may continue on that path until such time that you realize it is a detour that does not take you to where you wish to go or want to be. While you may have lost precious time, you may have acquired invaluable lessons along the way, or once you've realize you have detoured, you may return immediately to your original path and continue on.

During this journey, you will attempt tasks or take exams, only to find that you are unsuccessful at your first attempt or perhaps even at your second attempt. However, once you are determined and time allows it, you will succeed.

It is analogous to a game of baseball. Baseball follows the rule of three strikes, after which you lose your turn at bat—you're out. However, those three strikes, as you know (if you play the game), only occur once you have swung at the ball and fail to connect, or once that ball crosses the diamond within the strike zone. Once you're able to connect with the ball, putting it in play, even though it may have taken five, ten, or sometimes fifteen pitches, there is no limit on the amount of pitches you must take, just as long as you did not get that third strike. And although you may be out of that inning, you're still not necessarily out of the game until the ninth inning is completed, and also provided the score is not tied and based on how the game is played, you may get more or less chances at bat throughout the game.

The game will eventually end, and so will your turn at bat. Your team will either be declared winner or loser. Mastering self is like this analogy in its sojourn.

CHAPTER 10

SPIRITUAL LAW

Only those who have mastered self and have done so in obedience to spiritual and cosmic laws and in the teachings of God Almighty ascend to the etheric plane, a plane experienced through the senses of the soul in a dimension and consciousness far beyond physical awareness, and the etheric body is that gateway, a gateway to the three higher bodies: the I AM presence, the Christ self, and the causal body.

Spiritual Law

What life's food must we consume in order to ascend to this dimension of mastery of self? Obviously, understanding our purpose and adhering to spiritual and cosmic laws and principles are paramount. Understanding how the fruit of the spirit enriches us is imperative. "But the fruit of the spirit is love, joy, peace, long suffering, kindness, goodness, faithfulness, gentleness and self control, against such there is no law" (Galatians 5:22-23).[1]

Love, joy, and peace are internal manna. They characterize our state of being or mindset. Without these three ingredients, there is turbulence and imbalance in the lives of individuals and among all men, regardless of the public face displayed. Love, joy, and peace are intertwined and inseparable, for you cannot have joy without love and peace. Neither can you have peace without joy and love, and where there's peace and joy, you'll find love.

Our state of mind lays the foundation for the next three: long suffering, kindness, and goodness. These are external practices—what we must share and give as manna (food) to others. Long suffering refers to patience. Each of the three external fruit is not possible without first fulfilling the principles of the first three.

Loving each other begins with loving ourselves and then loving each other as we love ourselves, and to brotherly kindness, add love, the greatest gift of all. We must embrace and embody these nine characteristics to walk in spirit and to give light and power to the etheric body.

Exhibiting patience, kindness, and goodness provide enrichments in the form of humility to the spirit of men. Faithfulness, gentleness, and self-control signify our attitudes to God and in our requests for spiritual and material fulfillment.

In the enrichment of spirit and in the mastery of the spiritual self, the nine fruit of the spirit must become the spiritual foundation and principles—in essence, the law on which our lives are built and the etheric body is energized.

To walk in spirit, we must live in spirit, and to live in spirit gives manifestation to the divine destiny of self, which is, in ascending order, the lower self, the four lower bodies; at the next level, the Christ consciousness or higher consciousness; and at the highest level, the divine self, the I AM THAT I AM,[2] your perfection, and what each of us are striving for on this earthly plane.

The indispensables provide further credence and directives on how we apply spiritual law to our lives for the empowerment of our divine self.[3]

> But also for this very reason, giving all diligence, add to your faith virtue, to virtue knowledge, to knowledge self-control, to self-control perseverance, to perseverance godliness, to godliness brotherly kindness and to brotherly kindness love." (1 Peter 5:7)

The exercise of diligence and the examination of *virtue* provide us with the seven cardinals of how to live moral and upright lives: *justice, prudence, temperance, fortitude, faith, hope,* and *charity*—the foundation upon which the laws of earthly governments are based and the directives of the spiritual law upon which these laws rests.

Faith being characterized by belief, expectancy, and desire must be added to virtue; and to virtue, knowledge. We must first aspire for knowledge of self and add to this self-control or tolerance.

As we explore the four selves—self-concept, self-esteem, self-awareness, and self-disclosure (phase 2 of the second 4)—we will recognize the important role self-control plays in self-mastery. And to self-control, add perseverance, that is, determination, holding steadfast, and staying on course; to this, add godliness, that is, the God-ness or the Christ consciousness; and add to this brotherly kindness. Examine your life in relationship to these spiritual laws and determine where you stand.

Be vigilant of these spiritual laws, observe each one, and begin by having faith because your self-mastery has already begun. Believe, expect, and desire—it's that simple.

The spiritual laws under which we must live so as to attain the mastery of self were handed down in oral and written forms centuries before. A close examination of how these laws impact physiological and psychological changes in our lives and affairs will allow us to make correct choices as we exercise free will in choosing to live the lives we do.

CHAPTER 11

COSMIC LAW

As in spiritual law, the study of cosmic law[1] here helps students further understand how the four lower bodies can utilize the power that each possesses to develop and align itself harmoniously and how we can begin to recognize when there is misalignment and what may be the cause and the effect.

According to cosmic law, everything has a beginning and an end. Where it commences is considered its birth; thus, it moves forward in set progressions, periods, or cycles. The study of these cycles and the energies that emanate from the universe during these set periods or cycles creates in us certain impulses to do one thing or the other and to make one choice instead of the other.

The entire aspect of self-mastery as being laid out in these pages is based on the premise that we control our lives and fate does not. We create the circumstances we find ourselves in; they do not control us.

We are the sum total of all that we have accomplished and done, as well as how well we have chosen in obedience to spiritual and cosmic laws, whether accidentally or purposefully. We are connected to everything around us be it in our past, present, and/or future.

Those who have made the study of spiritual, cosmic, and natural laws a lifelong journey are to be credited with opening up portals beyond which we are able to examine with less condemnation that which science and the physical senses sometimes cannot explain but understand because of the effect of these energies upon us.

So in order that we may have a concrete way of measuring these emanations, we are provided with simple instructions that will give us a basis from which to begin to examine as well as track changes that affect us in definitive ways, that we have felt before now, and that we are powerless to control.

Understanding what affects these changes will help provide us with a better understanding of how we can best control the choices we make. If we divide our lives into periods of seven or into cycles of seven years, we will find that with each cycle or period comes certain definitive changes that will and must occur as natural law dictates, and these periods occur throughout our lives for approximately 144 years should we live that long.

Consider the cycles most women experience once at the stage of procreation, as dictated by the law of nature (natural law). For each woman, once their menstrual cycle begins, it will continue to occur at a specific time of the month, in general, at intervals of approximately every twenty-eight days. A breach in this cycle would signal an abnormality within the physical body caused by some occurrences of a physical or psychological nature. This alerts the individual to possible dysfunctions or phenomenons.

Yearly Life Cycles

The first seven years of our lives, according to H. Spencer Lewis from his book *Self-Mastery and Fate*, from infanthood to the age of seven is period 1. Our development in this period is both physical and mental. The educational and cultural foundations and fundamentals are laid down for us, mainly by our parents. This is a period of self-discovery for us. We learn how to talk, walk, and control our movements and, in general, how to relate properly to our surroundings and environment. All these actions are in preparation for the next period of seven years.

The physical body begins its work of garnering power, as the mental body is being guided as to how this power is to be harnessed.

In our discussion of the elements fire, air, water, and earth, the triad phase of the final four of the 4-4-4 connection and method to self-mastery, we will further explore and develop the relationship and connection between the earth and the physical body.

From age seven to fourteen, we witness a continued physical development, which seems almost accelerated. For men and women, these physical changes manifest themselves in different ways. For men, the development witnesses a more muscular frame; and for women, a more defined feminine form. This is considered the second period. These changes are further exaggerated if the individual male or female pursues rigorous regimens of exercise, diet, and nutrition. The result will be a more pronounced type of physique. Women are often on a faster track of physical development than are men. The mental development plays a secondary role at this stage or period.

Within this period is also the stage referred to as puberty. For males, it begins at around age fourteen; and for females, at about twelve. It is the natural progression to adulthood. Both can procreate at this stage of life. Physical awareness is heightened. Both genders become aware of their physical bodily changes and of the opposite sex. It is also a confusing time, for with this awareness comes a curiosity for carnal knowledge (although the mental side does take a secondary role to the earthly physical interests). Awkwardness and confusion in expressing emotions, as well as other changes, occur.

We are not yet in control of the emotional body; therefore, in general, reactions are almost always impulsive and unpredictable. It is during this stage that the preparation for the next period begins.

If the required changes do not occur before the end of the period, the individual is considered physiologically and psychologically underdeveloped. These signs therefore do signal normal progression within this cycle or period.

It is imperative that the child be instilled or be at the least exposed to teachings of spirituality during these first two cycles. Moral character must be molded, for this becomes the foundation upon which values will eventually be based.

For the earthly walk, the physical body must be fully prepared. Thus, the first fourteen years is a concentration on the development of the human as a physical being so as to begin the process of mastering the physical self and its environment.

Ages fourteen to twenty-one mark the third period. Character development takes precedent. The psychic development is accelerated, physical changes slow down, and psychological, mental, and physiological development occurs.

The development of the mental body is preeminent, and based on the foundations laid down within the prior cycle, the individual develops a sense of responsibility and begins to tune in to the higher vibrations of the mental self, developing and exhibiting stronger psychic abilities. The inclination to be emotionally impulsive is still prevalent; however, this is the stage where acquiring the skills and the knowledge needed to master the emotional body is procured.

Age twenty-one is considered the age of full emancipation, and with it comes legal responsibility. I say full emancipation because in some cultures, the age of eighteen marks this transition for some.

Individuals are considered to have reached the stage of maturation as independent adults at age twenty-one in the American culture and are thus considered legally and morally responsible for their actions. Spiritually, the age of maturation is when the individual recognizes and can discern right from wrong.

On close examination of this stage, which again is in preparation for the next period, we witness clearly the adaptation of spiritual laws to the precepts of earthly laws, where the employment of self-control, temperance, prudence, dignity, and other moral characteristics are expected to be adhered to by individuals considered to be socially integrated. This entrenchment is expected by the end of the third period.

CHAPTER 12

COSMIC LAW
FAMILY EFFECT/CYCLES

The emotional body is awakened and is now infused with power, and as members of the broader *human family*, we learn how to function as a unit and, over the next seven years, how to harness this power.

The functional skills at this stage of development is greatly defined by the *family* unit, the group of intimates who help us to develop a sense of group identity, loyalty, and emotion, particularly because the first friendships we experience are most likely to be with family members.

What is the role of the family unit, and how do we determine its functionality?

The family's primary role is to meet the physical, emotional, and social needs of its members, as well as supply comfort. The functionality of the family is determined by how well the primary goals are being met.

As part of a functional family system,[1] we learn how to *communicate our needs*; *interdependency, family rules*, and *goals*; how to *maintain balance* and *cohesion* within the unit; as well as how to *adapt to changes* in the environment and in the behavior of family members.

Collectively, we are all members of the human family. This large connective collective is then broken down into smaller and smaller units. These units are considered the primary units. Choices are made at various periods in our lives as to how new units are adopted into our lives. Therefore, how we set about in our quest to master self is a reflection of how functional our family unit experiences are.

As a functional family system, we learn how to correctly communicate and manage our needs.

Communication of Our Needs

Communication within the family serves three important functions: The first is *self-concept formation*.[2] Self-concept is discussed in more detail within the second connection of the 4-4-4 method to self-mastery, but clearly, verbal and nonverbal talks certainly contribute to the development of strong self-concepts in all family members. However, the verbal and nonverbal should not be incongruous but supportive of each other. Damaging statements leads to damaged self-concepts.

The second function is *recognition and support*, where interaction between members should demonstrate and supply both recognition as well as support. This helps to build confidence and a feeling of belonging within the individual, who would then feel a sense of security knowing there is a foundation and support system that can be accessed in times of need.

If support is not provided within the family unit, three choices of behavior are exercised: One is aggression, where we strike out at the source of our discontent; we may become passive and refuse to state our position or opinion, often submitting to the demands of others; or we may become assertive; that is, exercise power and speak up.

A group, a club, or an organization, such as the Boy Scouts, a sorority, a fraternity, or even a gang, provides a basis of support for individuals and hence the importance of societies, such as the Freemasons, as vital support units.

Keep in mind that family is not defined by blood relationships but by shared commonalities and interests, including strong emotional ties. Providing the individual with positive recognition and support allows for the building of confidence and positive development toward mastery of self.

A child would rather be praised than punished, but that child would also rather be punished than ignored, and that's how important recognition is to most.

The third function of communication within the family is for *behavior modeling*[3]. Members in positions of power are excellent role models for other members. Family members therefore should serve as role models. The responsibility for molding a foundation of respectability and developing moral character, including self-control, temperance, prudence, and dignity, is the parent's responsibility or who ever is functioning in that role.

An important behavior modeling characteristic is also conflict management, for how family members manage conflict will determine how the individuals within the unit manage conflict.

We utilize one of five choices in managing conflict. We withdraw, give in and accommodate, force our point of view or ideas on others, compromise, or collaborate. The choice we exercise determines how successful the conflict will be managed.

It is a more difficult task to respond effectively to conflict than to initiate it since it is the response that would escalate the conflict. For continued functionality of the family unit as a system, each member must understand the consequences of each of the choices available to be exercised.

Withdrawing, ignoring, or removing one's self from a conflict is the worst way to manage conflict, and it does not advance self-mastery, for the conflict will largely remain unresolved and the relationship will eventually decline. Choices of accommodating and/or forcing usually results in frustration because only one individual benefits from these actions. While accommodating satisfies the other person's needs, it can also result in the neglect of our own and does not preserve self-dignity.

Although accommodating might be an exercise in brotherly kindness, good judgment must be exercised as well to be sure that the insecurities of one person are not exploited in order to assure the continuance of that relationship.

Conversely, forcing often leads to reluctant acceptance and an uneasy relationship that does not promote tolerance nor uphold the dignity of the one forced into accepting. It builds neither character nor ideals for self-mastery. Forcing the acceptance of an idea or need is generally accomplished through the use of physical, verbal, or coercive methods, none of which are appropriate within a functional family unit and promotes an unhealthy respect for and negative effect on family values. One person is being taken advantage of, which eventually leads to conflicting relational issues.

To communicate our needs effectively, it must be fully addressed and issues resolved in a collaborative manner, making sure the lines of communication remain open throughout. If time is a factor in the effort, then compromise is a likely alternative that would at least offer each party some semblance of satisfaction and dignity. Practicing effective conflict management is akin to the practical applications of spiritual laws within the family unit.

Interdependency

Functionality within the family system means adhering to the spiritual law of brotherly kindness. We are indeed our brother's keeper. Interdependence means there is an interrelationship, a connection, and a dependency that causes the actions of one to adversely affect the subsequent actions of another member of the larger human family. Dysfunctional family unit members feel little or no connection to other members and act independent of the needs of the unit's members. Spiritual growth is stunted, often leading to behavior considered to be socially unacceptable.

FBI profiles of serial killers and other social deviants show in their characteristics a tendency to be self-indulgent and loners who are often isolated.

Family Rules and Goals

As previously stated, the primary goal of the family unit is to meet and ensure the safety, physical and social needs of its members.[4] In periods 1 through 3, the first three human cycles of existence, ages one to twenty-one, we see this clearly, including the influence of the family. The fundamentals of our culture and education are laid out for us.

In these periods, we undergo enculturation (learning the mores of the culture we were born into) from our educators—our parents, peer groups, schools, religious institutions, and government agencies. We learn values, beliefs, behaviors, and ways to communicate, including language, attitudes, and styles, as well as the group's artifacts. All of this information is passed on from generation to generation through communication.

In some instances, we also undergo acculturation (learning the rules and norms of cultures different to our native culture), again, with our care givers being our parents and other family members as principals responsible for the molding of our behavior.

The behavior expected and recommended by the family unit is determined by the roles within the unit, and the roles are determined by the rules, which are an outgrowth of responsibility. Some rules are passed down from generation to generation; other rules develop as necessitated by situations. However, there must be rules for each member of the family that must be adhered to.

Therefore, the early conditioning of the first three cycles are impactive indeed. The child is prepared to be an adult in the first three periods or first three cycles of seven years of life. How that adult fairs will be determined by the type of foundation that life rests on.

In a healthy family, self-maintenance provides for *balance*. Changes in family members are expected; therefore, constant adjustments and *adaptation* to those changes must be accepted as part of the process of growth. Spiritual guidance, love, respect, recognition, and support all play key roles. Learning how to deal with adversity, receiving emotional support, and harnessing the emotional power become very important for the next phase or cycle of seven years.

Within a functional family unit, these characteristics are paramount to the survival of the unit intact, and mastering these positive characteristics are key preparations for the next seven-year cycle. The individual not attaining this stage of development by age twenty-one is considered backward in progress and may be classified as incompetent or underdeveloped.

In the fourth period[5] of *seven years*, ages twenty-one to twenty-eight, development is strongly centered in the emotional nature. A sense of responsibility is further developed. Some dormant faculties like intuition and mental telepathy are beginning to awaken. There is more profound interest in relationships, and various kinds are fostered between family members and friends.

This is a period where temperance and self-control must be carefully exercised because of the infusion of power within the physical body, along with the strong vibrational influence of the emotions within this seven-year cycle. Hence, more volatility within relationships, more emotional upswings, and more psychological and physiological disturbances are prevalent.

However, concurrently, the strong vibrations within this period urge the gravitation toward the development of the higher intellect and higher mental faculties and the testing of mental skills, which helps to further awaken the etheric body and the Christ consciousness. Career choices are made, and social and financial stability is sought during this period. High interest in the arts, religion and more sophisticated things in life, leads to a softening of the carnal nature as preparation begins for the next seven-year cycle.

Ages twenty-eight to thirty-five mark the fifth period,[6] the launching pad for the Christ consciousness within. This period finds self-mastery centered on the creative mind. The ability to visualize, imagine, and mentally create is greatly enhanced during this period.

We clearly witness how the flow of power from the etheric body begins to influence the mental. It is from within this period or cycle that we see the emergence of future leaders, thinkers, philosophers, and others who, for the past four periods, have been honing their skills and developing the mind in preparation for their cosmic conscious awakening.

The physical body's power cells are fully charged. With high energy and zeal, the mental body's energy level is in perfect synchronization to the high vibrations and influences of this cycle, and with it is the mental ability to create, imagine, visualize, and bring into perfect alignment and then into reality whatever is imagined.

Imagination and experience are now on the same level. Everything is possible, and nothing impossible. Everything is seemingly attainable on any level.

The etheric body is at its awakening, for now the ideals of a higher mental and spiritual self, begun in the last cycle, has infused the etheric with its power.

The emotional body's use of its high energy charge is better harnessed and more in control due in part to the influence and experiences of the last period, along with a heightened interest in the arts, religion, and the higher things of life.

The four lower bodies are in perfect alignment for self-mastery to move forward and be accomplished within this period. Those seeking spiritual awakening also may be able to find complete synchronization.

History is replete with the accomplishments of individuals within this age range, some of whom have made their marks before age thirty-five, while others were able to set the stage for all the accomplishments that followed.

CHAPTER 13

COSMIC LAW
HUMAN SERVICES/CYCLES

It is not surprising that when we examine the Republic of the United States of America and its constitution, among the qualifications to become a public servant, that is, to serve in government, are age requirements. As a senator, for example, you must be at least thirty years old and for members of Congress, at least twenty-five.

At the beginning of the writing of this book, in 2007, out of more than 525,000 elected officials,[1] there were 814 under the age of thirty-five, that is, in their fifth cycle of seven years and in a state of readiness for the next seven years.

In the next period, between age thirty-five and forty-two, period six[2] witnesses the development of true knowledge through investigation.

There is a restless quality that surfaces and leads to the improvement of humanitarian and brotherly emotion. The desire is to explore and discover hidden facts of life and, further, to share this knowledge and information with others. Motivation is selflessness; many find themselves giving to charity and/or giving back charitably.

The period of true maturation is the development of the mental body's residual powers and the commencement of its eminent fusion with the power of the etheric body. This period is a continuity of the prior, with a furtherance of the spiritual awakening. It is the maturation of the mind to the knowledge of what is important and offers permanency in our lives.

Restlessness is created by the realization that it is not the pursuit of riches or the selfish attainment of worldly treasures that had been important factors, and while there is the understanding of the role earthly gains has played in our earthly journey, a new understanding and awakening directs us to be more selfless and to share what we have, whether it's just knowledge and our time or, if wealth is at our disposal, the sharing of it for the benefit of the masses.

I like to refer to this period as the period of the Epiphany, the manifestation of the Christ consciousness, and the essence of what true brotherly love really means. For those on the earthly journey of quest, searching but not knowing exactly what their purpose is or should be, this is a period of quiet reflection, thought, and meditation for them as well.

Many involved in interpersonal relationships find that within this period, especially after the age of forty, their minds are ready for permanency in a close relationship, if there was none present prior. While others have the feeling that they have found themselves, others opt for public office, feeling they can be of best service in that area.

In the seventh period,[3] ages forty-two to forty-nine, the self-mastery is centered on the philosophical development. There is a strong desire to rest and to meditate. This cycle is the beginning of the *new birth* or *the new person*. The mind is focused mainly on religion and philosophy, mainly on spiritual development rather than on worldly or business development. A new person is actually emerging, with new hopes and new desires. In fact, the work of the last seven years is in preparation for this new ideological viewpoint and goal to which the individual now launches himself or herself.

This new ideal is still strongly driven by the need to serve, and for this *new person emerging*, it's almost as if there is a chance to correct the ills of past years. It is indeed the rejuvenation of life and light within the cells, creating newly energized lower bodies and reenergized physical power within the physical body, along with the mental power surge in the mental body, with strong emotional desires to help and "save the world" so to speak. The emotional body is re-energized, and the urge to be better and to do better, with the mind turning sharply toward religion and philosophical matters, infuses the etheric body with renewed power.

Some feel that they can best fulfill the humanitarian need through public service in office. Money is not the object. In fact, several elected officials even refuse salaries because of this strong desire to serve, driven by the vibrations of that cosmic cycle, and so many do enter into public service.

According to the Constitution of the United States, to hold the office of president of the United States, you must be at least thirty-five years or older, in the sixth period, ages thirty-five to forty-two. Of the forty-three presidents of the United States, none who held office was under the age of forty. The youngest was Teddy Roosevelt, aged forty-three, and the oldest was Ronald Regan, aged seventy when the office of presidency was assumed.

All were in their seventh cycle and beyond, which begins at age forty-two, the period when *the new person emerges*. Seven presidents were actually in their forties, which is in the seventh cycle, ages forty-two to forty-nine. The fifth and sixth periods were the periods of preparation, where the power within the four lower bodies created a conscious awakening in the fifth and sixth periods, which then launched these individuals into the rebirth of a new person in the seventh period, thus beginning a new set of cycles all over again, albeit now in a continuance of spiritual and psychic awakening, thus furthering what had begun prior.

Over the past ten decades, the average age[4] of an elected official was forty-nine, which ends the seventh cycle and begins the next round of seven cycles or, for further simplification, the eighth cycle. The average age of the members of the House of Representatives was fifty-four, again, the eighth cycle (or the first cycle of the next seven), which begins at age forty-nine to fifty-six. Senators average 59.5 in age for those entering and serving in public office, the second cycle of seven years of the second round of cycles of the seventh or ninth cycle.

In the eighth period,[5] ages forty-nine to fifty-six, or the first cycle of the next round of seven years of seven cycles, there is a retirement from personal and/or selfish ambition.

Twenty-six US presidents ascended to office in their fifties, in the eighth cycle, ages forty-nine to fifty-six; nine in their sixties, which is the ninth cycle or the second round of the second cycle of seven years, ages fifty-six to sixty-three; and one president was age seventy, the end of the tenth cycle or the beginning of the eleventh cycle or the third round within the second set of seven-year cycles, which is from age seventy to seventy-seven.

There is less and less focus on physical attributes and prowess, which is, in turn, then compensated for by a highly developed and attuned psychic and mental nature. While the body changes physically, losing power as well as its great ability to fight diseases, the mental is infused with more power, fusing more and more with the etheric and gradually moving us from physical to spiritual beings.

Therefore, if we closely follow the cosmic law and the electrical impulses and energies of the cycles, we would find significant information and changes taking place, which not only can verify cosmic influence in our lives but, to some degree, also enable us to judge the approximate age of someone by observing their habits, thought process, and in general, their desires to do and to be, even if the means to do so is not possible due to their circumstances. This is not coincidental; this is cosmic law. Understanding it best prepares you for the future and your eventuality. Preparation + opportunity = positive results.

The next cycle[6] of seven years, ages fifty-six to sixty-three, the ninth period, witnesses a further declination of the physical power, as in the prior period, with an increase in psychic power.

The mental capabilities of the individual may fall off somewhat as well. However, the idea is that the individual in each proceeding seven-year cycle is more inclined to achieve certain levels of self-mastery as cosmic law dictates, with the psychic powers elevating to higher heights and the psychic and spiritual growth eventually arriving full circle toward the essence of our purpose and the return back to that from which we came and were separated.

By the time Ronald Regan left office in 1989, at the end of his second term of four years, and almost parallel to that, at the end of his ninth cycle of seven years and the beginning of his next cycle of seven years at ages seventy-seven to eighty-four, he had begun to show signs of advancing age and perhaps initial signs of Alzheimer's disease.

Those who have studied the history of the United States and its origins are privy to some of the seemingly strange phenomenons and so-called coincidental aspects of its history. The early settlers[7] used the Bible as a guide for the political organization of the early federation, borrowing from Galatians, Peter, Exodus, Deuteronomy, and Leviticus, initially seeking to create a republic much like the one described in the Bible about the Israelites, and the establishment of secret brotherhood societies helped to direct the course of the American Revolution. The United States is indeed steeped in mysticism.

In George Washington's[8] first address, he stated, "No people can be bound to acknowledge and adore the invisible hand which conducts the affairs of men more than those of the United States."

George Washington[9] was a member of the Freemasons (referred to as the secret society during the 1800s), and so were most of the signers of the Declaration of Independence and the Constitution of the United States. Of the fifty-six signers of the Declaration of Independence, approximately nineteen were known or referenced Masons, and as many as fifty-three of the fifty-six were actually Masons according to other estimates. Of the forty-three presidents of the United States, at least sixteen were known to be Masons.[10]

Other estimates are higher, as well as numerous U.S. senators, Supreme Court justices, medical and religious practitioners, U.S. military leaders, authors, publishers, business people, and foreign leaders. The Freemasons had a hand in the American Revolution, as well as in the unification of the early nation of seaboard states.

But what are the Freemasons all about, and what or how do they contribute to self-mastery? I will attempt to answer some of these questions by shedding some light on this and other so-called secret organizations.

CHAPTER 14

COSMIC LAW
FREEMASONS AND SYMBOLISMS

Freemasons[1] believe in the supreme being Christ and in a philosophy that holds man's spiritual life as being of utmost importance.

Like the Rosicrucians (another secret society), Freemasons have studied spiritual and cosmic laws and, in so doing, have acquired the knowledge of how to use what the universe offers every individual to the benefit of each of its members who faithfully adhere to the philosophical teachings symbolically embodied in the step-by-step, grade-by-grade teachings of spiritual evolution, thus regenerating through discipline to becoming a perfected man.

Freemasonry, according to W.L. Wilmshurst,[2] author of *The Meaning of Masonry*, offers among other things "a philosophy of the spiritual life of man and a diagram for the process of regeneration," which is quite similar to the stages that must be undertaken for self-mastery, the building and transformation of the soul from its lower nature to one of supreme light.

There are many conspiracy theories[3] involving Freemasonry, including it being a Jewish front for world dominion, the Illuminati or New World Order that secretly controls all aspects of society and government, supported in part by the fact that many political leaders are Freemasons as cited above, including the theory that the September 11 attacks were "astrological in nature, predicted as part of the hidden war between Masonry and Islam."

While many of the symbols in American society, such as the national seal (Great Seal) and the U.S. dollar bill, contain Masonic symbols, the architectural design of the nation's capital, Washington, D.C., some might suggest, is replete with satanic and occult diametrics. Their relationship to evil conspiratorial theories are promulgated due in part to the secretive nature of Freemasonry practices, supported by the fact that many in positions of power in the world are members of this order, even though membership is not exclusive to those of that kilt and is open to just about anyone.

Here are some facts. Masons were at the forefront in the building of the United States as a new nation. All except five of the fifty-five members of the Constitutional Convention were Masons.[4] All the leading generals in the Continental Army were Masons. The Constitution itself, particularly its freedoms, was a document that embodied the principles of the Masonic brotherhood.

The national seal of the United States is a Masonic fraternity emblem. None of the symbols are coincidental: the thirteen olive branches representing the rule of the Prince of Peace by the authority of God or in Hebrew, Jehovah; the Eagle, the spiritual vision for and of the American people.[5] The number 13 is repeated many times on the seal: thirteen arrows, thirteen olive branches, and thirteen pieces for the coat of arms.

The unfinished pyramid, with thirteen rows of masonry on the pyramid, is unfinished because of the spiritual work still to be done to align the soul and the spirit once more in the I AM THAT I AM Christ's perfection, our individual journeys to self-mastery.[6] The number 13 is a reminder that we are the twelve tribes, plus the Levites—the thirteen tribes of Israel, the *novus ordo seclorum* (new order of the ages).

Most of us, when developing and/or creating a new business, company, club, corporation, even a country, or nation, would incorporate our beliefs, attestations, symbolisms, proofs, signature, or evidence to it, for it signifies our work. The Masons felt this way as evidenced by these symbolisms on the national seal and elsewhere. Just as the Constitution serves as a reminder of her history and promise that has withstood many attacks, so too are the subtle and not-so-subtle symbolic reminders within and without.

The pyramids of Africa and its construction are a constant marvel for its geometric precision. Cosmic law is geometrically precise; nature and natural laws are geometrically precise. Science has always used geometry to measure with precision the success of formulas and various experiments.

Many so-called secret societies have borrowed from these geometric teachings and principles in Africa and Europe and have scientifically studied and used these laws to create a better world and planet in most cases. There are some who have used the same principles for selfish, self-centered, negative purposes and have thus paid awful prices, for within spiritual and cosmic laws is the law of compensation. Whatever you give to the universe, that will you also receive; whatever you sow, that will you also reap.

We have read about it. Some of us may have experienced it up close and/ or perhaps personal—"You live by the sword or gun, you die by it." If it's for the good, it will last. If ordained by God, none can destroy nor diminish it, for it will outlast even them. If any of these brotherhoods or societies or sects are not for spiritual awakening, they too will not last.

Throughout history, in Africa, Eastern Europe, Asia, and in other parts of the world, symbols have always been widely used in religion, social affairs, and in business as a means of identification and bonding with those who share similar philosophies and membership rites.

The Catholic Church, for example, has many symbols. Take for example the ring. Bishops adopted the wearing of the ring to symbolically show their service or dedication to their belief and to the service of the church. Bishops therefore received a ring at their consecration ceremony.

The pope's ring (referred to as Fisherman's ring) is a signet ring inscribed with the name of the pope, and this encircles a representation of Saint Peter in a fishing boat.[7] To Catholics and those who follow the faith, the ring attests to the status of that individual as head of the Catholic Church. To the pope, the ring symbolizes his papal belief, and because it is often used as a seal, the ring is destroyed after his death.

Other organizations (such as the Rosicrucian Brotherhood[8]) considered to be another secret brotherhood society; Greek societies, such as Phi Beta Kappa (motto: "Love of wisdom, the guide of life"), an academic honor society for college students that was the first to adopt a Greek-letter name (adopted it so as to secretly disguise the name and thus the purpose of the organization); and thousands of fraternities (male houses) and sororities (female) were created for social, literary, academic, and community service purposes and have all used secrecy, symbolism, and rituals as part and parcel of its membership.

Skull and Bones (Yale University) or Chi Delta Theta (Asian sisterhood out of the University of California) has at its base deep secrecy, rituals, and symbolism for its members. The military in the initiation of its recruits, while perhaps not necessarily acceptable as any military code of law or conduct, are aware of rituals and hazings by members for the initiation of new recruits.

The Mafia; other violent gangs, such as the Bloods and the Crips; and other religious and nonreligious sects and organizations in their practices have utilized symbols and symbolism, as well as secrecy, in their operations. This in itself is not enough to denigrate or deem an organization evil simply because the membership practices or rituals might be obscure. We must go one step further and examine the body of work of that organization and then make an honest appraisal and judgment accordingly.

The fact remains that the majority of these organizations were formed for the social, business, political, and /or religious unification and advancement of its members and for the purpose of community service, and many have done just that. There are a few who may have begun with high and worthy ideals but allowed some of its members to tarnish its reputation through selfish indulgence for personal gains.

Each of us must exercise the principles of our spiritual teachings: "Judge not that you be not judged, for with what judgment you judge, by this you will be judged" (Matthew 7:1-2).[9]

I am neither denouncing nor promoting any particular group. You ought to use your wisdom and exercise your own free will and judgment in this matter. I am merely stating what is factual. Each of these organizations have their challenges.

The fact is that it is spiritual wisdom that you must yoke yourself with those of like mind for positive upliftment and personal and spiritual wealth and growth if you are to attain self-mastery. "Do not be unequally yoked together with unbelievers. For what fellowship has righteousness with lawlessness? And what communion has light with darkness?" (2 Corinthians 6:14).[10]

You cannot play in mud and not get muddy, and once this has happened, all who witness would know where you have been and what you have done. Therefore, your associations will help determine and cast your fate, choosing wisely should not and must not be by chance. It too must be accomplished with almost geometrical precision, and if you have indeed exercised wisdom, which is based on true understanding or understanding of the truth and acting in accordance with it, you would have chosen wisely.

The journey to self-mastery is inevitable. Once we have begun to live, we have begun the journey. Each of us will eventually make the journey even prior to the consciousness that we are on that road. While some may delay the process through procrastination or by choosing routes and paths that may lead to dead ends and varying crossroads, we will, once persistent, eventually get to points of progress. Our choices determine the types of encounters we experience in our travels, as well as how soon we arrive or if we ever.

Those of us who give up and give in may see this journey end, only to begin again anew in another place and time. All the more why we must press on and persevere as shining examples for others of what perseverance begets.

Those who attain the level of mastership as spiritual leaders, Freemasons, Rosicrucians, Alchemists, or as members of other organized societies or sects, whether through personal trial, error, and eventual triumph, understand the importance of working in harmony with spiritual and cosmic laws and with the cyclictic energies that abound.

These masters know that self-mastery oftentimes comes with a price, and that price is often a sacrifice of some kind, but once determined, understand that it can only be achieved by working in harmony with the universe. Know this: when you desire something, the universe conspires in helping you to achieve it, and our destiny lies as a gift in our hands.

Keep in mind that the cycle of life herein referred to as the cycles or periods, like life, is continuous and as immortal as energy, having neither a beginning nor an ending but yet begins and ends at some points within the continuous concentric circle of light. It is indeed continuous and infinite. We only attempt to define or measure this time for our earthly purposes and business, for in effect, other than in our conscious states, time and space are nonexistent. My journey in this truth began when I discovered this fact. Stay connected.

CHAPTER 15

THE BODY CONNECTION SCIENTIFIC, COGNITIVE, AND IMAGINATIVE

For self-mastery, we must understand and fully accept that we're all masters of our own destinies and not merely victims of fate. The outcome of our lives rests in our hands. Our choices oftentimes determine our fate. Our fate does not determine our actions as some have falsely believed, and because we have the power of choice, we must live with and by the choices we make.

As we journey up the road to self-mastery, the importance of elevating humanity to the level of cooperative, healthful, and harmonious living becomes paramount and requires the research and the analysis of all available information—scientific, cognitive, and imaginative—and so we must like hunters always be in search of the truth wherever it may lead us. And so we arm ourselves with *belief, expectation, desire, hope, faith, honesty,* and *emotion.*

Belief Trust and confidence are in part ways to define belief, which is an ingredient of faith. Acceptance has already taken place. It has been established. In programming, what you wish for yourself, there must be the acceptance of it even before it is wished for. Therefore, belief places imagination (what you envision) and experience (what you already know by doing) on the same dimension or level. You cannot have mastery over anything without belief.

Expectation Goes beyond belief because it is unquestioning. Expectation fosters preparation, even in the absence of evidence, for it is faith demonstrated in its most potent state. The power of expectation is seen in the effort of preparation. One feeds the other, creating an emotional charge of a cause-and-effect nature. Because the results of expectation are based in the future, it helps to nurture faith.

Desire We cannot accomplish anything without desire; therefore, we only attempt to accomplish when desire is present. Desire provides the emotional and physical charge necessary and needed to begin, follow through, and then fulfill tasks. Desire is the spark of the lower bodies' fire, particularly the emotional body. Some refer to desire as a wish, the effort of acting in faith out of a need to act; thus, desire is a characteristic or ingredient of faith.

Hope This is the combination of expectation and desire. It inspires success and is the promise of what is anticipated from the work that was done. Success is eminent when hope is positive. Therefore, the presence of hope is always a good sign for success. Hope, while not a characteristic of faith, must embrace faith in order for inspiration to remain a strong forceful presence. "But hope that is seen is not hope; for why does one still hope for what he sees? But if we hope for what we do not see, we eagerly wait for it with perseverance" (Romans 8: 24-25).[1]

Faith The substance of hope, but more than hope. It is "the substance of things hoped for, the evidence of things not seen" (Hebrews 11:1)[2]. There are more references to faith in the Bible and in spiritual laws than to almost any other characteristic. Self-mastery is enlarging faith in self.

The things seen in the world—in fact, the world as we see it—is largely made of the things that are invisible. Whether you believe the framing of the world came out of the concept of the so-called big bang theory or by the word of God. Even if you were to argue for the concept of the "big bang" as the way the world was framed or the beginning of time, the very elements that became the synthesis of this eruption had to have had its origination from *somewhere*.

To evolve predicates out of that which was before and that which was before it and so on, and even if evolution were to be the standard of your belief, it still rests on the evidence of things not seen, which in effect is what faith is and therefore what you believe in.

John 1:1-5 tells us what that *somewhere* was. It was the *word*, "and the word was God and was with God, and . . . all things were made through him and without him nothing was made that was made."[3] My point is not to convince you on the fallacies of the evolution theory—those fallacies are self-evident (science has its place)—but rather to point out that in order for us to persevere in life, we must exercise faith, that is, the belief in a future not evidenced. That is the true testament of faith as we pursue self-mastery.

Honesty Being fair and righteous in the way we behave and speak is the essence of honesty. Feigning feelings we do not have is being dishonest with ourselves and therefore dishonest with others. This is the beginning of the breakdown of healthy communication brought about through unhealthy communication patterns that involve hiding our true feelings and purpose. Hence, we block our pathway to self-mastery.

It is worth a moment for us to examine ethics in the way we speak and behave and how it assists in the mastery of self.

Communicating Ethically In the process of attempting to change the attitudes and/or actions of others, we must use persuasion. In order to persuade, we can use three tactics[4]:

1. *Reasoning*—appealing to the individuals' sense of logic; what is plausible or what makes sense.
2. *Credibility*—making a conviction based on personal expertise, trustworthiness, and/or likability. There must be consistency in actions and words, truthfulness, and full disclosure of information and facts. Making sure the information is kept in perspective.
3. *Emotions*—making sure the language used relates to the climate of the situation, therefore having personal knowledge of the situation, and being able to identify your personal feelings about the situation is a necessity.

Being ethical therefore means communicating in ways that gives others the freedom of choice without force. Being ethical (honest) therefore must be paramount in the journey to self-mastery if free will is to be exercised.

Emotion Utilizing the highly charged power of the emotional body to create force and vividness is what triggers feelings and all the components that forms the right attitude for the accomplishment of whatever tasks needs to be accomplished.

Our emotions engage us actively in the task, creating in us the right attitude. The more charged up we are, the more effort we will exude since the more important we will regard the task. The more seriously we regard the task, the better the results will be. Faith remains the mainstay of these seven characteristics.

CHAPTER 16

SILVA MIND CONTROL METHOD JOURNEY II CONNECTION

To find truth, begin your search with self.

—T. L. Fraser

My earlier astral projection experience pushed me to seek answers, mostly the truth about my existence. I decided to and did read the Bible almost from cover to cover at one point, plus countless other books regarding life, death, spirituality, and other dimensions.

Years later, while in college (graduate school), I decided to do a television show on hypnosis for one of my graduate college projects. This project ended up being a mind control course called Silva Mind Control. So as to have firsthand up close and personal experience as to the credibility and claims of the techniques, I took the course myself.

The course claimed to be able to allow individuals to function at higher levels of intelligence, thereby enabling them to control stress, improve memory, and recall and master tasks that require great effort and will. I wound up being able to put into perspective some of my earlier astral projection experience and connected the dots to projection from this two-day intensive course.

On the final day of the course, we were paired for what was known as a "healing at a distance exercise." Everyone was asked to bring the name of someone they knew personally who had an ailment. The only information required was the name, age, sex, and general address of that individual. An orientologist (each individual of the pair took a turn at this role) would then guide or orient the performing psychic (the person you were paired with; each person took a turn at this role also) through the meditation process to detect and correct any ailments.

Let me assure you that this was not a game we were playing. Everyone took this seriously, for this was, for everyone who took the course, the proof that the techniques worked. My case was a nine-year-old girl. I was asked to place her on my "mental screen" (mind's eye or work area) and detect and correct any ailments I perceived.

I followed the instructions of the orientologist and perceived on my mental screen a little girl with a plastic tube tied tightly around her chest. It seemed to be constricting her breathing. The end of the tube leading into her chest was black. I mentioned what I observed to the orientologist who had brought the case to me. She asked me to correct what I observed and to continue examining the subject.

To correct, I visualized the defective area of the body of the subject surrounded by white light. I also visualized that person in a situation having full and normal use of that defective organ or part of the body. In this case, I visualized the young girl without the tube around her chest and saw her breathing naturally and easily.

I continued to search for other possible ailments. I then noticed that one side of her jaw seemed to be misshaped as if it were swollen. The orientologist indicated that she had no information about any type of injury or ailment in that area. I immediately corrected this defect.

After coming out of my meditational level, the orientologist and I discussed the findings. The young girl was her niece, and she suffered severely from asthma. My reference of this ailment was the plastic tube tied tightly around her chest, constricting her breathing. Initially, the orientologist indicated that she had no information regarding the girl's jaw, and then suddenly, she exclaimed that weeks prior, her niece had fallen off her bike and injured her jaw.

This exercise and the information blew me away. There was an intelligence that enabled me to gather the information consciously and with complete awareness. I did not know the girl, never saw her in my life, and in fact, I'd never seen the orientologist in my life prior to this exercise and have never seen her again since.

Remarkably, this individual was able to correctly detect the ailment in the case I presented to her when it was my turn as the orientologist. This was the first of many cases for me, and the level of my accuracy has been astonishing since then.

This approach to self-mastery covered techniques on meditation, imagination, visualization, and projection, referred to as extrasensory projection (ESP),[1] with various useful techniques for problem solving and eliminating bad habits. Some of these techniques will be discussed as they relate to self-mastery.

The roles of projection and imagination in this course were vital.

Projection: It is picturing the end results or the success of a venture just the way it was envisioned. We picture ourselves in those future situations that, in effect, help to bring about the successful changes in those future situations. "How so?" you may ask. Well, remember the framing of the world. From the invisible came the visible, and if we really stop for a moment and think about it, *all things now visible were once invisible until its creation*—the world, mankind, and things like the airplane and cell phones.

By the power vested in each and every one of us through the Christ consciousness within, we are able to create the visible from the invisible, beginning with just an imagination of that which we wish to create. The stronger, clearer, and more vivid those projected images, the sharper, more focused, and clearer the creation.

There are many books on the power of visualization; therefore, this is not a new concept at all, even though many of us fail to apply this principle righteously in our lives. The dangers of drugs and television (which is a drug) are real, although let me quickly qualify it when I say television programs, for it is not homogeneous since not all programs stifle the imagination and dull the senses, disabling our creativity and lulling our minds into a passive, almost senseless stupor.

Minds in nullified states cannot create and/or expand. So Silva Mind Control utilizes visualization and projection to stimulate the brain in a mental state of constant active alertness.

The projection exercises[2] gives students visualization practice by allowing them to project into substances like metals, plants, animals, and other inanimate objects. Impressions are gathered and interpreted till eventually there is a backlog of imaginative travel and inner experiences that then becomes vital for the interpretation of sensations that may be experienced later in life.

Silva Mind Control thus uses projection to help students develop the imagination by actively participating, sensing, feeling, touching, and examining with our mind's eye, as we would, any visible scene in the tangible world in a real situation. Eventually, an inner world is structured and created, where the individual can go to work on projects that allow them to work on self. Projection then is a necessary tool for self-mastery, visualizing what you wish and then achieving it as was visualized.

As you may recall in my astral projection, I visualized prior to the exercise exactly what I would do and how, and as I envisioned, so it was.

Imagination: If you cannot imagine, you cannot dream, and for those who cannot dream, I wonder what life must be like for them.

All actions begin with thoughts, manifested by the word, which gives it life and then the action that brings it into being tangible. This exercise of the use of picturization or imagination thus becomes extremely important in self-mastery since mastering self is knowing self first, so we must bring into view how we see ourselves, and this requires picturization.

Some of us may try for years and never see ourselves as others see us, or we may see ourselves in a state of total denial, and unfortunately, this may be our reality.

Imagining is daydreaming or forming images. In the book *Mind Play*, by Jerome Singer and Ellen Switzer, several benefits of daydreaming[3] are discussed, such as control over undesirable habits, increased empathy, sexuality, heightened self-awareness, and increased awareness and appreciation for the high arts, such as literature, art, and music, and while projection awakens our inner life making more vivid impressions, the more we project, imagination forms a reality all its own at an inner dimension, causing as well as reflecting inner experiences and thus an inner life.

Therefore, by utilizing imagination, where the process of creating begins, the world can now be examined from three perspectives, each having its own reality: *our senses*, outward reality, sensations, or senses; *science*, where theories and experiments are utilized to draw factual conclusions; and *imagination*, where we create from the invisible that which is visible and tangible.

We cannot and should not therefore discredit the imagination simply because it differs from science and our senses. In fact, if we believe in anything, then that thing really does exist for us. This belief then becomes reinforced with results. This is how we evaluate both science and our senses and this is how we have to examine imagination.

Psychics are able to take the invisible and sense at inner dimensions that which has, is going to, or will transpire. How? By being receptive at both the outer and inner dimensions.

The Silva method showed students ways of identifying the inner sensations from our external experiences by using points of references for these imaginative sensations.

Imaginative impressions, as it is pointed out, reflect reality from a different perspective, which we learn to interpret as we move closer and closer toward self-mastery.

Meanwhile, I continued to explore others avenues to self-mastery and to understanding our existence.

A small group of us, including the professor who had encouraged me to take a look at the "mind control" classes for my television show, met on a semiregular basis. The group explored the philosophy that quite possibly our future and the future of mankind was inexplicably and inescapably intertwined with our ancestors; thus, to discover the truth in this present lifetime, we must connect with our ancestral past and bridge the gap.

What I learned from the two meetings I attended was that we all have tremendous spiritual energy that must be harnessed and focused. I also learned the importance of belief, faith, and open-mindedness, which in effect helps us to truly be accepting of people and ideas and to examine and evaluate those ideas without prejudice.

I did produce a thirty-minute television show on "mind control," and included as my guests were a lecturer and a student from the mind control school. The studio audience were enthralled with the techniques demonstrated, and I was equally impressed, for not only did I continue to practice the techniques, but I have also used many of them as teaching tools wherever and whenever practical in my higher educational teaching. I have since designed and continue to teach various self-improvement techniques based on some of these principles.

There are those who are spiritually advanced and possess the gift of clairvoyance. Children, because of their unpolluted spirits and souls, are true examples of the display of faith required for self-mastery. "Assuredly I say unto you, unless you are converted and become as little children, you will by no means enter the kingdom of heaven" (Matthew 18:3).

CHAPTER 17

PROGRAMMING SELF-MASTERY
OTHER CONNECTIONS

We must nurture all the gifts given to us. Children, if encouraged and directed positively, would be great teachers of adults, but unfortunately, we are taught to fear and oftentimes despise that which we do not understand, and thus we lose our blessings.

I've had many conversations with individuals who are spiritually gifted and/or enlightened. Some of them understand the importance of having the gifts they possess; others are fearful of it.

A former client falls in the latter category. She has the gift of clairvoyance but was very fearful of herself, not understanding how to positively utilize or even harness this ability. She related to me what to her I'm sure must have been a terrifying ordeal when still in her childhood at her aunt's home one afternoon.

Standing in the doorway, she saw what appeared to be two red beams of light, which in fact, turned out to be eyes peering at her through the darkness (from the other dimension). Suddenly, from across the room, the neck of that entity stretched from across the room (as if it were made of elastic) and peered curiously at her. She could not leave the building fast enough and, after that incident, prayed that the ability (gift) to see would be taken away from her.

Most recently, I had a conversation with the aunt of one of my self-mastery students. The aunt (who we will refer to as Sylvia) worked at a beauty shop for hair and nails. While to some, her experience would be described as frightening and traumatic, yet there was calmness to her experience, even in the way she recalled the incident, and this speaks perhaps to her faith and/or peace of mind.

She told me about one of her clients, whom we will call Mary. Mary was a regular customer at the beauty shop.

Sylvia, while waiting for her customer, rushed outside to park her car properly and discovered a somewhat somber spectacle in the parking lot. Everyone was standing around silently. In her haste, she never stopped to inquire about the spectacle. However, on her return to the shop, she was informed that there had been a fatal accident in the parking lot, and suspicions were it could be Mary. It turned out to be Mary, for as Sylvia ventured once more into the parking lot, she could actually see the partial body of a female under the wheel of a large van.

Mary never arrived for her appointment that day. However, the very next day, as Sylvia sat in her bathtub, suddenly out of nowhere, Mary appeared with two other individuals. Sylvia described their appearance as nonfrightening and nonthreatening. She was not drinking nor was she sleeping. This was not a vision in a dream. Sylvia was fully conscious and aware.

Mary was standing a few feet from the bathtub, just as she appeared in life, blond and beautiful. Behind her was a female with dark hair; and behind her in the distance, a male dressed in a suit.

For some odd reason, Sylvia said she felt no fear at the presence before her. Mary addressed her, asking of her what she considered to be a strange favor. Mary wanted Sylvia to pass along a message to her daughter whose nuptials was only weeks away. The message was that her daughter should not marry the man she had planned to.

Sylvia's response to Mary's request was disbelief, as she thought to herself and then aloud to Mary that the family had just recently lost a loved one. Mary's daughter was now motherless and, here it is, she was being told by this deceased woman to deliver another emotional blow to the grieving daughter.

As Sylvia listened to Mary's request, she was struck by it. This was not an ordinary request. This was a life-altering decision to break off her engagement and wedding plans.

Sylvia did not know Mary's daughter. In fact, she did not know her family at all, except for the deceased woman's sister-in-law, and their relationship was purely business since the sister-in-law also had her hair and nails done at the same beauty shop. Sylvia curiously inquired of Mary as to why she was chosen for this task, Mary's response was that Sylvia had walked through her when she had ventured outside to view the accident. Perhaps at that moment, there was a spiritual connection and Mary felt or knew Sylvia could assist her with the wish she could no longer directly fulfill.

Mary insisted and, in fact, implored Sylvia to fulfill what seemed to be a final wish. Meanwhile, the woman standing behind her kept on urging Mary to hurry up, stating that they needed to leave at once.

Sylvia inquired how she would be able to pass information on to someone she did not know, and most importantly, why would her daughter believe all this that was happening. Mary simply told her not to worry and that her daughter *will* believe. Sylvia promised her that she would pass on the message on one condition: that she never visits her again. She agreed, and as they had entered, they disappeared.

Days later, Sylvia reiterated the story to the sister-in-law of the deceased, who was then able to verify the identities of Mary's companions, based on her descriptions. They were her deceased sister and brother. The brother died years before. The sister died years after. Mary's daughter never married her fiancé. She believed Sylvia.

Another friend recalled her experience while working as a nanny for a family in New York. This friend of mine has the gift of sensing. She eventually quit the job because the situation had become too traumatic for her. The grandmother of the little girl she attended (the mother of the woman who had hired her) kept the spirit of her deceased mother around the house.

The woman's spirit, now a ghost, was not at rest and not very happy at the prospect of someone else taking care of her granddaughter and felt the need to express her anger at the new temporary resident of her room. To the occupants of the home, the presence of the entity did not seem unusual nor did it appear to disturb them in any way. In fact, to the little girl who she was being paid to care for, the presence of this entity was just another nuisance, and she would indicate this by making quips, such as "It's back again."

According to Shakespeare in Hamlet's soliloquy, "Conscience makes cowards of us all," and perhaps it is the fear of not knowing what we may face that disquiets our souls, and this discomfort is based on the experiences of our present life and the ways in which we may have handled our adversities.

Mastering self is overcoming our fears, and our greatest fear is the unknown. Gypsies and fortune-tellers have made wonderful careers off of the fears of others. Many have paid millions to know the unknown about themselves and then use that information as though someone else knows more about them than they do of themselves.

Unfortunately, even if told factually about the unknown, many would still not believe, requiring verification from their senses and/or scientific proof. For this reason, many have followed blindly leaders who have led them down rocky paths to utter chaos and destruction, believing unwisely that their future was secure in the hands of such leaders. We have numerous stories and examples of those tragedies. Fear then is just one more obstacle to overcome in the journey to mastery of self. "Yea though I walk through the valley of the shadow of death, I will fear no evil for you are with me, your rod and your staff they comfort me" (Psalms 23:4).[1]

Under spiritual law, the only person to fear is he who have power over your soul, God.

Our greatest enemy is our selves and the less we know of self, the more fearful we are or will be. Therefore, understanding how to live prosperously lies in how we treat evil, our fellow man, and ourselves. Keeping God's commandments gives us a good understanding of how to please God and become wise. The fear of death is the pretence of wisdom; the fear of God is the beginning of it.

T. Lobsang Rampa, writer and clairvoyant, talks about sitting by his window late at night and watching the wonderful sight of thousands upon thousands of earthly spirits in astral flight, their spirits attached to the physical bodies at the navel via blue silken cords that stretched and soared through the air in different channels and currents of energy as they lay in dreamy slumber, asleep to the physical world but quite awake to the spiritual.

This blue silken cord is the only link between that physical body and the soaring spirit. Once that cord snaps, the spirit is permanently separated from the physical body and the soul goes free.

As we become more advanced in our mastery of self through self-discovery in fervent prayer, supplication, affirmation, and practice, our spiritual awareness becomes lifted and sharpened. We are less fearful of self and are eventually able to have the mountaintop experience as we discover the place where the lower self is wed to the higher—the experience of flow where matter and spirit merge.[2]

Being able to trust and depend on our subconscious or on our sixth sense to provide us with the information we need for correct problem solving takes us out of the realm of one-dimensional existence. For those who are fortunate to have the gift of clairvoyance, recognize it is a gift. You're not insane, but you must use it wisely and only for the betterment of humanity.

You must pray for understanding, wisdom, and guidance in using this gift, and remember that the only person to be afraid of is yourself. You're always in control. No one can take away your power except if you give it to them. For those of us not as discerning, we can and will learn to be so through our self-mastery efforts.

A persistent type of behavior results from habits formed through repetition and other ingraining factors, referred to as programming, and this reinforces habit. Therefore, growing in the art of mastering self requires good programming, and good programming[3] consists of four principles:

1. Talking to yourself
2. Becoming highly conscious of self
3. Awareness of the subconscious as a source of information
4. Listening to yourself

Talking to Yourself: We do this constantly, and this is primarily how we program ourselves to do and be. These conversations or internal dialogues must mirror the types of conversations we would engage ourselves in with one another regarding things we wish to achieve and accomplish; therefore, self-dialogue must be courteous, respectful, gracious, positive, and truthful. "A good man out of the good treasure of his heart brings forth good; and an evil man out of the evil treasure of his heart brings forth evil. For out of the abundance of the heart his mouth speaks" (Luke 6:45 and Matthew 12:35).[4]

Internal conversations reinforces the beliefs of that individual, and those beliefs become manifested first in words and then in the actions of that individual. Our thoughts therefore are the silent conversations we have internally, which could be negative or positive based on our mindset. Therefore, keeping the heart with diligence is important, "for out of it spring the issues of life" (Proverbs 4:23)[5].

Talk to yourself. It is important, but the dialogue must be respectful, adhering to a high standard of morality and human kindness; gracious, being thankful and not thankless, expressing gratitude and not complaining; positive, conversing about what can and will be accomplished, and what can and will be successful; and truthful, not feigning or pretending to have feelings that do not really belong to us or hiding our real purpose from ourselves.

Becoming Conscious of Self Being conscious of self means becoming more aware of your habits, patterns of behavior, feelings, and how you respond to situations. We test our fortitude and character in times of adversity. How we react and behave speak to our character as well as to our awareness of self.

We begin to become conscious of self by the way other's react toward the things we say and do. The more we recognize and understand our behavior, the more conscious we are of self. In programming self-mastery, we must become aware of our triggers (what precedes an action, what follows it, and what transpires in the process). Ask yourself, "Who am I really?" and write down ten specific things you know about yourself. Be honest with your list and with yourself.

Create a list of between five and ten "good habits" and a separate list of "bad habits." Make sure they're habits and not characteristics; for example, smoking is a habit and not a characteristic and being soft spoken is a characteristic and not a habit. On the other hand, speaking loudly is a habit and not a characteristic. Therefore, habits come under our direct control and are ingrained through practice but can be gotten rid of by being conscious of its existence and being aware that it is an unattractive habit that you'd like to rid yourself of.

Some of these habits are a bit more complicated like lying. Not telling the truth can become habitual. It is therefore cultivated and then becomes characteristic, so too is honesty.

Because our culture allows us to practice diplomacy and graciousness to protect the feelings of others, we oftentimes would opt to not tell the truth about something others may have done or said or about a particular behavior of someone else that may be unpleasant; thus, we may develop the characteristic of being diplomatic, thoughtful, or gracious in our words.

The sometimes-brutal honesty in children is characteristic of children and is second nature to them. Honesty is also very important in programming self-mastery. You should not feign feelings you do not have since doing so breaks down healthy communications and, more so, healthy programming. Besides, you're only fooling yourself and no one else.

Honesty begins to become modified when children begin to learn the cultural mores of acceptability in speech and deeds. Thus, while it is an admirable trait, the natural characteristic of honesty in children is curbed to the extent where that truth is subjected to the position of political correctness in order for certain behaviors to be socially acceptable.

Becoming Aware of Your Subconscious as a Source of Information: The human mind seems to exist on two parallel yet connected levels: on the conscious and subconscious levels. The conscious level operates on the external, having outward awareness and utilizing the senses, while the subconscious operates on an inner consciousness level, with a separate awareness of its own. All external activities are recorded on the subconscious mind that has perfect memory; thus, we have conscious and subconscious actions.

The sum total of our past experiences is our subconscious, and what we think, feel, and do forms the basis of our experiences. These experiences[6] are then stored in the form of impressions. These impressions react with other impressions we have stored to produce tendencies. A tendency to do one thing or another is based on how the subconscious has analyzed the impressions. The exercise of these tendencies becomes character and identifies us from others, thus distinguishing our character(s) from someone else's. The tendencies lay dormant until the right condition comes about.

Therefore, two individuals from the same family or group will react to the same situation differently based on their character or based on the nature and strength of their character. Once the correct conditions are in place, then the fulfillment of the necessary conditions becomes responsible for activating impressions in the subconscious mind, and once this happens, what will follow is a particular behavior based on specific characteristics of the individual.

Although we all have free will, the free will act we exercise is in accord with our experiences or our character, that is, that sum total of all our past deeds, thoughts, and feelings. We may certainly act "out of character"; however, for the most part, we have a tendency to act "in character" based on our tendencies.

To change and to begin to approach self-mastery means recognizing that our subconscious is a great source of information we can utilize, and to help us in our efforts, the content of our minds must change. As we change the conscious mind, the subconscious mind receives new impressions. While the old impressions may still be present, it is pushed aside to make way for these new impressions. I take you back to my discussion of mental house cleaning,[7] ridding yourself of bad habits and programming new ones.

Therefore, it is necessary to tap into our subconscious for answers we cannot seem to fathom in our conscious aware states, for the subconscious has the power of deduction and the subconsciousness, while subordinate to the conscious, controls our bodily functions and our innate activities.

Thus, developing our self-awareness is paramount to successful and complete self-mastery. Self-awareness makes us pay closer attention to the urgings of our subconscious mind.

Listening to Yourself: The next chapter deals with listening and talks about the importance of listening in general, distinguishing between hearing and listening. Listening to yourself involves following the Christ consciousness within, the so-called sixth sense of discernment. While many of us may talk to ourselves, many of us seldom listen. We do not heed our own advice or even tune into the voice within. "If you would only learn to listen and be still, knowing I am God within."[8] Cosmic law principles tells us that within certain cyclictic frequencies, certain things are most likely to happen at a given time than others due to cosmic vibrations and alignments.

Understanding these vibrations by studying them through the patterns and impressions they leave behind in our lives and then tuning in to them and making mental notes as to when and how they occur would provide for us a blueprint to follow.

Nothing is coincidental in life. There is cause and effect, and while it helps to be in the right place at the right time, still we must be prepared when the opportunity presents itself, and part of that preparation is understanding how to enhance our chances of success while simultaneously decreasing chances of failure.

By tuning in and listening to self, we become more aligned with the voice of reasoning. Decisions are no longer made haphazardly but guided by inner awareness, utilizing the knowledge of unseen vibrations, cosmic urges, spiritual guidance, and experience. Sometimes we know because we just know, and that's when we are really listening.

CHAPTER 18

LISTENING

The only time learning occurs is when listening is present.

—T.L. Fraser

We could make listening our greatest friend and the most important and rewarding factor for self-mastery or our worst enemy, diminishing our capacity to love, trust, and live complete lives, depending on our understanding of how it works to promote change in our lives and how we utilize this skill.

We now understand that to program self-mastery and change, we must *listen to ourselves, talk to ourselves, listen to our subconscious,* and *be aware of our deeper consciousness, habits, responses,* and *reactions. Tuning* into our subconscious and following its instructions enable us to avoid costly mistakes and mishaps. Listening also involves these characteristics as well as complete awareness, and choosing the best possibilities for our self-mastery and success promotes efficacy in the listening experience.

What is listening?[1] It is the process of receiving, attending to, understanding, remembering, evaluating, assigning meaning to, and responding to aural and visual stimuli. Poor listeners have the inability to exercise sufficient control over or focus attention on any one thing at a time, and unfortunately, most of us are poor listeners.

Hearing is not synonymous with listening, although we tend to believe it is. We can hear and not listen; however, it is virtually impossible to listen and not hear. So what's the difference between the two? Hearing is effortless or automatic so long as the physical capability exists. Without even realizing it, we have virtually made a decision prior to the commencement of the process as to the importance of what we will hear and listen to.

Listening, on the other hand, requires engagement and effort. In fact, it requires work on our part. We must be discerning, analytical, and perceptive. Therefore, the approach to listening and hearing is quite different. We do employ various listening styles but do not necessarily categorize them as we are engaged in the process.

Appreciative Listening

This listening style[2] is employed when it comes to aesthetic values, such as listening to music. We would then make a judgment or determination as to its value to us. This determination is made almost immediately and could last a considerable length of time in its appreciative value to us. We demonstrate this by the frequency and the amount of attention we pay to the specifics of that object or subject when we are engaged with and in that particular act of listening.

Empathic Listening

This style[3] concentrates on feelings or attitudes rather than on the message. When the message is secondary within the listening process, then the emphasis is usually strongly emotional, either on the part of the speaker or the listener. In this instant, as the listener who has employed empathic listening, it suggests that the speaker is expressing feelings or attitudes that require you, the listener, to soothe, comfort, or at least provide for the speaker some clarity that you understand or share the emotional experience they are undergoing, for example, listening to a friend's problem.

Discriminative Listening

This style[4] involves the drawing of inferences from what the speaker has said and has not said to discern the total meaning of the message. The type of listening exercised in discriminative listening is also measured in terms of depth and surface listening efficacy. Focus is on both the verbal and the nonverbal, as well as on the content and relational messages. Attention must be paid to the literal as well as the hidden meanings from the cues the speaker is providing and as you evaluate the reasons for the message.

For example, being told of the benefits of a particular product but not being given all the facts about its side effects is an example of discriminative listening.

Analytical Listening

This style[5] involves listening for deeper meaning to understand, interpret, and analyze the message. Therefore, this listening style goes beyond the mere content of the message. It involves breaking down the message itself and its various meanings so as to determine the truthfulness of the content as well as its long-term effects. Being analytical should be exercised in a manner of honest search for truth rather than in an effort to be argumentative for its sake.

For self-mastery to begin to effect changes in our lives through the listening process, we must first be able to *focus attention* (tune in), disregard a multitude of distractions, and attend to what is important. We do this by first eliminating *physiological* and *psychological impediments.*

Psychological impediments or blockages affect our concerns, needs, and desires. We instinctively follow these urgings and will satisfy them first and foremost as listening priorities. Therefore, other messages we are supposed to pay attention to become less important and often take a backseat if the psychological impediments are not eliminated.

Similarly, eliminating the physiological impediments simply means removing any physical barriers, such as an object, a thing, or a person, that create a condition not conducive for maximizing listening, for example, a radio or loud voices or perhaps an object blocking your view physically. Additionally, learning how to relax and then applying those techniques to listening habits greatly enhances our capacity to improve listening and to improve self.

Certain techniques enable us to refocus our energies inwardly. Techniques that help practitioners create virtual getaways to their ideal place of relaxation is one positive way to make sure our listening conditions are well maintained so that we avoid and eventually eliminate distractions. But the questions still remain. Why are so many of us poor listeners? Why do most people stop listening, and how can we improve and/or master the art of listening?

I have created acronyms for the reasons why most people cease to listen in a simplistic way so that it could be easily retained and remembered.

Listening barriers are ADDD and APPN (two acronyms, nonmedical terms).

ADDD—(1) AD, Our *a*ttention *d*rifts: We normally and naturally drift in and out of the listening process and seldom retain the same intensity throughout. (2) D, We become *d*istracted: There are many distractions we must constantly deal with that are both external, such as someone distracting our attention by an action, or internal. Perhaps we are hungry at the moment and begin to think about what to eat. We can adjust to distractions or tolerate it, so that the distraction is no longer bothersome. (3) D, We *d*isagree: Once we disagree with the information being presented, we become unwilling to consider any aspect of the message we are receiving, and we eventually cease to listen.

APPN—(1) A, Too many *abstractions*: For the information to be attention grabbing, it must paint vivid images. We must be able to visualize the effects or results of what we hear. When this fails to happen, we tend to form our own opinions. (2) P, *Prejudiced*: Each of us bring into a situation our hang-ups, beliefs, feelings, and notions about things, and some of these beliefs we feel pretty strongly about. Therefore, we are quite inflexible about shifting positions concerning them and therefore, because of this prejudicial view, we oftentimes cease to listen.

PN—*Preconceived notions*: We draw impressions from appearances of others, and those appearances tend to color how we pay attention to messages. We are predispositioned to listen to who and/or what we may consider important, and if our impression of the messenger is not positive, then we will fine-tune our listening accordingly.

If we constantly fake attention, then that can become habitual, and without realizing it, we will tune out a speaker and allow our minds to wander as we pretend to pay attention. Consequently, we must be diligent about how we pay attention.

Overcoming Poor Listening Habits

Overcoming poor listening habits[6] means fine-tuning our listening skills. We learn to master various areas of our lives by exercising diligence in practicing the skills necessary to overcome the poor habit. We must, however, regard what we are doing seriously, and thus we must take listening seriously if we are to improve this skill.

First, we must *get ready to listen*. Even before we engage in the process, we must create the mindset that we are going to be fully engaged in listening. Do not prejudge the speaker or speech. Consider all speeches or discussions to be useful, whether it's interpersonal, intrapersonal, public, or mass communication forums.

Minimize misunderstandings. A determination must be made through querying whether the message we have heard is the message intended, and also whether it is the message others have heard. This is accomplished through active questioning. Additionally, we must identify any reasons for misunderstandings.

Don't be distracted. Leave them behind. Focus should be on the speaker and the speech or discussion and not on mannerisms, such as physical idiosyncrasies. If listening is viewed as a responsibility, it will be taken seriously and our engagement will be at high, intense levels.

Don't prejudge. There exists the temptation to prejudge the message even before hearing it based on simply how we feel about the topic and/or the speaker. Response must be toward the message; therefore, suspension of judgment is vital to avoid rushing to judgment. Hearing a person out before reacting must be practiced diligently.

Content first; delivery second. While meanings are in people and not merely words, the content of the message must provide meaning, therefore must be adhered to. So, as a listener on the pathway to mastering self, this must be lesson one. The content. Delivery is how those words are imparted—the action that says what we mean in a demonstrative way. This could simply be the words we choose to emphasize. Content must be separated from delivery.

Charismatic speakers or great salesmen have mastered styles or ways of making their points, sometimes at the expense of content—substance versus style.

Focus first on ideas (these must be sound or at the least reasonable) and then on delivery, that is, how these ideas will be presented. For individuals who have not yet mastered the art of speaking, it is sometimes difficult to listen to a speech and to separate its content from the delivery. The natural tendency is to stop listening altogether. However, if listening rules are adhered to and applied in concert, then mannerisms merely become temporary nuisances.

Record contents effectively. Listening more effectively often requires active engagement in the act of listening, and active engagement means recording the ideas heard. This often means effective note taking using diagrams, sketches, scales, or charts, and in our modern, technological age, in the twenty-first century, the use of audio and video recordings onto cassette tapes and CDs have proven effective.

Utilizing a numbering system can prove effective since it allows for remembering in a sequential manner. In fact *loci and peg systems*[7] enable listeners to memorize large volumes of information through a combination of numerical and key word memorization.

The act of writing or note taking assists in recording information in long-term memory just simply by the act of writing it down. Because practice makes perfect, until we have mastered the act, we must make the act of recording information habitual and, in conjunction with it, find more effective ways to cultivate effective listening habits.

We exist and function in a technological era where expediency and immediacy has had a costly impact on the way we communicate, resulting in a deficiency for details and detriment in quality in both our spoken and written forms of communication.

Our access to larger and larger volumes of information is exponential, and perhaps because of this, there might be the feeling of this urgency to (as quickly as possible) access this information and rapidly retrieve and communicate what we need. To enable this process, we have adopted abbreviated forms of communication.

The danger of this practice of abbreviated forms of text messaging, Internet language, and communicating in general has crept into standard writings on the higher educational levels, lowering the standards even further. College students, for example, in formal essays are writing the letter U instead of "you," "b4" instead of "before," and "U R" rather than "you are." Additionally, many fail to distinguish the difference between *then* and *than*. It seems to be enough to many of these students that it sounds the same—a listening problem specifically and a communication problem in general.

While some may feel the need for purpose of expediency to process information quickly due to the sheer volume of it, a disastrous precedent is being set, and we have begun to witness the denigration of acceptable standards in general and of written language in particular, creating the decline in our standards of acceptability. This can be disastrous for achieving self-mastery.

Be an active listener.[8] An active listener is engaged verbally and nonverbally through actions and activities in the process of listening. This listener understands that the mind has considerable amounts of time to engage in being overanalytical, to theorize, and in general, to wander. Therefore, to minimize this problem, we must be engaged actively and constructively.

Evaluate.[8] Note what you agree and disagree with and why you agree or disagree. Observe carefully the general content and delivery of the speaker's words and actions and provide feedback actively before, during, and after the conversation and/or speech.

Take notes.[8] This helps to focus on specific as well as on the important points, plus the act of note taking reinforces the information.

Anticipate.[8] it is almost like a game, anticipating what the speaker will say next. Anticipating keeps you fully engaged and interested.

Relate.[8] Relate the comments of the speaker to your own experiences and knowledge.

Define.[8] Seek out the core idea of the speech or discussion and define it along with its supportive points. Address the "So what's the point?" issues.

Understanding the Classical Barriers

The classical barriers to listening are twofold, physical and psychological, both as old as the listening process itself and both within the scope of our control, which means that we are not helpless to defend against their debilitating effects.

Physiological impediments or limitations include anything that would prevent the physical reception of the message from the possibility of being hard of hearing to incidental noises within the environment.

The cessation of physical movement and, in certain situations, maintaining eye contact are other ways in which we learn to tune in physically. However, for improvement to occur, we must always create the best conditions for the most effective listening situations.

Learning to be still through meditational practice rather than through stimulants has a long-lasting calming effect, whereas the usage of drugs of any kind would have a counter-effect.

Psychological impediments are more difficult to control because they are all around us in various forms we cannot often discern. These psychological impediments occur as random thoughts, some of which may be unfulfilled wishes.

We most certainly can control our thoughts by redirecting them. Controlling our thoughts is controlling our destiny.

> *Watch your thoughts, they become words.*
> *Watch your words, they become actions.*
> *Watch your actions, they become habits.*
> *Watch your habits, they become character*
> *Watch your character, it becomes your destiny.*

(Author unknown)

Our needs, interests, concerns, and expectations determine what we think about at crucial times. Our experiences help determine how we think and what solutions we apply to the issues we face. We *must* listen to ourselves.

Programming Listening

Even when in deep meditation in complete relaxed states, random thoughts flow in and out of our subconscious minds. We must become aware of these occurrences and cultivate the habit of hearing everything before we process the information.

We must listen to ourselves.

Understand this that the moment we begin to process an answer, we have stopped listening. We cannot focus with the same intensity on everything we hear or choose to concentrate on. We must therefore adjust our listening (focus) goals to the current or particular situation and decide for ourselves the importance of that situation, and based on how important we determine the situation to be, fine-tune our listening accordingly.

If we strongly believe in what we're about, no other voice is louder than the voice within, no matter what others may say we are or are not.

Many successful individuals were told they were failures. Albert Einstein's parents thought he was retarded. He was even advised by his teacher to drop out of high school. Pablo Picasso was pulled out of school at age ten because he was failing at almost everything. In fact, even his tutor quit on him. Charles Goodyear discovered rubber by pure accident, an accident he caused. Henry Ford barely made it through high school. Bill Gates dropped out of college and was selling computers from his garage. They were all listening to another voice—their own—and they never gave up.

We must talk to ourselves.

We can program simple phrases to help us in difficult listening situations. One such phrase is "I will have superior concentration and understanding in this situation [name the situation and add]. Noises will not distract me. I will be able to recall any of this information I desire at any time."[9] Repeat this prior to and again after the listening situation.

We must become aware of our habits, attitudes, deeper responses, and reactions.

Once we have improved our focus, we must now listen for *understanding*, that is, be able to analyze, interpret, and develop the ability to decode the message by correctly assigning to it meaning. To improve understanding is to become observant of both the verbal and nonverbal cues of others and, most importantly, of ourselves. We must examine the message for total meaning.

We must employ active listening, that is, ask questions and paraphrase the responses, ensuring our understanding of the information. The capacity to structure and organize our affairs outwardly must parallel that capacity to do so at an inner dimension, mastered only through the application of specific techniques, dedicated practice, and active listening.

Phase three in programming listening is *remembering*[10], retaining and returning information you have focused on and understood. The difference between someone who does and one who does not remember is simply technique (all else being equal). Remembering therefore requires the conscious application of techniques that imprint ideas on our memories.

There are three workable techniques employed in remembering, and if used effectively, an individual can raise his or her IQ by at least 50 to 75 points: *Take notes, repeat information,* and *construct mnemonics or memory aids.*

Techniques and a Practical Experiment

Repeating information allows it to be stored in long-term memory. I've advised students of the technique I used in college. I had two notebooks for each class. One was for class work or work in class. This was my scrapbook. The other, my real notebook, was kept at home. I would write almost every word my professors would say into my scrapbook and then transcribe the information neatly (no crossouts) into my real notebook, the one at home. Afterward, I read what I had written and closed the book until the next lecture and then repeated the process all over again, always reading the old and the new notes for continuity.

With my technique, I heard all lectures at least twice and through repetition retained most of the information, so at midterm, I knew most of the facts without even attempting to study any of it. I graduated summa cum laude. The students who have adopted my technique have raised their GPAs. C students are now B+ and A students.

Taking notes is an active process that allows you to take a more creative role in the listening process. The technique is not to try to write all the details but rather the main points—brief list of key ideas—and a few significant details is all you need. The key is to make sure it is in your language, not the professor's.

The Use of Visualization

Constructing mnemonics or *memory aids* revolves around two major systems, loci and peg. The. loci system[11] is an ancient Greek system formerly used by Greek orators and politicians to remember long speeches. This system uses visual associations with familiar locations and visual associations in a particular order. Unusual associations are easier to remember. The system can be adapted to locations at your workplace, at your home, or even locations on your body. You simply create a visual association. The peg system employs key words represented by numbers.

In Silva Mind Control Method, the peg system[12] is employed, where, for example, 1 = T, and then the loci system is also employed where you mentally visualize a glass of tea. 2 = N for Noah, visualize a man with a long white beard. 3 = M for May, visualize a calendar. 4= R for ray, visualize sun rays. 5 = L for law, visualize a judge or policeman. 6 = J for jaw, visualize a judge with a square stern jaw. 7 = K for key, visualize a large gold key. 8 = F for fee, visualize winning one million dollars. 9 = B for bay, visualize land and water. 10 = T and S for toes, visualize ten toes in the sand.

The self-mastery key is to *listen to our subconscious*. In our subconscious minds is stored information that we can call on to provide us with most, if not all, the answers we need.

In order for this system to be effective, the peg words need to be learned well, they run in sequence from 1 to 100, so therefore, once you've memorized the peg words, you can then associate any random information with the numbers and words in the sequence in order to remember the random information. This amazing system can't give you the appearance of being a genius, but rather it brings out our genius.

Evaluating[13] is the listening phase that requires the critical analysis of messages you have received, remembered, and understood in order to determine its truthfulness and authenticity. Because this phase involves the critical use of our perceptions, we must identify any biases, self-interests, or prejudices we may have that would unfairly color our analysis. We must also seek clarification on any issue we feel is objectionable.

Again, *be cognizant of your attitudes, deeper responses, and reactions.*

Listening and Keeping the Message in Context

Critical to improving our ability to judge what we have heard is to be able to separate fact from inferences. Keeping information in context is key to this determination.

Answers to three critical questions would accurately evaluate inferences as facts: (1) Is there factual information to support the inference? (2) Is the factual support relevant to the inference? (3) Is there any other information that would prevent the inference from being considered a fact?

We must answer yes to the first and second questions and no to the third for the inference to be considered a fact. Again, the key to improving our evaluation techniques is to remember to keep it in *context.*

In this story, illustrating inferences, we see a man dressed in a long white coat, standing in the parking lot of a college campus, holding a bloody butcher knife. In this isolated context, individuals viewing this scene would most likely be fearful and disturbed and would perhaps call security to intervene.

Let's change the context by placing a sign that reads Mike's Butcher Shop beside that same man in the bloodied white coat. Suddenly the scene is less threatening. There's an explanation for the blood and the knife. No longer do we see someone who has possibly committed a crime. Instead that individual becomes a butcher who has opened a temporary meat shop in the parking lot.

The scene, now slightly more amusing and a bit odd, changed our perspective. We heard the message, listened and evaluated its content, and then responded based on the context.

The *response*, also referred to as feedback, determines the effect of the message on us. Our response generally occurs in two phases: while the speaker is talking and after the speaker has stopped talking. At this juncture, we would employ our understanding of what was said.

As with most techniques, we are interested in results. Self-mastery is measured by its results. Although the response phase can be considered as a separate activity from the actual skills and techniques emphasized in the listening phases, it is just as essential to the improvement of listening, for it provides the speaker with critical data for self-evaluation.

Understanding how to listen effectively promotes greater self-awareness, which in turn assists in the eventual acceptance of others and self. The total acceptance of self is the epitome of self-mastery. When we can examine and evaluate ourselves noncritically without judging and be equally accepting of our frailties and strengths, we have achieved the zenith of self-acceptance.

Other Objectives of Effective Listening[14]

1. *Listen with empathy and objectivity*—Be able to feel with the person, to put yourself in the person's place, and at other times, to put aside empathy and listen with neutrality and detachment.
2. *Use nonjudgmental and critical listening*—Listen with an open mind, that is, avoid filtering out those difficult messages and messages we dislike.
3. *Use surface and depth listening*—Listen for total meaning, which means we must pay attention to both the verbal and nonverbal messages. Evaluate not only what we hear but also what we did not hear.
4. *Use active listening*—Express what we've understood in our own words and ask questions for clarification. Fully participate, remembering it is a process and each step is meaningful to the entire process. One misstep and the process fails.

Our total self-discovery lies in our ability to be actively involved. We must listen to ourselves, listen to our subconscious, and tune in to our intuition—that nagging voice that keeps saying over and over "Don't, don't" or at other times "That's the way to go" or "That's the right answer" while we're taking that important exam or involved in making crucial decisions.

Because effective listening is such an important aspect to mastering self, it is imperative that it be an integral lesson in this discursive. So many have failed and continue to fail in their listening effort—a clear indication that there's much work to be done. We spend most of our conscious moments listening and yet have not managed to master the act. We repeat the same errors time and time again and yet expect the results to be different. Heed first self and then others.

The subconscious mind provides us with information, allowing us to know without knowing. Sometimes we may feel as if we're just guessing, and if allowed in, fear will displace trust. We must remain open-minded, listen and trust self, and know that sometimes the truth is more absurd than the greatest lie a man can tell, and while nothing is more debilitating than fear, fear evaporates when we understand that our life stories and the history of the world were written by the same hand. Just keep remembering that "the only time learning occurs is when we are truly listening."

CHAPTER 19

SELF-CONCEPT
PHASE 2: THE SELVES

And why do you look at the speck in your brother's eye, but do not consider the plank in your own eye.

—Matthew 7:3[1]

Self-mastery begins and ends with *you*, and in your mastery of the four selves—self-concept, self-esteem, self-awareness, and self-disclosure—each play dominant roles in determining the success or failure at most tasks and in every phase of our lives. Collectively, these are life's DNAs, the concepts of self and the psychological traits that makes for our personalities and characteristics, and they are all learned.

Who we are and how we see ourselves and others are greatly influenced by our self-concept and self-esteem. This in turn influences the way we communicate, our responses to the communication of others, how positive or negative our lives are and will be, and how we improve our lives and relationships. No matter what we do or do not do, self-mastery will evolve. It is, however, so much better for us if we're able to control this development and not leave it to others. While Matthew 7:3 refers to judging others, it also points to the fact that before you can help others, you must first help yourself and before others can help you, they must first help themselves.

Self-Concept

Self-concept is the mental image or idea we have of our selves[2], that is, how we perceive ourselves. Therefore, self-concept is wed to our social perceptions. How we perceive or feel about our skills, knowledge, competencies, personality, abilities, and limitations are all, in effect, our self-concept.

Our self-concept is developed through our experiences, whether they are good or bad, or negative or positive. Therefore, the more positive our experiences, the more is the possibility of developing a high self-concept, the opposite being true for negative experiences.

Personal successes raise our self-concept. The more we have, the more confident we become and the higher our resulting self-concept will be. Personal failures impact this self negatively.

Secondly, what others say about us and how they react and respond to us help to develop and subsequently reveal our concept of self. Obviously, who the individual is and our relationship with them play a vital role as to how we respond.

The more important our relationship with these individuals, the more of an effect their reactions and responses will have in helping to shape our self-concept. The shaping of our self-concepts occurs slowly over time. Changes are sometimes subtle but once formed, are very resistant to change. Others help reveal to us images of ourselves, and seeing images of ourselves in others may lead to negative or positive mirroring; that is, we may dislike someone because we dislike *that* personality or trait in ourselves, or conversely, we may like an individual because we see that positive image of them in us.

The third factor influencing the development of self-concept is the comparisons we make between ourselves and others. In order to discover how good we are at a task, we would compare ourselves with others we believe to be more competent than us at that particular task. We want to know how well we measure up. This is positive imaging.

However, to make us feel better about our incompetencies, we sometimes compare ourselves with peers who are less competent than us. This leads to negative imaging. It temporarily makes us feel good about ourselves, especially our negative traits.

Comparisons are generally made with individuals who are distinctly similar to us in various ways, in age, ability, or level. We therefore tend to make comparisons with our peers.

In learning self-mastery, we learn that to compare ourselves with others is to seek satisfaction outside of ourselves and our abilities. This behavior invariably may leave us to become vain and bitter, for there always will be lesser and greater than us in ability and competency, and because of this, we may engage in blame displacement. Thinking that all that is positive is a result of our own doing and the negatives are a result of someone else's.

Self-mastery programming techniques teach that we must do our own house cleaning, and when we program habits for success, look first to ourselves for answers as to our progress or lack of progress and examine how we are applying what we have programmed, what our goals are, how honest we are with ourselves, and how realistic are the results we seek. Once we have examined ourselves thoroughly, then we can examine the external influences.

Another common problem of comparison is false consensus effect,[3] the tendency to overestimate the degree to which others share our attitudes and behaviors. We assume that what we are doing, others are doing it too. This goes to the heart of the strong impulse for us to be socially integrated. In fact, according to communication writers William J. Seiler, Melissa L. Beal, and Sarah Trenholm, in understanding self-concept, self-concept may be organized into levels or compartments, some of which are higher than others.

The hierarchy of self-concept[4] may be organized into many different levels of beliefs, images, feelings, and characteristics that help determine who we are. Among these levels are psychological, social, and physical self-concept, and according to Carl Rogers, a personality theorist, people with high social self-concepts tend to function better in interpersonal situations than people with low social self-concepts.

These levels determine how we act toward others and how susceptible to change certain characteristics and personality traits are. The further down the level of hierarchy, the more specific and susceptible to change these characteristics are.

The highest level is where our strongest and well-established self-concepts are. On the second tier are the elements that form our self-concept and self-image. It is therefore easy to see how elements on one tier or level could affect elements on the other level.

Cultural experiences also determine how we react to certain events and situations, and it affects our self-concept and how it is developed. Our culture is everything we are—how we speak, what we eat, how we socialize, the way we dress, what fuels our drives and ambitions, who we choose as friends, and to some extent, our career paths.

Our behavior is culturally driven. Our values, beliefs, and attitudes are all characteristics of our culture, and our self-concept is therefore determined by cultural norms and behaviors.

Determining one's culture would help determine that individual's approach to self-mastery. Some cultures stress individual goals while others emphasize group or collective goals. Cultures that emphasize individualism tend to measure success based on how much they have accomplished in comparison to other family members and peers. The general measurement used is monetary wealth and educational achievement. Collectivist cultures[5] most likely would shun the "I" concept for the well-being of the group. If the group is successful, then the individual feels rewarded.

When individuals are placed in intercultural contexts or situations, problems arise, especially in communication. This can create cultural conflict and may eventually lead to redefinitions of self-concept by these individuals as a way of allowing functionality within the confines of the new culture.

The process of adjustment that would eventuality lead to balance and improvement is acculturation,[6] learning the rules and norms of a culture different from your native culture. Your native culture is modified. The more educated and younger you are, the quicker the adjustment or acculturation.

I conducted an exercise in one of my classes where several foreign students were asked to take specific and opposing positions on acculturation. One position was that acculturation was good; the other position was that acculturation was not good at all.

The major points students made in support of the position that acculturation was necessary was that in order to succeed in business and scholastic life and to be and feel accepted by members of that culture, acculturation was not only necessary but beneficial.

The opposing position was also just as strong. These students felt that not only was acculturation detrimental to the traditions of those individuals who are forced to set aside their culture and beliefs for the sake of acculturation, but it also presented grave conflicts between parents and children (children tend to acculturate very quickly), thus creating not only a generation gap but also a cultural gap within the family unit that can eventually lead to dysfunctionality with the family unit.

The major barrier to cultural self-mastery remains to be ethnocentrism, the tendency to see our culture as superior to other cultures that are different from ours. However, avoiding assumptions, overcoming your fears, and recognizing and embracing the differences in people are four major ways of ensuring cultural self-improvement to the point of self-mastery and uniformity between culture and self-concept.

A fifth factor influencing self-concept as it relates to self-mastery is gender. While gender[7] is transmitted genetically, it is still considered a cultural variable because it is learned. We teach boys and girls different attitudes, beliefs, and values. In other words, we teach boys how to be boys and girls how to be girls, and any variance in their expected behavior is considered abnormal.

Gender identity occurs when it becomes a part of our self-concept. We identify as being male or female on a permanent basis somewhere between ages four and eight, and once this occurs, our perceptions of self are affected by our beliefs about those tendencies and our values and beliefs regarding gender.

I would oftentimes test some of these gender theories out on my eleven-year-old son. For example, we may be walking through a department store shopping for a pair of sneakers, and I would intentionally point to a pair of pink or orange sneakers and say, "Do you like these? Let's get them." He would react by saying in no uncertain terms, "Noooo," or give me an incredulous look as if to say, "How could you ask me something so ridiculous. These are not for males."

Without a doubt his identification of being male is firmly in place, and while the seven-year-old may not be as sophisticated about it, clearly his concept of gender is also defined.

Barriers affecting gender and the mastery of gender relate to gender expectations and the resulting gender stereotypes that result from these expectations.

Researches do believe that the differences between males and females are superficial and grossly overstated, and the magnitude of differences are far less than what the prevailing stereotypes suggest or imply.

A theory is that all progress is brought about through conflict of opposing forces. This conflict is inevitable and necessary. According to German philosopher Georg Hegel, the change is the result of the mixing of three elements[8]: thesis, antithesis, and synthesis.

Change begins with a thesis and consequently generates an antithesis or opposing view or force. The two will inevitably interact, producing a synthesis, which then transcends both. This synthesis, in turn, then becomes the new thesis, and the process is repeated over and over, again and again. So it is with male and female relationships and good and evil.

To understand this clearly in the dynamics of self-concept and self-mastery, consider the divine or spiritual plan for a moment since this is the ultimate quest of self-mastery.

The power or will to be is the thesis. This is represented by the male or masculine polarity[9] (+). Wisdom is the antithesis or the opposite polarity as represented by the female of feminine polarity (-). The intermixing of the two creates the synthesis, love, which then becomes the new thesis, thus producing the many manifestations of males and females. This is further exemplified in the make-up of our chromosome, the Xs and Ys.

In the Hindu tradition,[10] the male and female principles are given names and are looked upon as gods. Father is thesis, and Mother is antithesis, and the whole of their creation is the synthesis. Their reason for being is reproduction, for it is only in this union can the creative purpose of their being be fully realized. Hence, man's dual nature of having both male and female charges is not only reasonable; it is also necessary.

For improvement in communication and relationships between and among men and women, it is helpful to avoid categorizing behaviors as being exclusively male or female. Psychologists suggest in their findings that androgynous men and women,[11] having both male and female traits, are most likely to be successful in their interactions and careers than the individual who is masculine or feminine in their behavior.

No, it does not mean that we should all be androgynous in our sexuality, but rather behaviors considered distinctly male or female prevents us from mastering all aspects of self through the very categorization of these behaviors.

According to the compiled text *Communication Making Connections*, by William Seiler and Melissa Beall, and *Thinking Through Communication, An Introduction to the Study of Human Communication*, by Sarah Trenholm, five guidelines[12] to improving self-concept were put forth, and they include the following:

1. Deciding what you would like to change about yourself, and to do this, you must describe as accurately and specifically as possible using the empowering "I" statement—what you wish to change about yourself.

We are our worst enemy because we can convince ourselves about almost anything and believe it to be true. I say almost anything because the only thing we cannot convince ourselves that we are not is being alive; that is, once we are breathing, this is a reality we are cognizant and consciously aware of every moment of that consciousness, although on the flip side of this, there are those who may have departed and still believe they are of this world or dimension, but that's for another conversation.

The point is that there are times when some of us wish to be other than what we are and where we are and sometimes pretend to be what we wish to be for many reasons, paramount of which is usually because we cannot face the truth about ourselves.

Pretending is not the same as daydreaming or imagining, for pretending is having a false or twisted sense of what our reality really is, falsely claiming what we are not, as opposed to daydreaming or imagining, where we can and are able to separate one reality from the other, being clearly conscious of the two realities and the differences between them.

Therefore, the first point to improving our self-concept is to describe specifically and accurately what we would like to change about ourselves. An honest appraisal about the specific thing we dislike and wish to change about us must first be made, and we should and must be able to describe what we wish to change in a full, complete, and concrete statement, beginning that statement with the word "I."

For example, "I wish to lose ten pounds" (specific and concrete), not merely "I wish to lose weight" (vague) or "I want to be able to speak up immediately when someone does or says something that I believe to be distasteful and not just ignore it or pretend it did not happen."

The "I" is empowering because it makes you take control of your actions. You claim the feeling as yours and can no longer pass it off, and the more specific you are, the less there is the chance of misinterpretation or misrepresentation.

2. Making a commitment to improve yourself by acting on it and accepting small incremental changes over time.

Once a clear, accurate, and articulated statement is made, the logical next step is to act on it with dedication. A committed act endures time, therefore making a commitment to improve involve acting with determination and not being deterred by initial failure but deciding to try until there is success, even when our motives are called into question.

This is the most difficult task we will face both in mastery and in the improvement of self, having the dedication to endure and, even when we falter, to get back on track. The need and the desire determine the level of commitment, and desire provides the motivation to act in accord with the commitment.

Recognizing and accepting the changes we may not always be able to measure must be understood as part of the equation. Changes in our lives are mostly obscure, especially to those closest to us. We also seldom notice those changes ourselves. Time, however, is the teller.

These changes are synonymous to comparing photographs of yourself at various periods in your life. You don't see the changes until you compare the images side by side, and then again, we only see one dimension of change in those images—the physical—which is usually the most obvious.

Continued acceptance of self allows for the acceptance of the subtle difference we, from time to time, may notice.

3. Describing why you feel the way you do about yourself, that is, begin to recognize why you feel the way you do if you're unhappy and who is contributing to you feeling this way.

4. Deciding that you're going to do something about the problem, specifically over time, keeping in mind that there are things that can change overnight.
5. Setting reasonable goals for yourself. Understanding that some things take longer to accomplish require more effort and change slowly.
6. Associating with people who will support and help you; that is, you must yoke yourself with people you like and trust.

An additional technique to be used along with the six guidelines are affirmations as a constant reinforcement of our goals. Therefore, critical to the mastery of self-concept is the total understanding that we are all that we are and also all that we are not, and to accept ourselves without being critical or judgmental.

Affirmations are prayers, mantras, or programs we can use to reinforce what we wish and desire in our lives. Used during meditation, it can serve as a form of self-hypnotism. Remember: the keys to effectively programming beneficial habits is to *believe, expect, desire, hope*, have *faith* and *emotion*, and be *honest*. Each and every programming effort begins with your thoughts—how you think of yourself and of others.

Here are several affirmations you may use for various purposes: for motivation, for success, for protection, for faith. You can create your own affirmations like poetry and use them wherever and whenever you desire. Here are a few.

I refuse to be intimidated by the way things appear to be
I tenaciously cling to the inner conviction that the divine and invisible power and presence of God
Has worked things out for me in a perfect and miraculous way,
I am grateful

I cannot fail, for God cannot fail.

I am surrounded by the pure white light of the Christ,
Nothing but good can come to me,
Nothing but good shall go from me

Positive thoughts bring me benefits and advantages I desire

My increasing mental faculties are for serving humanity better[13]

Every day in every way, I am getting better, better, and better[14]

I am not moved by *fear*, therefore, *fear* moves

You can also substitute any other adjective : *hate, emotion, anger,* and so on. So for example,

I am not moved by *anger*, therefore *anger* moves.

I have superior concentration and understanding.

This is programming self-concept. It is simply reinforcing thoughts, behaviors, and eventually habits at deeper and deeper levels until they become you and you become them, and they become character and destiny. Therefore, it is vital that these programming phrases be all positive and uplifting.

CHAPTER 20

SELF-ESTEEM
PHASE 2: THE SELVES

Personal self-esteem[1] refers to the degree to which you have a favorable impression of who you are, that is, how much you like yourself, how competent or good you think you are at a task, and how valuable you think you are.

I distinctly mentioned personal self-esteem since there is also group self-esteem. Group self-esteem influences and affects personal self-esteem. This goes back to what I've previously stated as our universal purpose, which is to meet the needs of each other. We cannot exist in a vacuum, and so we constantly evaluate ourselves and our progress based on our impact, good or bad, on others.

Viewing our membership in a group, whether it's an ethnic group, business membership group, political group, social group, gang, or sports team, if we view the group positively, then there will be a certain amount of pride in being part of that group and hence high and positive group self-esteem, which will subsequently lead to great personal self-esteem.

Many factors do affect and contribute to our overall self-esteem[2]. These include (1) personal successes and failures. Failure lowers our self-esteem; success raises it. (2) The culture we were raised in. Some cultures emphasize group values, while others emphasize independence, competition, and uniqueness.

In group cultures, interdependence is taught and valued. Members are taught to get along and to help others. It is not so much that these values aren't taught in the independent cultures, but rather they are not emphasized.

Self-esteem, then, will depend largely on how many of your goals are achieved as selected by your culture (our culture seems to select the specific goals), and because our culture selects our goals, we base the accuracy of our self-esteem on the accuracy of the perceptions of others about us. This accuracy is relative to the importance of the person making the assessment about us.

There is a reality gap between what we believe our self-esteem to be and what others say it is. Others do play a vital role in the final determination of the accuracy of this reality.

Therefore, how others constantly react to us will over time determine our real self-esteem as well as self-concept. The question is how is this reinforced and finally determined to be our reality?

While our self-esteem is culture relative, maintaining it is not. *Self-fulfilling prophecies[3] and filtering* provide the reinforcement. Self-fulfilling prophecy helps to magnify our self-esteem. It does not determine the positive or negative aspects of it but simply takes what's there and magnifies the picture.

A prophecy is something foretold but that has not yet come to pass. It is predicted, and a self-fulfilling prophecy is largely self-created or imposed mostly through our actions. In other words, as a result of something we talked about, expected, and/or foretold (the prophecy), we made it happen through our actions (self-fulfilling).

There is a downside, which is, because of our belief in a position held, we will have a tendency to act in ways that will reinforce us and/or fulfill that belief, thereby fulfilling our own prophecies. For instance, if we predicted a particular outcome, we may act in ways that would reinforce our belief in that position or outcome. Therefore, it is because we believe in that prediction that we acted in that way to begin with. Thus, it comes to pass, and consequently, we fulfilled our own prophecy.

In our discussion of self-concept, I mentioned the role of self-fulfilling prophecy as well as its potential downfalls or barriers, one being the potential to influence another's behavior so that it confirms our prophecy and the other, to distort perception by influencing us to see what we predicted rather than what's really there.

In the relationships theory, predicted outcome value, which is one of the theories psychologists put forth as a motivation for forming relationships, it is suggested that whatever we predict will be the outcome. Therefore, as an example, if we predict a greater outcome or that the outcome of a relationship will be successful, it most likely will be since our tendency will be to work toward what we seek or predict. If a greater outcome is predicted, then there will be more success in the relationship than if the prediction was negative.

Those of us with high self-esteem will attribute our success to pass successes and with an expectation of succeeding in the future, whereas those with low self-esteem would more often attribute any success to luck or chance as opposed to personal effort and therefore would predict success, again, hoping for a lucky break. There's no such thing if you're in control of your destiny.

Our expectations therefore are a powerful force and shaper of our self-concept and self-esteem. All the more it is important to understand and remember the keys to effective programming and mental reshaping of our thoughts, which are worth repeating at this juncture: *Believe*, *expect* and *desire*, have *faith* and *hope*, be *honest*, and exude *emotion*. Enthusiasm is infectious.

We must expect others to succeed if we are to experience success. We must not limit ourselves. Therefore, we cannot place limitations on others. However, we must be realistic in our expectations, both for ourselves and for others.

Honesty becomes an important factor, for dishonesty or excessive flattery or praise will provide an adverse effect, such as an inflated ego or self-image, which in turn may remove objectivity from the perspective of that individual who has had praises heaped on them. With objectivity negated, objective truth becomes barren.

Filtering messages simply means hearing messages accurately but not listening to or perceiving them equally. We tend to listen to those messages that helps keep our egos intact—the messages that reinforce our current self-image.

In the listening process, we hear what we wish to hear and discard or at least filter out that information that tends to contradict our position or view, and this is regardless of the truth. This is a major barrier to achieving the absolute oneness of self, the total acceptance of who we are, and hence self-mastery.

The need to insulate ourselves, to protect other's feelings as well as our egos, and to deflect any information that would change the perspective of our secure world causes us to engage in filtering. Pretending to be someone we're not is an example of filtering to preserve an ideal self and maintain a certain self-image. The moment we begin to let information (comments) pass our filters, we begin the process of changing our self-image and eventually we will begin to develop a new self-perception.

Because we have an almost automatic reflexive response to certain language and comments, once new situations are experienced and are allowed past our filters, they seem to lend themselves better to expediting the process of changes in our self-esteem. Three such situations are *drastic changes in our social environment, transitions of life*, and *profound experiences*.[4] These situations must provide the individual with experiences that are positive and gratifying in order to produce desired positive changes.

Examining drastic changes in our social environment, we observe that in attempts to institutionalize and reintegrate recalcitrants, it often necessitates their removal to an environment completely different from the one they are accustomed to.

For example, one of my students reported in a speech presentation his involvement in gangs when still in his teens as a member of the Crips. He was heavily involved in drugs, murders, and other gang-related atrocities. He somehow managed to escape death and imprisonment but knew that someday this would be his fate. At that time, he lived outside of New York State. Most of his friends and family members were either murdered or imprisoned for gang-related crimes in the state in which he had resided.

He was involved in crimes and made a name for himself until his mother decided that she wanted to keep him alive, and so she removed him from that environment. They moved from that state and city and relocated to the suburb of New York City, a totally different environment than what he was familiar with. It helped to force change.

In that previous environment, he believed and did say it that he was destined to fail. Everyone around him did fail. The change removed him from the gang, the people, and the toxic environment and gave him an opportunity to start over.

He never thought he would make it to age twenty-one, much less college, and for him, it was a major achievement to be in college, pursuing a degree. His self-concept and self-esteem changed drastically, mostly because of the profound change in his social environment.

Exposure to new filters creates readjustments in our attitudes and therefore a reevaluation of our self-esteem.

Life transitions is leaving behind that which we have outgrown and find no more usefulness for because we have moved beyond it in knowledge, wisdom, maturity, and experience.

One of the fastest ways to get someone to mature is to give them responsibilities. When we no longer feel responsible for just ourselves but have others dependent on us, our demeanor changes. We are forced in some situations to behave more responsibly and mature exponentially.

When children begin school or leave home are other examples where filters are dropped and the absorption of new information commences. This is necessary not only for our survival but for our growth. Our self-esteem undergoes change.

Profound experiences always bring about changes. My first astral projection created a change in me, and so did each one thereafter. Each experience creates an action and a reaction. The first time I had a gun pointed at me was during a robbery in Brooklyn by three young men (myself, also being a young, progressive man at that time). I always believed I walked in the spirit. I was never afraid and never was or felt threatened by anyone, but my self-concept and self-esteem were sorely tested after that incident.

It was a spring evening, in April, not too cold but not warm enough to be without a coat. That evening, I was wearing my imitation fur. I loved that coat (my friends and I affectionately referred to it as my dog fur coat). It was a warm coat and looked expensive (it wasn't fur and wasn't that expensive)—paid less than $75 for it, but I always received compliments on it.

Although unafraid, I am never the less always on guard, perhaps not as on guard as I should've been that evening. I was less than two blocks from the brownstone where I lived in Brooklyn, just strolling along, enjoying the evening after visiting my girlfriend at the time. And as I walked adjacent to the park, approximately one block from my home, I heard the patter of footsteps behind me. I turned around, only to be confronted by three bandits, one wielding a gun and demanding my coat, my jacket, and my wallet.

It is not a habit for me to carry large amounts of cash nor is it a habit that I would carry two wallets. But that evening, I was carrying two wallets. One contained one Canadian dollar currency and my driver's license. The other contained, as I recalled, an insurance check for over $800, several credit cards, and over $100 in cash, in addition to an uncashed paycheck. Altogether, I had approximately $1,500 in that wallet. I believe it was the anticipation of having to carry this sum of money why I opted to have two wallets that evening.

As I turned around, after hearing the steps behind me, I was confronted by three bandits. The one with the gun demanded my coat, which I immediately relinquished. He then demanded my wallet as he visibly shook nervously (and I suppose I was as well) as he pointed the gun at me, while his accomplices observed in silence.

I quickly handed over my wallet, the dummy, which I had placed in the left inside pocket of my jacket. The other wallet was secured in the other pocket. He then demanded my jacket and my keys. "Naw, man, we don't want your jacket or your keys," his accomplice quipped. "Just turn around and run and don't look back."

I ran track. My distances were the 100 and 220 meters, and on occasion, the 400 meters, and from where I was standing, it was approximately 100 meters to my house.

My personal best in the 100 meters was ten seconds flat. I was in top shape then, trained every morning in that same park I was now standing in front of, confronted by three bandits brandishing a gun.

That evening, I don't believe any of the top sprinters would've out-distanced me. I took off and never looked back. I'm positive I did that 100 meters in maybe five seconds. They took off in the opposite direction with their take of one Canadian dollar and, of course, my imitation fur. I still have that wallet (minus the credit cards, my choice) to this very day.

Did this incident affect my self-esteem? Yes, for a while it did. I am sure I would've been nervous around black men with guns for sure, and for a time, I was a bit uneasy if a young black man around the age of those bandits (late teens) approached my direction, but there's more. There was a second robbery.

In spite of the fact that I was much more cautious and aware of my surroundings, I did not allow that incident to control my way of life. Because the second incident occurred in the same neighborhood, let me premise this incident by saying that the neighborhood where I resided at the time was a wonderful one—lovely brownstones lined most streets, and the neighbors were very friendly. The Children's Museum was two blocks over.

However, neighborhoods change, and the neighborhood was beginning to change. Approximately ten blocks over was Atlantic Avenue and Bedford Stuyvesant, which lay north of Crown Heights, a striving neighborhood of working-class people, while Bed-Stuy was struggling.

It was about two years later, I was again less than seven blocks from the brownstone where I lived. I had just left the gym, parked my car, and was about to enter the brownstone where my girlfriend resided.

These bandits were definitely laying in wait to victimize someone, and I just happened to be that someone. They must have seen me as I exited the car and entered the building. However, the dimly lit street provided ample cover for these two teens. I spotted them running across the street, waving what appeared to be a gun and quickly approaching the house and the door I had just entered.

I slammed the outer door; unfortunately, it did not lock automatically, and there was a second door that I had to enter to gain entrance into the building.

For a brief moment, it was a tug o' war—two against one, they pushing in while I'm pushing out. They were eventually able to push the outer door open and demanded my wallet and money. I did not have a dummy wallet for them this time; however, I did outthink them and was able to reach into my wallet, in my back pocket; retrieve $10; drop the wallet behind the door which I was leaning against; and give to the one closest to me the $10.

The scariest moment for me came after this when the punk holding the gun on an unarmed man says to his accomplice, "Let's shoot him. Let's shoot him." For a brief moment, my life flashed before me. I felt my stomach churn and my bladder gave way. I urinated on myself, and as I yelled, "No, no," they turned and ran.

Shortly after that incident, I picked up a pistol license application, and for two or three years, I did not fill it out, just carried it around with me while struggling with my fear and uncertainty (self-esteem).

Then one day, I decided that I would either have to fill the application out or discard it. I filled it out, got my pistol license, and bought a handgun. I was now 100 percent American—I owned a gun and even joined the NRA.

Although I knew that having a gun did not really protect me, it did, however, give me a false sense of security.

I've owned a gun now for over eleven years but never fired it, not at a range or anywhere else. In fact, I've never fired a real gun. I regained my sense of self. I knew I would have to make a decision very soon—take shooting up as a hobby, join a range, or not renew my license. While I still do retain ownership rights to my gun, I have since turned it in to the police department for safe keeping. If I ever do feel a need for it, perhaps I will renew my license.

Self-esteem is truly driven by experiences good and bad. My experience pushed me to apply for a pistol license and subsequently purchase a gun.

There are those who after volatile or traumatic experiences, in desperation, do not bother to follow the dictates of the law and (in the case of obtaining a gun) indulge in illegal activities to obtain one or, as in the movie *Death Wish*, take the law into their own hands out of the feeling that the wheels of justice turns much too slowly.

There are others who never recover after grave experiences and become bitter. Their self-esteem almost completely destroyed. Without intervention, their lives become a living hell.

Time is the greatest arbiter of self-esteem, for over time we can gradually buy into a reduced or increased sense of our possibilities, and accomplish and/or achieve our goals, or not, as our self-esteem dictates.

In programming habits, to change our self-esteem, we must first make a commitment to start believing in our selves; that is, to generate a higher self-esteem, first think it, write it down, and then list the ways you believe you will benefit from a higher self-esteem.

Reach for self-actualization by releasing unrealistic standards and views. Fortunately, I realized that obtaining a gun would not do me any good in my situation. I could not shoot every black kid I felt threatened by, thinking they are about to rob me. Therefore, reach for goals and standards that are achievable and realistic.

Be mindful of what we think and say. Remember: Thoughts are one or two steps removed from the act. In programming habits, we undergo mental house cleaning, which is necessary to rid ourselves of harmful thoughts and therefore harmful habits.

If you tell yourself you cannot, you will not; therefore, strive for balance, talk to yourself, know yourself and your deeper responses, find out what works for you and what works well in your life, don't be so modest that you underrate your achievements, accept compliments as compliments, and recognize that you are responsible for your achievements.

When programming habits, trust yourself. Remember: *believing* is key to succeeding and for programming to take effect. Asking for direction is different from asking for advice; therefore, *you* must be creative in finding solutions that work for *you*. Trust the choices you've made once you've examined the soundness of it.

An excellent advisor would not give you all the answers but will give you the creative freedom to invent your own solutions. Your tendency to use your solutions to further develop your self-esteem is greater than the possibility of using another person's solution.

Measure your success by your progress, not by someone else's, for always there will be lesser and greater than yourself. The danger with comparisons is that it also leads to self-doubt, which in turn lowers self-esteem.

I teach because for me, it's a way of sharing knowledge. I'm on stage each time I step in front of a class. I'm the grand performer, and in the process of doing this, I also obtain knowledge and find better and better ways of explaining a concept or theory, sometimes even borrowing from my students and being able to return it, whether it's knowledge or love as it was obtained. I find this to be very enriching.

Finally, for self-esteem to develop properly, we must withhold critical judgment, be gentle, and accept improvements in very minute increments but expect success, and to expect success, we must have success along the way in our efforts. Success breathes success, just as failure can breathe failure if we did not learn from the failure how to succeed the next time.

To reiterate, for an improved self-esteem, rid yourself of self-destructive beliefs, especially negative statements; use affirmations, which are positive reinforcements for your success, strength, and virtuous qualities; avoid those who bring you down—the pessimists and the negative people; and tackle first those things that will result in success before working on the difficult projects because success breathes success.

Self-esteem therefore depends largely on achieving our goals, and by doing so, we boost our self-esteem.

We must therefore indulge in the following for the mastery of self-esteem:

1. Attack self-destructive beliefs. All negativity is self-destructive.
2. Engage in self-affirmation. Remind ourselves of our successes, and focus on our achievements not our limitations.
3. Avoid toxicity. Avoid people who are pessimistic and negative and who do not make us feel good about ourselves. Align ourselves with nurturing people.
4. Work on our successes first. Select the projects we know we can complete successfully before tackling the more difficult ones. Past successes breathes future successes.

CHAPTER 21

SELF-AWARENESS
PHASE 2: THE SELVES

Having full knowledge of self is *self-awareness*. The more you understand self, the more self-control you'll possess, and following the concepts of effective programming, is greater self-awareness.

Once again, effective programming requires *talking to yourself, listening to yourself, being conscious or aware of your habits, feelings, and deeper responses;* and *listening to your subconscious.*[1] Awareness denotes total consciousness, and having total consciousness can only be achieved by being completely in tune with the conscious and recognizing the subconscious self.

According to *The Group Processes: An Introduction to Group Dynamics, Third Edition,* by Joseph Luft, self-awareness can be explained through four different areas of self[2]: open self, blind self, secret self, and unknown self, explained through a quadrant referred to as "The Johari Window." Information is communicated in some form at each window, some more effectively and completely than others.

The *open self* represents all the information, behavior, attitudes, feelings, desires, and ideas you know about yourself and that others know about you. Communicating is easy and open.

This information incidentally includes your physical appearance as well as your personal values. However, this does not mean that the individual has no secrets, but rather the openness varies depending on who is being disclosed to as well as what is being disclosed, but in general, significant information that would otherwise hurt or derail a relationship is oftentimes disclosed and discussed with the relevant individual or individuals. As we develop a better awareness of self, we better understand the significance of (sharing) information.

The *blind self* represents information about yourself that others know but you don't know they know. These may include tendencies, mannerisms, habits, and idiosyncrasies.

Communication can be difficult in the blind self or window, unless individuals have the same basic information about each other. To paraphrase, if parties know each other's blind spots, then the likelihood of surprises within the relationship while it may exist may not be as devastating. There will always be information about us that others know but we don't know they know. The idea is to eliminate or decrease the information that would harm the relationship or communication.

The *unknown self* represents information or parts of yourself that neither you nor others know.

The development of the unknown self is significant in self-mastery. The sharing of information here is paramount, and just as significant is how the information is shared and dispersed.

Trust is essential, and developing good habits is critical. The idea is to gain useful insights as to who you are; therefore, the sources from which you gleam this information become almost as important as the information itself.

Your unknown self can sometimes be revealed to you through hypnosis, regression, drug experiences (not recommended), dreams, and traumatic or pleasant experiences. If the experiences and revelations are with trusted friends and/or family, then the possibility of gaining effective insights would be heightened.

One of the goals of meditation is for individuals to get in touch with their inner selves, the place where information is buried. One of the four keys to good programming is listening to your subconscious. It reveals significant information about us and to us.

The *hidden self* represents all that you know about yourself but keep hidden from others.

It is not only okay but also necessary to have secrets. However, the aim is to strive to be a selective discloser. When we discuss self-disclosure, we will talk about the rules of disclosure. The general rule here is that the more you hide yourself, the less you will learn about yourself and others.

Self-awareness grows when the four keys of effective self-programming are applied to it.

Talking to yourself—No one knows you better than yourself, yet we constantly seek gratification outside of ourselves. This is because we seldom ask ourselves about ourselves.

When you're alone, do you speak to yourself? Most of us would answer yes. When you do speak to yourself, who hears you? Most of us would say, "We hear ourselves." Are you embarrassed if someone happens to walk in on you having a soliloquy? Most would say yes, somewhat, the reason being that the individual observing the behavior may have a different opinion about us from that encounter. They may think we have taken leave of some of our senses, even though they may indulge in similar kinds of behavior.

Practice talking to yourself out loud. Be sure it is positive and encouraging. Affirmations are brain dialogues, for example, a simple statement such as "I know I can do this" to one's self is talking to yourself or "Who am I really?" and then finding the answers is significant for self-discovery.

We are constantly in discourse with ourselves anyway, mostly in silence but sometimes out loud. The observance of children at play makes this point eloquently. They are not afraid to be creative and pretend that toys (especially the Transformers and Power Rangers) are exchanging dialogues as they battle or plan the next adventure. In fact, that child becomes so engrossed in this make-believe world that you cease to exist, although you might be standing there trying to get their attention.

Listening to yourself—The deliberate act of focusing attention on what is being said and following through actively.

Listening to yourself amounts to tuning in to your inner voice, the sixth sense we all have referred to as our intuition. This is our inner guide—the revelation of what God's plan is for us momentarily and through our lives.

Our intuition alerts us to danger and/or providence and gives us answers to events and questions that our five senses do not necessarily discern. The intuition thus operates on a higher mental level, in immediate communication without reasoning with our mind, providing insight to that which is unknown to us through inexperience. In order for this sense to be fully developed and useful to us in the mastery of self, we must pay attention to it, and paying attention to it means tuning in and listening to ourselves.

Our subconscious is a store wealth of information, and when we tune in, we discover answers to issues we may have had for years. We may also discover why individuals behave the way they do and even why we behave the way we do.

While listening to ourselves follows the same principles as listening to others, unfortunately, the practice of listening to one's self does not necessarily translate into us being better listeners or in recognizing the difference between hearing and listening.

Hearing yourself but not heeding amounts to ignoring the intuition, and since the intuition serves to alert and sometimes protect us, not tuning in could be detrimental. Listening to self and heeding or acting accordingly is intuitive listening, and the more we practice listening to ourselves, the more in tune with self we become and vice versa. The less we tune in, the less in tune we will become.

Following our own advice is often easier said than done, for we do have tendencies to act in ways expedient to the circumstances, for example, a parent telling a child not to smoke as they light up. In this instance, the parent is being hypocritical and not heeding his or her own advice.

Our greatest enemy happens to be ourselves. Why? Because the urge to sometimes satisfy a need or desire overrides or takes precedent over the consequences we know that could and may follow our actions. It sometimes derides logic, but logic is not a weighed factor when an emotional or physical urge is present. We relent to this need, knowing full well that we should not. The remorse sometimes comes after, but oftentimes even the feeling of remorse is not enough to stymie the action from occurring again. We are not listening to ourselves but rather feeding an urge.

Carl Jung, the Swiss psychiatrist, mentions *the collective unconscious*, which he references as a storehouse where all knowledge is accessible, including that which we would consider intuitive knowledge. Based on this theory, it would suggest that our subconscious minds can be a provider of information we may not even believe we have access to based on our current experiences. This is information we would not normally comprehend, much less listen to, but the theory also suggests that there are times when we must and sometimes do suspend logic.

Listening to yourself is mastered with patience and through practice. Most importantly, it is trusting yourself and your intuition.

We will revisit Jung's theory again as we examine the fourth key of self-programming for the growth of self-awareness.

Being Conscious of One's Patterns

Habits, feelings, and responsiveness: The triggers that compel you to do and say the things you do and say. All learned behavior that becomes reinforced at deeper and deeper levels, creating habit formation.

As human beings, we learn through repetition, and this repetitive behavior becomes habitual and patterned. All human beings learn behavior this way—through consistent repetition. It is true: "Practice makes perfect."

All habits are acquired, and a habit constitutes a fixed pattern of behavior. Good and bad habits are acquired the same way. Because habits are acquired, they come under our control.

There are distinctions. Breathing, for example, while it is repetitive and consistent, is habitual but not a habit, because we do not have immediate control over this function, as it constitutes part of the structure that is natural to all human beings, in fact, all living creatures, if they wish to remain that way. Of course, we can purposefully and consciously hold our breath for periods of time, and with practice, we will be able to do this for longer and longer periods. However, we will and must eventually exhale or we suffocate.

Blinking the eyes while habitual is also not a habit in the sense of it being acquired, even though it is repetitive and consistent, for as like breathing, it is natural and necessary to our existence.

Therefore, when we speak of habits, we are referring to all learned behaviors, such as smoking, drinking excessively, and overeating, which become part of our lives. We have brought this behavior into existence because of some form of reward it seemingly tends to offer.

These patterns of behavior become imprinted on our brains through consistent repetition; therefore, our immediate control over them becomes mitigated. We therefore feel we have no control over them and accept the behavior as being natural to our existence like breathing.

Once there's clarity in understanding what constitutes a habit, we must also understand that to break that habit constitutes changing the pattern of behavior, in other words, giving our brains a different orientation regarding that habit.

Because our brains operate in a consistent manner based on goals and rewards, habits then become part of this functional equation of real or imaginary satisfaction from that habit. We cannot just erase impressions that are engrained. Our brains just do not work that way. We must find out why we hold on to certain patterns of behavior regardless of their consequences.

Through behavioral consciousness or awareness, we begin the process of orienting our brains regarding a certain habit and give our brains a different orientation, if we wish to change the behavior. We become more acutely aware of a behavior at the point we recognize that we wish to break or change that behavior or habit.

How is it accomplished? If we know that the urge to smoke is greatest after a meal, do we avoid eating? No. This is not possible nor practical. However, first, we need to recognize what triggers the behavior we wish to change. In this case, it is the reward offered at the conclusion of the primary behavior. What's the reward a smoker gives himself or herself at the end of a meal? A cigarette. This to the smoker represents dessert, the hearty meal being the trigger and the reward, the cigarette. So we change the reward since it is not practical to discontinue the action that triggers the behavior.

In this instance, the reward needs to be replaced with one that is more healthful, instead of a cigarette at the end of a meal—something healthier—perhaps a fruit each time. This new behavior or orientation would then become ingrained, forming a pattern and eventually a habit. We would have given our brains a different orientation. Care must be exercised not to replace one bad habit with another; This defeats the purpose.

How do we react to stressful situations? What happens if we go to certain places or hang around certain individuals? Are these situations or people triggers to behavioral patterns we wish to change? Remember that it is the satisfaction we seek, imaginary or real, why we engage in certain habits.

Being conscious of our patterns, habits, feelings, and responsiveness is simply being aware of how we react in and to certain situations. What behaviors act like triggers to other behaviors we wish to change?

1. Once we understand what triggers certain behaviors, we can either avoid those situations altogether or
2. change the orientation, replacing it with a more healthful one.

To change our habits and become behaviorally conscious, we must examine the *cause* (How does it occur?), the *sequences* (What leads to it occurring?), the *needs* (What satisfaction is derived from the behavior that keeps it in play), and the *circumstances* (What are the collective situations or situation that causes its occurrence or triggers it to happen?).

1. Determine the reason or reasons why you have established and held onto the habit.
2. Determine the advantages and the disadvantages of changing or not changing the behavior.
3. Replace or find another healthier way of satisfying or eliminating the needs that are presently resolved in undesirable ways.

Consider Our Subconscious as a Storehouse of Knowledge to be Accessed at Anytime

Carl Jung, the Swiss psychiatrist who contributed to the psychological theories of introverted and extroverted behavior, describes three aspects of the psyche, primarily as it relates to dreams. However, in this discussion of the subconscious as an aspect of self-awareness, his theory relates.

Jung describes the psyche or mind as containing three layers: consciousness, personal unconsciousness, and objective or collective unconsciousness.

Consciousness contains the individual's attitudes toward his environment, including his awareness of the world and how he copes with it.

Personal unconscious is the repressed consciousness (either deliberate or unknowing), the urges forgotten or repressed, including your personal fantasies, dreams, and ideologies.

Collective unconscious is the memory seat and deepest area of the mind. All knowledge and wisdom of the past is contained in the collective unconsciousness, and this is the knowledge and wisdom of all humanity.

The collective unconsciousness is therefore akin to the storehouse where all knowledge is accessible[3], including that which we would consider intuitive.

How are we inspired? Where is the inspiration itself derived? Does it begin internally, or is its influence of an external source? Is the subconscious and unconscious the same? I surmise that inspiration comes from within, even though there may be, in some instances, external influences creating the spark.

What Jung has declared in his theory on dreams is the fact that the information within the unconscious already exists. We must, however, drill for it and tap into its source, the unconscious being that well.

The difference between the unconscious and subconscious is in the theoretical levels of awareness, the subconscious being a greater level of consciousness or awareness than the unconscious. On the subconscious level, while the mind is not fully conscious, it is still able to influence actions, whereas in the unconscious, while awareness may be present, theoretically, the mind is unable to influence actions.

It is more than just theory, however, that the visible is created from the invisible, which means the invisible already exists within our subconscious minds. We take from it and create that which needs to be made manifest.

The ability to create is a gift from God, that is, to be able to bring that which wasn't into being. Without this ability, mankind ceases to exist.

To a psychic, when information or an event is sensed, it is oftentimes unknown whether it is in the past, present, or future, for sometimes the past or future is experienced as being the present. This is because the sensation is of an inner dimension and concerns itself with events beyond the reach of outward perception. Psychics learn to trust themselves and those visions or feelings.

How are psychics able to discern that which they have no prior knowledge of? They possess the ability to tap into that well of the subconscious and perhaps the unconscious and access information at any time.

Theoretically, all individual experiences, whether they occur at conscious, subconscious, or even at seemingly unconscious levels, are stored. The ability to retrieve and utilize this information is what separates us creatively and otherwise. We can all achieve levels of mastery of this ability as well.

We can be inspired at any time and in any instance to do one thing or the other, and in doing, you too must consider the subconscious as a storehouse of information to be accessed at any time.

Increasing and/or enhancing our self-awareness amounts to practicing the following five aspects[4]:

1. *Self-dialogue.* Engage in self-dialogue. Question who you are. Ask yourself about yourself. Ask, "Who am I?" and then complete five to ten specific and brief statements about yourself. Begin each one with "I am . . ." These statements must be both positive and negative. Your name is not who you are, neither is your career or title.

2. *Listen* especially to others. People constantly tell us about ourselves, but we're often too busy to listen or too busy filtering. When you ask a question or make a statement, you are providing feedback about yourself; therefore, listen to what others say.

3. *Blind reduction.* Actively attempt to reduce the amount of information others know about you that you don't know they know. Less skeletons in your closet means less embarrassing moments and less secrets you have to cover up for.

4. *Observe different selves.* It is very difficult for us to see ourselves as others see us. The partial lyrics to one of my favorite songs goes like this:

> When you look in the mirror, tell me what do you see?
> Is it who you think you are, or who you want to be?
> (Jimmy Cliff)

Learn to see yourself as others see you, especially those individuals with whom you interact frequently. In order to accomplish this, you cannot filter out information you dislike or have a shields-up (defensive) attitude. Being open to criticism and to change is of importance.

5. *Increase open self.* Ironically, as you begin to reveal yourself to others, you not only learn more about others, but you also learn more about who you are. You become multidimensional and gradually more accepting of a variety of comments from others. Filters are no longer obstacles preventing you from seeing yourself from various perspectives, and even though you still may not always see yourself as others see you, you're, however, much more analytical and accepting of comments from others, including those comments that are nonflattering.

Increasing your open self is a natural segue to self-disclosure as you will observe.

CHAPTER 22

SELF-DISCLOSURE
PHASE 2: THE SELVES

Self-disclosure[1] is communication in which you reveal information about yourself. These include your thoughts, feelings, ideas, and behaviors.

Each time we communicate verbally and/or nonverbally, we disclose something about ourselves. Some of this disclosure is voluntary; that is, we choose to reveal certain data, while withholding other information. While, again, some disclosure is involuntary. No matter what we communicate, simultaneously, as we communicate, we reveal or disclose information about ourselves unintentionally.

Mastering self-disclosure is important because in building relationships, revolutionizing changes in communities, within ourselves, our society, and the world requires the free exchange of ideas and the ability to eloquently and effectively express ourselves and our ideas and adapt to changes.

Mastering the other aspects of self and not revealing personal and oftentimes intimate information about yourself is virtually impossible since others reveal to us much about ourselves, and we, in our journey to self-mastery, in effect revolutionize the self (abandoning the old and taking on the new). Self-disclosure is constantly at work in this effort.

Three primary factors[2] influence self-disclosure: *who you are, who your listeners are,* and *your topic or what you are disclosing.*

Who You Are

There is the tendency to disclose more to those individuals we believe are more like us; therefore, *culture, age, affiliation, gender, competence, self-esteem* and *social status* are some of the factors greatly influencing how much we would disclose of ourselves.

Culture

Culture basically sets the standard for much of our behavior, and because of this, much more is revealed to the in-culture (those of similar culture), and over a shorter period of time, than to the out-culture (those of a different culture), and what is revealed also differs, with more personal information being shared within the cultural in-group.

These cultural tendencies and behaviors cross all boundaries; that is, the behavior is commonplace not only from one group to another within a community but also from one country to another, and the type of culture determines the behavioral mechanisms. For example, Americans are very outspoken and tend to disclose more personal information about themselves than do people from Germany or Japan.

Culture must be examined seriously on the path to self-mastery, for culture may oftentimes subconsciously lock us into particular patterns of behavior that can hinder us in the mastery of self. We must therefore be consciously aware of these tendencies if we are to rid ourselves of these unwanted habits.

Age

In most cultures, age is associated with maturity, adulthood, privilege, status, expectancies, and influence. For example, in the United States, the age of emancipation (achieving adulthood or independence), in some states, is at the age of eighteen; in other states, the age is twenty-one.

Various laws are written specifically with age limitations, such as the age requirement for the consumption of alcohol or a license to operate a motor vehicle. Senior citizens are granted certain privileges based on them achieving a particular status associated with their age at sixty-five.

In self-disclosure, people tend to self-disclose more to their peers; that is, people of their own approximate age more than to those much younger or older.

There are assumptions of shared common interests and similar experience levels that play a definitive role in these aspects of self-disclosure.

Affiliation.[3] Strong bonds develop among family members because of their close association or affiliation to each other as members of the same unit. Disclosure tends to be more personal and intimate. The same might be said of members of clubs, associations, companies, and organizations.

Competence and self-esteem.[3] When you feel confident, your communication generally reflects this attitude. Competence refers to having what it takes or being adequately equipped. When you are, you exude confidence in your conversations and actions.

Competence and high self-esteem are intertwined. One leads to the other, and high self-esteem cannot exist without competency. Competent individuals will disclose more and more often than those with less confidence.

Gender.[3] It is more than rumor that women talk (disclose) a lot more than men do, but one of the reasons for this is that women are disclosed to more than men are. Women are perceived to be better listeners (they are), more compassionate, and offer more empathy, and so the tendency is, if you wish for solace, empathy, sympathy, and support, disclose to a woman. If you wish for practical solutions without the frills, disclose to a man, although it does not mean that men are dispassionate.

Ironically, more women prefer men as friends than other women. This is because men are less judgmental, less emotional, and guard information better than do women. Women therefore feel more confident that their disclosures would remain confidential with men than with a woman.

Social status.[3] Social status is bestowed upon those having achieved certain levels of accomplishments, whether it is within their community, country, or within a company or organization.

To use an example, the president of the United States holds the highest executive seat within the country, and with this status come certain responsibilities. These responsibilities accompany certain personal and public disclosures that are necessary to determine public trust and to judge whether the president is worthy of the status bestowed upon him. Hence, the intense scrutiny that is involved with someone running for or heading this office or other public offices.

On the other side of self-disclosure, however, is the fame that accompanies achievements by so-called celebrities. With their status comes an intense need by the public (fed by the press) to know more about the intimate details of the life of the individual to the point where it perhaps becomes intrusive, and subsequently, the private life of the individual is played out in public disclosures.

More often than not, those of equal status have more in common with each other, thus making it easier for disclosure to occur and relationships to develop between them. It is therefore no surprise that we often hear disclosures of intimate relationships between accomplished musicians, athletes, actors, and others of similar status and career interests played out at times in the form of titillating public and private disclosures sometimes called "news."

Who Your Listeners Are

Who you are disclosing to weighs heavily on what you would most likely disclose, and I will qualify this by saying in most cases.

Exceptions are made due to the fact that we do exist in a highly technological age, where information gathering, managing, and dissemination are now a masterful art available at our fingertips.

There are those who manipulate information for economic, political, and/or social gain, making the disclosure, while seemingly meaningful, merely sensational so as to create a diversion from the real event and/or disclosures.

The qualifying factors[4] influencing disclosure to select listeners, include *trustworthiness and likability, relationship status, affiliation status* (in-group), *group size*, and *competitiveness*.

Like and trust

There is more self-disclosure between those we *like and trust* than to those we do not, and this seems to be a natural occurrence. The more we like and trust someone, the more we disclose to them and the more personal the disclosure usually is.

In the mastery of self, personal disclosure improves the open self and indicates confidence and high self-esteem on the part of the disclosure, providing that the disclosure is truthful and the discloser trustworthy.

The development of trust in a relationship where there is personal disclosure hinges on four key issues: (1) *Dependability*, both individuals must be able to be relied on at all times and in all circumstances; (2) *responsiveness*, actions of each person cannot be self-serving, but instead it must be geared toward the interest and needs of one to the other; (3) *conflict management*, the ability to amicably resolve conflicts in constructive ways and not gunnysack (hold on to grudges) is desirable and necessary; (4) *faith*, feeling secure in the relationship, especially under adverse situations and circumstances.

Listener–Discloser Relationship

Relationships in general can be classified or categorized into four areas:

Acquaintance—Someone with whom we have a casual relationship. Our interactions with that individual is limited both in quantity and quality of time.

Friend—Someone who we have negotiated a closer relationship with. We share feelings and information, as well as disclose to them. There is also a level of commitment.

Close friend—An even closer relationship is formed, and secrets are shared. There is a high level of trust involved in close friendships.

Intimate—Someone with whom we share our deepest feelings. There is a definite bond and personal disclosures, usually exclusively.

The level or category of the relationship between the listener and the discloser will determine the disclosure. A more intimate relationship means more disclosure.

In small-group situations, as well as in in-groups, disclosure is more likely since the level of comfort rises as the groups become smaller and more manageable. The familiarity of in-groups takes precedent over an out-group when it comes to the disclosure of personal information and feelings, and this is due to the level of trust within the in-group.

Competitive/noncompetitive situations

Finally, in discloser-listener relationships, in noncompetitive situations, where neither party (but especially the discloser) feels threatened, intimate self-disclosure easily occurs and the level of self disclosure is high.

Topic

In early relationships, we are more selective as to the topic of conversations, choosing to have "safe" conversations, communication in which personal information is not exchanged. A safe conversation might be a casual conversation about the weather, political views, or about a sports team.

If the conversation is safe, and this is generally determined by either party, then most likely, self-disclosure will occur. However, as the conversation becomes more personal (less safe) as topics such as sex, personal finances, or personal relationships are explored, self-disclosure is approached with more caution.

What complicates the mastery of self-disclosure is its timing. When do we disclose to remain in the open self and be truthful, and how much do we disclose to move the relationship forward and at the same time not overload? The answers to these questions are not as simple as it may seem because we are constantly trying to negotiate our relationship with others, strike a balance within that relationship, and ensure that true friendships develop.

Some may be of the opinion that disclosure is instinctive, and perhaps to some extent it is. However, there are guidelines *for* self-disclosure as well as to self-disclose that helps us avoid most of the negatives in disclosing that could degrade communication and consequently the relationship.

Guidelines for Self-Disclosure[5]

1. *If the other person does not disclose, then you should not.*

If the individual you are disclosing to mistrusts you, have secrets to hide, or lacks interest in you or in the present conversation, they may hesitate or altogether refuse to disclose. Use their unwillingness to disclose as a guide for *your* actions and responses.

If the type of disclosure is intimate, then the same rules apply. Only if the intimate disclosure you have made is reciprocated should you continue it. Otherwise, you need to seriously consider limiting the amount of disclosure of this nature you make.

2. *Only disclose the kinds of information you wish others to disclose to you.*

Generally, others will follow your cue in disclosure and you should follow theirs.

If you're meeting someone for the first time, you should not share deep, intimate information. It may cause overload (too much information too soon to be processed adequately), resulting in mistrust of the information and the discloser. Safe information disclosure in the beginning until the relationship has been built.

The relationship must be balanced in its development for it to be meaningful to each party. Therefore, following this guideline helps to maintain an adequate balance.

3. *Disclose more intimate information only when you believe that disclosure represents an acceptable risk.*

Any information you provide can be used against you in whatever way the person deems fit. You increase the risk level with each piece of intimate or personal information you provide. Therefore, build trust and employ sound judgment in your disclosure of intimate information, especially information you perceive to be detrimental, illegal, or having negative consequences.

You may want to resort to disclosure rules 1 and 2 before disclosing information that may be considered risky.

4. *Self-disclosure of a personal or intimate nature should be gradual.*

Your disclosure to others as well as other's disclosure to you should not surpass your expectations or theirs. If the information you have received makes you feel uncomfortable or if you sense discomfort in others with the revelation of information you've provided, you have most likely violated the intimate self-disclosure rule on graduality.

As a relationship develops, the depth of disclosure increases. If the depth of disclosure does not match the level of the relationship, then there may be issues within the relationship and with the self-disclosure.

5. *Intimate and/or very personal disclosures should be reserved for established and ongoing relationships.*

Some falsely believe that truthfulness (in self-disclosure) means revealing all there is to reveal about one's self, with the belief that these revelations help to establish your relationship with that individual, but very personal self-disclosures should be for those with whom you have established a personal relationship. Therefore, you must make sure that your relationship has been established and secured because you may falsely believe you have a relationship where none exists.

Is it dishonest to not disclose everything about yourself when you're attempting to establish a relationship? It depends. If the nondisclosure could adversely affect the relationship and/or friendship, while it may not be dishonest to not disclose information (unless you were asked directly and lied about it), it is deceptive because the withholding of that information might be important in determining the type of relationship that can be or will be established. Each of us is allowed to have secrets, providing that the secrets do not negatively impact the relationship or the potentiality of a relationship.

In general, early self disclosure may create hostility and embarrassment and could be quite burdensome on others who are not quite ready for the information or who may have a different view than you have of the relationship.

6. *The disclosure must be appropriate and well motivated.*

The initial question that you must inquire of yourself after a disclosure has been made is "Why am I being told this, or why am I disclosing this information, and is it appropriate?"

The time and the timing of the disclosure is a good yardstick in determining appropriateness, and a careful examination of the first five disclosure guidelines would help.

There are numerous motives for someone wishing to disclose information considered very personal or intimate to inappropriate individuals. To unload personal guilt might be one motive, to gain an edge in a competitive situation might be another, and to gain attention or sympathy might also be a motive.

Extreme exuberance over a particularly wonderful occasion or situation, while it may motivate spontaneous self-disclosure, may not be appropriate since it could lead to unwanted or inappropriate attention. Whatever the motive, it must be honest, without hidden agendas, and nonmanipulative. It must meet the appropriateness of the situation, the discloser, as well as the audience being disclosed to.

7. *The best conditions must be provided for an open and honest response to a disclosure.*

You must have a clear sense as to whether the situation is ripe for a particular disclosure because the conditions could take the wind out of a joyous disclosure and make it one that you may wish you had never made.

An example to consider might be the birth of a child, usually a celebratory occasion. However, if the disclosure of that birth is to someone who did not expect the announcement or who just recently suffered a miscarriage or great loss of a child, it would be inappropriate and not the best condition for an open and honest response to the disclosure. If you wish to have honest and open responses to your disclosures, choose the right time, place, and situation.

Self-mastery in self-disclosure is knowing when to disclose, what to disclose, and how to disclose that information, and equally important is knowing what to do with the information disclosed to you.

When mastery of self-disclosure occurs, you will find yourself being called upon regularly for advice or to help resolve conflicts. The level of trust others have in you will rise considerably, and so would your level of honesty and integrity. As important in mastering how you disclose is mastering how you handle disclosure.

Your response to the information as it is disclosed to you will determine your sincerity and integrity and whether you can be trusted. The following guidelines when *responding to self-disclosure*[6] may prove helpful as you approach self-mastery of self-disclosure.

1. *Activate your listening skills with effective and active participatory engagement.* If you're interested in hearing the disclosure, act that way by asking appropriate questions, including follow-up questions, remembering to let the discloser speak. If there's need for clarification or to ensure understanding, appropriately paraphrase or ask other questions.
2. *At all times, reinforce and show support for the discloser.* The most difficult aspect of disclosing is the thought that what you're about to reveal might be laughed at or ridiculed or you may be thought of as being less intelligent. Disclosers therefore oftentimes clam up in fear of this.

The discloser is highly sensitized to the reactions of the listener; therefore, responses that are less than sincere or supportive are devastating to the discloser and, if of a low self-esteem, may destroy the confidence of that individual altogether.

In listening to the discloser, *eye contact* must be maintained to ensure the discloser that you as the listener are paying full attention and that you're really interested in what is being said.

Maintain *relevancy* in the questions you ask. This will indicate to the discloser that you were really paying attention to what was being said. If you're really listening to the discloser, you will ask relevant follow-up questions and not make the mistake most listeners do in listening situations—*rehearse or plan their responses.* Don't. Good listeners are aware of this trap and avoid it by planning to listen even before they get to the listening situation, and you must also demonstrate physical listening skills. Do not make assumptions but use surface and depth listening behavior, listening both for content and intent or meaning.

3. *Maintain confidentiality.* Always regard self-disclosure as a personal affair. Someone has chosen to reveal to you things they would not to others because of the level of trust and respect they have for you and your opinion, and breaching this would be detrimental indeed.

Utilize the rule doctors have with their patients, lawyers have with their clients, and journalists have with their sources—protect the discloser, and protect the information. Therefore, *never reveal information to others you have learned through someone else's self-disclosure.* If they're interested in letting someone else know, they'll tell them personally. Regard it as an honor that the discloser chose you to confide in.

My rule regarding secrets as an aspect of disclosure is that I will not allow someone to disclose to me what they would consider a secret. Therefore, if the information is qualified to be or considered a secret, I would politely decline the invitation to hear it. However, if the information being disclosed is considered confidential or exclusive, with no strings attached to the material, except my own inclination to adhere to its confidentiality, then I'd have no qualms about hearing the information and offering my feedback, using my judgment in determining what aspects of the information, if any, would be considered useful as a brief or extended example without the names attached.

Quite often and especially during arguments or breakups in relationships, individuals would resort to informational blackmail, *using the personal or intimate information they have regarding someone they know as a weapon against them,* thus betraying their trust and confidence. The law of compensation reveals that whatever you sow, that you shall reap as well, and if you betray someone's trust in this manner, then at some point in your life, your trust and confidence may also be compromised.

There is an upside and downside to self-disclosure; you must decide for yourself which is more rewarding.

Self-Disclosure: The Rewards

1. *A new perspective through self-knowledge.* Increased self-knowledge means increased awareness and hence heightened mastery of one's self.
2. *The ability to cope better.* Each of us have varying thresholds regarding stress, conflict resolution ability, and generally, how we cope with guilt and other life issues. Our coping abilities largely depends on our personal history of resolving conflicts, and the habits we have developed that ties into how we tend to resolve those conflicts.

If you gunnysack (hold on to grievances) and seldom express how you feel, then there would be difficulty in resolving issues when they arise. If there is a tendency to speak up and address conflicting issues in an honest attempt to resolve them amicably, your ability to cope would be on a much better level.

Regardless, there are many reasons why some individuals do not self-disclose their feelings. Among the most common are fear and guilt and being afraid of harming the relationship and of being thought of in a lesser capacity. Sometimes, there's guilt that their feelings of anger, hurt, jealousy, or resentment exist and are inappropriate.

Self-disclosure does not allow for a buildup of emotions since it is constantly being expressed; therefore, when an issue arises, coping with it becomes easier.

3. *Improved and more effective communication.* Practice makes perfect, and if you practice in the open self and honestly express your ideas and feelings, as you do, you'll discover better ways of expressing those ideas and feelings, and before you know it, you will have mastered self-expression and considerably improve your communication.

4. *Establishing meaningful relationships.* Communication and conversation are the building blocks of good relationships, and meaningful conversations and communication determines the kind or type of relationship built.
   Establishing in-depth, meaningful relationships means you must allow the other person to get to know who you are and vice versa, and the only meaningful way to do this is through self-disclosure.

Self-Disclosure: The Drawbacks

1. *Difficulties in your personal life.* Rejections of your ideas and feelings may lead to a lowered self-esteem and self-concept and, subsequently, intrapersonal difficulties. It is important that rejections are qualified and that individuals understand that a rejection of his or her idea is not a personal rejection, or your nonsupport regarding a particular situation does not mean general rejection or nonsupport of that individual.

   Proper communication is crucial so as to avoid these intrapersonal difficulties that could arise.

2. *Loss of trust and position within an in-group and personal rejection by friends and intimates.* If an in-group feels that a trusted member has betrayed the group, regardless of whether that betrayal corrected an immoral act, there will be resentment from within that group against that member. This resentment may lead to total rejection by the in-group, leading to the eventual ostracizing of that member.

   If close friends and/or intimates believe that personal disclosures were inappropriate and compromised them or the discloser, regardless of the morality or honesty of the disclosure, those individuals may feel that the breach is enough to sever ties with that individual.

   At the end of the day, we must follow our conscience and make decisions based on our moral beliefs, regardless of the known or unknown consequences, and when you're able to do so with no regrets for the decision made, you're one step closer to self-mastery of self-disclosure.

   Mastering self-disclosure, once again, does not mean saying what you feel as you feel it, without regard for the listener or for the effect of what you say; therefore, the correct strategy must be employed if the desired effect is to be achieved.

   The most effective strategy for self-disclosure is to *describe your feelings*. It gives the discloser several clear advantages. While this is the most effective strategy, it is not the only one employed.

   Two other strategies used in self-disclosure are *masking* and *displaying* feelings; these are ineffective for various reasons.

   Masking—Pretending you don't have the feelings you do have, you give no verbal or nonverbal credence to the existence of these feelings.

   There are individuals who are quite good at this type of disclosure or nondisclosure, being extremely affable while simultaneously holding a grudge against you, and you will have no idea of their ambivalence. This behavior is inappropriate and quite unhealthy for the masker or masquerader, for this pattern of behavior ultimately leads to internal blockages, which lead to various forms of diseases.

I often use the example of the college worker I once knew several years ago. I will not mention the name of the person nor the college, but it was an individual I had to communicate with in requesting materials for my classes. Each time I would make a request, I would always receive the same unfriendly response. At first, I thought it was personal but soon found out that others with similar requests received the same unfriendly welcome.

On this occasion, I entered the building with my request. I approached the individual, and almost before I could complete the verbal request, the response was "Don't have it." My reply was "But you did not even check your logs." The retort was "Don't have to. Don't have it." Of course, I never received the materials, and I left there feeling sorry for the individual but understanding that it was not personal and that it was nothing that I had done.

The following semester, relieved that my hours worked out favorably so that I did not have to request materials through that area, I just mentioned it in passing to someone else handling my request. The response astounded me when I was told that the individual had died a few months earlier. My heart sank. I felt empathy and a sense of loss. They found the body a day or two later. Internal medical causes as I was made to understand—a blood vessel erupted internally.

The point is masking or withholding your feelings simply means, outwardly, you give no credence to them. At an inner level, this negative energy must be released somewhere and, if internalized, would center itself in one of the seven energy points of light areas of the body (see page 193, chakras).

Negative energy centers itself internally on the weakest internal organ or area of the body. Blockages occur, light is denied to this area, cells begin to die, and as in the story above, there is the possibility of implosion, leading to aneurisms and a multitude of other diseases, such as heart disease, ulcers, and liver failure.

Do not deny your feelings by keeping them inside, for while you may falsely believe it denotes strength, it does not.

Displaying—Expressing how you feel emotionally through the manipulation of your facial muscles in facial reactions and/or through other physical bodily reactions.

Displaying emotions as opposed to masking them is more appropriate. However, for your self-mastery journey, control of the emotional body in concert with the physical, mental, and etheric is vital for self-mastery to occur within the lower bodies.

The tendency to display your feelings is giving the emotional body control over the other lower bodies in expressive ways to show how you feel. However, if you have not mastered control over the emotional body, then strong and even overwhelming emotions can lead to the loss of control over the physical and mental bodies, which can then lead to inappropriate displays of emotions.

While this behavior serves as an escape valve ("for letting off steam") and provides for a release of energy, it could also be physically destructive and very damaging to a relationship.

The strategy of displaying your feelings, while it is better than masking them, must be displayed with appropriate controls. However, emotional behavior does not always follow the course of its intent, and this strategy may be just as damaging as masking if the situation is emotionally caustic.

Describing—The most effective strategic approach in expressive self-disclosure is to describe your feelings.

Naming the emotion without judging it increases the chances of reaching a meaningful climax to an emotionally charged situation because it provides the opportunity for positive interaction and decreases the chances of the communication being disrupted or cut off through withdrawal or due to a breakdown in the process itself.

The four major advantages[7] of describing your feelings when disclosing are

1. It allows you, the discloser, to exercise measured control over the behavior of others toward you, mainly by making them aware of how their behavior affects you negatively or positively.
2. The discloser is able to explain the personal effect of the particular behavior, thus teaching others how to treat him or her.
3. It removes the expression out of the realm of emotional display of feelings to a calmer description of how the particular behavior impacts them.
4. You don't have to label your behavior, that person, or their behavior.

In describing your feelings, first indicate clearly what has triggered the feelings; that is, clearly identify the behavior that has resulted in you feeling the way you do. It may have been something that was said or done. Once you have clearly identified the trigger, then describing your feelings is less difficult. It is therefore important that you immediately identify the trigger as the situation occurs or try to recall the trigger as you're experiencing the emotion.

Secondly, you must be able to specifically identify in a nonverbal descriptive manner what you're actually feeling internally; for example, I have feelings of sadness, anger, embarrassment, or rejection.

Thirdly, you must verbally own the feeling and lay claim to it. What that helps you to do is self-disclose in ways that gives power to your descriptive statements while allowing you to take responsibility for those statements and that feeling you're describing.

Finally, you must verbally state what it is you're feeling and state it in ways that clearly show you own that feeling. For example, "I feel sad," "I feel anger," "I feel embarrassed," or "I feel rejected." Owning the feeling means framing it with the use of "I" statements, thus identifying yourself as the source of that feeling, thought, idea, and /or emotion.

The psychology behind someone self-disclosing is that the discloser needs sympathy, advice, or just for someone to listen; therefore, a response is expected.

In addition to the practical guidelines for responding to self-disclosure, understanding that there are only two types of responses a discloser often hears, especially when the disclosure is of a highly emotional nature, helps you to frame the response in a language that is affirmative, consoling, and empathetic. The discloser often hears either positive feedback (praise) or negative feedback (criticism), and as a discloser and/or disclosee, understanding the effects of praise and/or criticism on the psyche is crucial.

Praise (positive feedback) is when someone's positive behavior or accomplishment is described. Comments are focused on the effects that behavior has on others, and it is done as a means of reinforcing that behavior. The praise must be specific and in accordance with the significance or value of the accomplishment; otherwise, that individual can become arrogant, boastful, or even egotistical. Remember that important to self-mastery is humility.

Criticism (negative feedback) is describing the specific negative behavior or actions of someone and the effects that behavior has on others, done as a way of dissuading the behavior. As disclosure feedback, criticism should always be *constructive* and *specific*. It should be restricted to that person's most recent behavior. It should be described accurately and not labeled good or bad. Negative statements, harsh or bad criticism, should always be prefaced with a positive statement. Start with praise and always suggest positive changes to the behavior being criticized.

Self-mastery does not mean you must be perfect; instead, you must always be willing to move ever forward toward mastering the errors of the past, correcting your mistakes and making every effort to not repeating them again in the future.

Self-mastery of disclosure means knowing what to say, when to say it, and how, never having to apologize because you did not engage brain before putting mouth in motion but being able to acknowledge when you have said too little or too much, too soon, or at an inopportune time.

CHAPTER 23

CULTURE
EFFECT ON THE FOUR SELVES

From the previous chapters, we learned that personal experiences play a major role in the development of the four selves, and these experiences help to mold the ways in which we view the world.

However, what influences how we react and communicate and what influences our attitudes and the way we behave in particular situations are more than just our experiences. Culture plays a dominant role.

We will examine how culture affects the four selves and ways in which we can use culture effectively in the mastery of the four selves.

Always in examining culture, we must avoid ethnocentrism, the belief that one's culture is superior to another. It is dangerous and has always and will always lead to catastrophic results, as have already been witnessed in various parts of the globe where ethnic cleansing has occurred. Forms of ethnic cleansing has its roots in the belief that one group holds cultural superiority. This fallacy invariably leads to genocide and wholesale slaughter of those whom the superior group deem inferior and whose lives the ethnocentric deem to be worthless.

Culture[1] is the values, the beliefs, the ways of thinking, the ways of behaving, the art, the artifacts, the laws, the religion, the styles, the attitudes, the language, and the ways of communicating by a group of people. Culture therefore is everything we are.

The culture of the group influences the individual culture and is passed on from one generation to the next through communication. Therefore, culture is a learned process.

Our physical attributes, such as skin color, eye color, and shape of our eyes, lips, and nose, are sometimes confused as being cultural variables, for these attributes are often so closely identified with specific ethnic groups, which in turn is closely identified with ways of behaving or with a language and hence a culture. However, physical attributes are transmitted genetically and not through communication and therefore are not cultural characteristics.

On the other hand, gender, though transmitted genetically, is considered a cultural variable because cultures teach boys and girls different attitudes, beliefs, values, and mores (learned behavior).

Enculturation and acculturation are the two processes by which we learn and acquire our culture mores, enculturation being the process by which we learn the culture we are born into, and acculturation being the process by which we learn the rules and norms of a culture different from our native culture.

Because of demographic, geographic, economical, and technological changes, culture has taken on a more meaningful and prominent place in the lives of us all, and in the mastery of self, its effect must be strongly considered.

The access to technology and the increasing speed at which we are able to transmit data and information have not only increased communication capabilities but also narrowed the cultural divide and made our national economy a global economy, bringing foreign and different cultures right into our living rooms.

Today, global culture is very relevant, and it affects our self-concept, self-esteem, self-awareness, and self-disclosure in unique ways, yet through this, we have discovered how similar and connected we all really are.

Individual and collective cultural variances is one way our four selves are affected.

Individual culture

In cultures that emphasize individualism like the United States, the values are more single-minded and more self-centered. Individual goals and values are promoted over group goals and values. Individual members are encouraged to excel, to be different, to stand out from the crowd, to be responsible for self, to compete, and to win at all costs.

Because total independence is emphasized, there is a feeling of obligation on the part of the parent and the family to prepare that child for the world by the time they acquire the age of eighteen and most definitely by age twenty-one.

At the age of twenty-one, that individual is considered emancipated and no longer a child and is encouraged and, in some cases, forced to venture out on their own and become totally independent, and what, you may ask, is wrong with this view? From a cultural standpoint, nothing. In fact, there's nothing wrong or right about any culture since no culture is better than any other.

In fact, not so long ago, in Western cultures, a woman was considered old by age twenty-one and was married by age thirteen.

The group sets the standard for the cultural behavior, and each cultural group would behave differently in similar situations. Does this mean, then, that there are different standards for self-mastery since culture plays such a vital role in setting these standards? The answer is no because there are things that know no cultural boundaries because of the universal laws that govern each and every one of us—spiritual and cosmic laws.

Secondly, the universal or common emotional expressions of feelings—anger, sadness, happiness, fear, disgust, and surprise—have no cultural boundaries. We all feel these common emotions and express them in similar ways, regardless of language or other barriers.

Thirdly, the four lower bodies—the physical, mental, emotional, and etheric—are a common inheritance to all human beings, regardless of the amount of arms or legs that individual may possess or the mental state, emotional makeup, or spiritual beliefs. At some given point and time in everyone's lives, each of us will have to determine its role in our lives.

Fourthly, the elements under which we all exist and must rely on for our very survival—earth, air, fire, and water—know no cultural boundaries. We cannot live without these elements but must learn how to live with it and prosper.

Collective Culture

In these cultures, in parts of Asia, India, Japan, and China, for example, tradition and conformity are expected; therefore, group goals supersedes individual goals. Ambition based on individual drive is sacrificed for the common good. Success is measured by the individual's contribution to the achievements of the group, and individual members are responsible for the entire group; therefore, if the group succeeds, the individual members succeed.

One of the major attributes within the collectivistic culture that furthers the development and mastery of the four selves seems to reside in the fact that cooperation, not competition, is fostered. Extreme identification with the in-group would sometimes allow the rights of those outside of that group to be violated if not checked.

High and low context cultural variances[2] is another way our four selves is affected by culture.

High Context Culture

These cultures usually exhibit collectivism. They are traditional in their outlook. High context simply means that the context of information sharing is limited. The information exchanged is usually vague or nonexplicit; that is, members hold on to information and are very secretive. Even when the information is known by all, the participants seldom state it explicitly. You have to read between the lines.

There is a reluctance to say no because these cultures don't believe in offending, disappointing, or embarrassing anyone. Therefore, in conversations where there might be the possibility of an argument or conflict, individuals within this cultural group would do whatever they could to avoid arguments, primarily for fear of causing the other person to be shamed.

Members of high-context cultures spend quite some time building personal relationships, even in business transactions. To members of this group, a handshake is more important than a written contract since they consider their word sacred.

Trust and dependability, above all, seem to be major contributors to the development of the four selves within high-context cultures.

Low-Context Culture

These cultures exhibit individualism. Power and achievement are among the primary drives. Countries like Sweden, Germany, and the United States are examples of low-context cultures.

Low-context cultures emphasize that expressive communication; verbalized, explicit explanations; and written contracts, rather than verbal agreements or a handshake, seals deals.

Because less emphasis is placed on face saving, arguments are often used to persuade and win points. Being able to say no when no is meant is a sign of strength and indicates an ability to confront reality. Because less time is spent on personal relationships, there is much less shared knowledge between individuals.

The major contribution to the development of the four selves in low-context cultures is the ability to separate personal feelings from business decisions, to be practical, and to be able to set aside personal fears.

High and low power distance cultural variances[3] is a third way the four selves is affected by culture.

High Power Distance

There is great divergence between the haves and have-nots and between those holding power and those who are powerless. The greater the void, the higher the power distance, as seen in countries such as Mexico and Brazil.

In cultures where high power distance is a cultural norm, authority is respected to the point of being feared. It is expected that those with less power be polite, modest, and respectful. Consequently, being assertive or aggressive is looked down on and viewed negatively.

Maintaining the status quo and conforming to the cultural mores are strongly enforced and quite rigid; therefore, for example, forming relationships outside of your cultural class is frowned upon, and much pressure is brought to bear on those who do not conform.

A key contribution to the development of the four selves seems to be the healthy respect for authority, which might be equivalent to having respect for God and self to help further the mastery of self.

Low Power Distance

Power is more evenly distributed between those in authority and those with seemingly less power.

In the United States, the constitution has been quoted and referred to often and has served as a reminder to ordinary citizens that they too have inalienable rights to certain freedoms, such as free speech, liberty, and the pursuit of happiness. This document, more than any other, has empowered the citizenry of the United States with the courage to stand up and address inequality and injustice wherever it may be found.

For the development and mastery of the four selves, the reminder is that we are masters of our own destiny and must act accordingly. Thus, empowerment raises self-concept and self-esteem creates more self-awareness, and when we feel empowered, we act empowered and are not afraid to speak up and speak out. Self-disclosure becomes positively impacted.

Masculine and feminine cultural variances[4] is the fourth way culture affects the four selves. In these cultures, there is either the predominance of males or females, and which predominates helps to determine what the important issues within that society are.

Masculine Cultures

In these cultures, males set the rules and the standards for the rest of the society. Governance is largely by males; the rules and the standards are also set up by males.

Males would most likely hold certain positions in business and work in fields that are more physically demanding. Hence, you'd find, for example, construction workers being mostly males, while domestics or nannies being mostly females.

The socialization of members in a masculine culture is for males to be assertive, aggressive, competitive, ambitious, successful, and strong, both emotionally and physically.

In areas of conflict management and conflict resolution, there is an attitude of the last man standing is the winner; thus, a win-lose conflict strategy is adopted.

Direct confrontation is expected, and in fact, almost desired if the male is to be respected. In the Latino culture, this attitude of being tough or hard is referred to as *machismo*.

Countries like the United States, Japan, Austria, Jamaica, Great Britain, parts of Latin America, and Germany exhibit predominantly masculine cultures.

While there seems to largely be a negative effect of masculine cultures on the development of the four selves, with males being overly aggressive, which can lead to the eruption of violence, this type of culture mirrors the family structure of hierarchy and subsets necessary for the maintenance and functionality of the family as a system, with the male being the head of the household in most societies.

Feminine Cultures

In feminine cultures, the female's point of view is more valued. The focus within these cultures is on quality of life, and a gentler, softer approach is adopted to obtain the desired results. Modesty is valued in both men and women.

Interpersonal relationships is valued in both masculine and feminine cultures; however, it is emphasized in cultures that are feminine in nature.

Conflict management and resolution utilize compromise and collaboration in the negotiation efforts.

Unlike the masculine cultures, in feminine cultures, there is less competition and, because of it, less aggression.

In feminine cultures, the development of the four selves benefits from the conflict resolution approach.

While within these culture, conflict may not arise as much as we think, the real conflict comes about when these opposing cultures clash; therefore, the approach in intercultural situations would be to anticipate and plan in advance, recognizing that there are cultural differences that may result in conflicts.

Effort must also be made to reduce ethnocentrism and to embrace the differences in us. Travel, explore other cultures, venture outside of your comfort zone, and be global and think globally, especially as ethnic boundaries shift and populations within communities change proportionately.

CHAPTER 24

EARTH
THE FOURTH QUADRANT OF MATTER

The Lord by wisdom founded the earth; by understanding He established the heavens;
by His knowledge the depths were broken up, and clouds drop down the dew.
— Proverbs 3:19-20[1]

What does earth have to do with self-mastery? In fact, what is our connection to earth? We know our physical walk must take place here in development of and in preparation for our spiritual walk.

Here is another important factor, the earth element embodies the other elements of fire, air, and water, and the unification of those three elements is what is responsible for our physical walk in the development of the "I" consciousness of the human being—the ego.

There is a strong correlation between earth the fourth quadrant of matter and the physical body, and while it is the lowest aspect of the spiritual/cosmic development, it is on this plane the individual develops egotism and other instincts, including selfless or selfish attributes that often characterize human behavior in its most base form or toward its manifestation of higher principles. And basic to these human characteristics is self-preservation, an instinctive attribute for which the earth element bares a direct responsibility, for it is here we foster and develop this attribute.

Self-mastery through the 4-4-4 connection methodology explores the relationship of the four lower bodies—physical, mental, emotional, and etheric bodies—to one of the four corresponding elements of earth, air, fire, and water.

The physical body corresponds to earth, the mental body corresponds to air, the emotional body corresponds to the water element, and the etheric body corresponds to the fire element. The real self or the Christ consciousness overshadows the lower bodies. Being attuned with and understanding clearly, the interdependent relationship between the corresponding four lower bodies, the four selves, and the four elements brings us closer and closer in the discovery of the real self.

References are made to the four elements[2] as they relate to the lower bodies as the first, second, third, and fourth quadrants[3] of *matter*.

Fire, the first quadrant of matter, is responsible for energy, might, and passion and relates to the etheric body.

The second quadrant of matter air relates to the mental body. This element is responsible for memory or the intellect, providing the human being with the ability to reason, analyze, judge, and differentiate.

The third quadrant of matter water correlates to the emotional body, bares the responsibility for the development of our intuition and our conscience, which in turn enables us to discern right from wrong and, for the most part, prevent us from exercising our most basic animalistic instincts.

The fourth quadrant of matter earth as previously described correlates to the physical body, and vice versa, this body relates to the element of earth.

Of the four lower bodies, the highest is the etheric (i.e., the highest plane in the dimension of matter), followed by the mental body, the emotional body, and lastly, the physical body.

Matter is everything around us. Simply put, molecules and atoms are compositions of matter, and solids, liquids, gases, plasma, and Bose-Einstein condensates are scientifically identified matters. Examining earth and its relationship to self-mastery illuminates the importance of matter, energy, and our physical development as it relates to our existence on earth. If matter is around us, then matter is also in us. We are therefore comprised of matter.

We, as referring to humans, are energies that cannot be destroyed but only change form or state. Figure 1 capsulate what Science 101 teaches us about the various composition of matter at various states of energy.

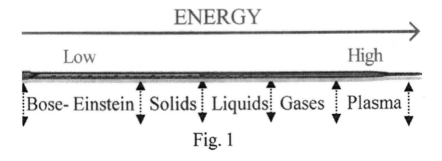

Fig. 1

We know water freezes at 32°F and boils at 212°F (F for Fahrenheit). On the Celsius scale, water freezes at 0°C and boils at 100°C.

In the examination of the energy scale in (figure 1), at the lowest energy level would be the Bose-Einstein condensate, followed by solids, a little higher in energy; followed by liquids; and then gases, and the more excitable and energetic of matter is plasma.

Think of water being boiled and then cooled; it changes state or loses energy as it cools and would slide up or down the scale, respectively. What has really changed is the density, pressure, temperature, and other physical properties of the water; however, the basic chemical structure remains the same.

In our examination of the physical body as it corresponds to earth, the physical body changes in relationship to the energy expelled or expounded. However, the chemical structure remains constant. Similarly, the earth's physical properties changes according to its exposure to pressure, density, temperature, and other elements.

Much has changed over time on this planet called Earth, and it is important to understand how these earthly changes affect us individually and collectively and how understanding our relationship to it all, as it relates to our drive to self mastery, helps us in this quest.

All material on earth consists of at least one of these three states or properties: solids, liquids, and/or gases. Each can be altered in form, and each in its form can be described as having its own property and hence can be grouped together accordingly into categories of solids, liquids, and gases.

The atmosphere or air around us is comprised of gases. Approximately 78 percent of it is nitrogen, and about 21 percent of it oxygen. One percent is a mixture of various other gases.

Pollution and other environmental factors have contributed to the increased emission of greenhouse gases (such as increased carbon dioxide) in higher concentrations than in previous years, causing the earth's temperature to climb way above past levels. The warming effect of the earth's atmosphere has created serious imbalances in the environment like melting glaciers, changing rainfall patterns, changing sea levels, and other disturbances, which in turn has created havoc and severe ecological imbalances on the planet.

Climate changes affects all life on the planet—humans, plants, and animals—and according to the U.S. Environmental Protection Agency (EPA), "some observed effects include the rise in sea levels, meltings in Arctic regions, seasons lengthening and in some cases, shortened seasons for plants, ice on rivers and lakes freezing later and breaking up earlier, and the thawing of permafrost."[4]

The warming effect in the earth's atmosphere occurs because gases become trapped as fossil fuels burn and other industrial erosions occur. The heat cannot escape into space, thus causing the "greenhouse effect" within the earth's atmosphere.

There is a balancing act that takes place on planet Earth. This balance adheres to natural or nature's law, and imbalances occur when there is removal or alteration of a natural resource, without it being replaced or repositioned so as to create equilibrium once again.

Using the laws of the jungle as an example, animals and insects prey on each other, and while it may appear to be cruel to us higher animals, it is a necessary and natural cycle and way of life, and if left alone (and barring some natural disaster, although it does not count as an intrusion), a balance is maintained within that domain, irrespective of how many are preyed upon.

The moment there is unnatural intrusion (human intrusion), for purposes other than altruistic, the equilibrium changes, often times permanently, and animals, birds, sea life, and other creatures become extinct. The earth itself undergoes a well-maintained and balanced cleansing process, a natural occurrence under natural law. We humans have created the imbalances.

According to the EPA, although scientists are uncertain as to by how much the greenhouse gases[5] would change the composition of the earth's atmosphere, they are certain that the changes will be detrimental to all life on the planet, creating (as it has already) severe health and environmental problems if not altered.

Globally, the problem is finally being viewed seriously, albeit in my opinion, with not enough urgency. However, (in 2006), an intergovernmental panel on climate change (IPCC) was convened to study the effects of future temperature changes, precipitation, storm and sea level changes, and their effects globally. The jury is not out as yet as of this publication.

Part of cosmic and natural laws involve cycles. These cycles occur in every facet of life on earth and create patterns that influence behavior. Understanding the patterns allows us to make life adjustments. In general, the cycles of life—birth, life, death, and birth—form a continuum and adhere to cosmic law, and all life form on earth is part of this experience.

Depending on the region of the world in which you reside, the seasonal cycles are fall, spring, summer, and winter. With each season, specific physical earthly changes occur. Even in regions where only one seasonal occurrence is experienced (such as summer all year round), there are still cycles within these regions' inhabitants come to expect and do experience regularly, such as hurricanes, rains, tornadoes, and other related changes.

Within the plant kingdom, there are fixed cycles from the time a seed is planted to its germination and then its growth into a flower or plant and eventually into a tree bearing fruit in its cycle. This is so with all plant life.

Within the animal kingdom, the gestation or period of development of the embryo varies widely. In dogs and cats, for example, it takes approximately 63 days; in elephants, about 624 days; and in humans, about 280 days. And within each group, the cycle remains identifiable, predictable, and certain. Any precipitous changes in the natural occurrence would suggest an abnormality.

Among Rosicrucians and in their teachings, it is common knowledge that there are cycles of disease and sex, earthly cycles, daily cycles, cycles of life, business cycles, health cycles, and yearly cycles, with each period of the cycle producing some effect on the physical, emotional, mental, and spiritual bodies. Each cycle works in harmony with nature or natural law and has the same occurrence or reoccurrence of a situation within that period.

An observable example of cyclictic occurrences in humans is noted in the menstrual period of women. This cycle is consistent and persistent. For each woman, the occurrence, while it may commence at a different time during the course of the month and its duration may vary, the period's occurrences are constant in its cycle, approximately every twenty-eight days.

Changes in the cycle give notice to the person of an anomaly and draws attention to the fact that something extraordinary may be occurring. It is imperative for the health and the equilibrium of women that this natural occurrence takes place until its course has been run. At a given age, this occurrence ceases and the woman will no longer experience this phenomenon, and this also is in accordance with its cycle.

There is medical research currently being explored, and drugs are being market tested to control the woman's natural cycle by lessening and, in some cases, stopping its occurrence. This, I dare say, will produce catastrophic results in the end for those women who are knowing or unknowingly challenging natural law.

Without the observance of earthly cycles, there is no way to measure with certainty occurrences and changes in our lives and the regularity in which they take place, and nature will always win a challenge.

Counting fifty-two days going forward from your birthday charts each person's individual yearly earthly cycle and, with each period, the cosmic vibrations influencing individual business and personal affairs.

Understanding how to work in harmony with the cycles enables individuals to become masters of their own destinies. Understanding how to achieve the most from the universe and work in harmony with the offerings of the earth begins with understanding that there is no bargaining with God or the cosmos. You cannot make deals with that which is greater than you are and no respecter of persons in meting out justice, for the sun shines equally on the just as well as on the unjust.

This all begs the questions "What should our relationship to earth be?" and "How does the physical body correspond to the fourth quadrant of matter, earth?"

There are 195 countries in the world,[6] with 6.6 billion people. About 70 percent of the earth is liquid (water), and approximately 30 percent is land. This also corresponds to the makeup of the physical body, which is 70 percent water. In fact, at one point in our history, the earth was a connected land mass that slowly eroded, broke off, and separated. Parts of Europe, for the most part, has remained a connected land mass. However, most of the world is today separated by vast oceans, rivers, and lakes.

There are numerous regions, languages, customs, and cultures on earth that seem to divide the 6.6 billion people into small communities, making it seemingly harder for us to work cooperatively for the common good of the earth and the planet, but all of us have one thing in common—there is but one earth, and we are its keepers.

More and more, especially with the growth in technology, we are now able to make global connections instantaneously. We hear mention of global economies and global technological innovations and advancements. Our relationships to each other should be and has become more global, not only in the outlook of achieving and maintaining a global economy but one universal view and mindset in the earth's preservation.

The separations of nations—politically, economically, and culturally—has provided the disconnected view that what is done to the earth in one part of the world does not affect those of us in other parts of the world. Consider this analogy of "the unkept lawn." Here you have neighbors living side by side in a small community, and each is responsible for mowing their lawn. All the neighbors, except one, mow regularly. The weeds begin to grow among the grass on that unmowed lawn. Not only does it make the neighborhood look bad, but soon the weeds would begin to spread to the mowed lawns as the wind directs it. After a while, even on the manicured lawns (if diligence is not exercised), there will be weeds.

We are stewards of the earth and, as such, are responsible for the upkeep of our portion of the earth, and that includes the preservation of all life on the face of the earth. As in the analogy, if we fail to do our part, then soon, everyone begins to pay the price.

The earth's erosion began centuries ago with the industrial revolution and continues to this day unabated simply because we are driven by economics, industrialization, and the unquenchable desire and need for quick results and returns. This has been the philosophy irrespective of what happens to the earth in the process; thus, we create waste, fail to conserve, cut, burn, pollute, and do not clean up after ourselves, and consequently, we now have a global problem.

There is no survival without the soil, where our food is derived; without the air, by which our breathing is sustained; and without water, which is indeed liquid life. However, erosions in the soil through the use of pesticides in the air and water through pollutants have made us all poor stewards and have created the estrangement we now witness in the global relationship of humans to the earth as it is with human to human.

Our estranged relationship with nature in the twenty-first century is perhaps most obviously witnessed by the rampant diseases on earth and the toxicity in foods, including the many food-borne diseases and allergies.

In small pockets of the world—in some places far removed from so called civilization, in small rural villages deep within some jungle or rain forest, and among people "developed" nations would regard as backward and uncivilized—there are those still clinging to traditional ways of life, utilizing nature to track, hunt, heal, feed families, and upkeep their villages and towns. They remain close to nature, utilizing it to predict drastic seasonal changes and disruptions, anticipate natural disasters like volcanoes, tornados, earthquakes, and tsunamis, but they too are becoming modernized.

As globalization spreads, allowing us to reach into the once-inaccessible areas of the world, and as these areas begin to come into the twenty-first century, the ability to be one with nature and to listen to the wind and hear and understand nature's language—for the inhabitants of these regions—the observance of cosmic law becomes a phenomenon of the past.

During the 2004 tsunami in the areas of Malaysia and Indonesia, not a single animal perished. They listened, heard, and heeded nature's dire warning, and because of their eminent relationship to nature, these beasts were able to interpret the low rumblings underneath the seas as a call to move to higher ground.

We cannot halt progress and advancement; none of us have the singular ability to make that happen. We can, however, deter some of the damning effects with wiser choices. We are masters of our destinies and have the freedom to choose, and this choice is all that separates the wise from the foolish.

The utilization of nature's gifts, along with our advanced knowledge of the earth—plant life, for instance, and the utilization of its roots, vines, barks, leaves, flowers, and seeds for medicinal purposes and to promote healthier living—has always been available to us. We need only to become conscious about working in harmony with cosmic and spiritual law.

Each generation has always borrowed from the prior its ability to utilize earth's natural resources in the effort to promote qualitative living. There is now an urgency that much might not remain for future generations at the rate of earth's decay.

Our relationship to earth therefore must be one of a procurer, protector, and preserver, and *herein lies the corresponding relationship of the earth the fourth quadrant of matter, to the physical body.*

As *procurer*, we have been entrusted with the earth and all its resources for our physical living and well-being. Having been given dominion over every living creature both on land and sea, there is a true responsibility that comes with this procurement, and there must now be a consciousness of this responsibility if we are to truly be self-masters.

A quotation from *A Manifesto for Earth*, in effect, captures in essence what makes our relationship to earth so unique and important.

> "We are born from Earth and sustained by it throughout our lives. In today's dominating industrial culture, earth as-home is not a self-evident percept. Because we are issue of the Earth, the harmonies of its lands, seas, skies and its countless beautiful organisms carry rich meanings barely understood." (Masquin, Ted; Rowe, Stan; *A Manifesto for Earth*, April-June 2004).

The Sioux and other natives have referred to earth as the universal spiritual mother or Mother Earth. They understand that the earth belongs to no one and to everyone and is of utmost importance as the physical repository of every life form within it.

Ed McGaa, in his book *Mother Earth Spirituality*, talks about reconnecting with the earth as a means of self-healing, as well as for the healing of the earth itself.

Ted Masquin and Stan Rowe, in their manifesto for earth, declares,

> "We humans are conscious expressions of the Ecosphere's generative forces, our individual "aliveness" experienced as inseparable from sun-warmed air, water, land, and the food that other organisms provide. Like all other vital beings born from Earth, we have been "tuned" through long evolution to its resonances, its rhythmic cycles, its seasons." (Masquin, Ted; Rowe, Stan; *A Manifesto for Earth*, April-June 2004; http://www.ecospherics.net).

Therefore, as procurers, we must, for our sakes, be wise in the collective choices we make with our habitation (earth). As we modernize and advance into this new and daring technologically era, we must seek to utilize the best alternatives harmonious to our continued existence on earth. Otherwise, the end result will be predictable and disastrous for all its inhabitants.

As *protectors*, we must begin to believe that the earth is worthy of our protection. This means, we must recognize that the earth's air, soil, and waterways are endangered, and if it is, so is the health, longevity, and sustenance of each and every one of its inhabitants. The physical journey on this planet, though temporary, is important to the development of our higher selves and, if it is to be meaningful, must also be in harmonious rhythm with earthly vibrations.

If we divide our lives into rhythmic periods of seven years, with each period of seven years contributing to our physical and spiritual development, while marking the gradual decline of our physical bodies, according to Rosicrucian teachings, each of us are supposed to live at least 144 years, but, most of us don't. Why? Because of our violation of cosmic and spiritual laws and our intransigent relationship to the environment.

In the book *The World's Greatest Treasury of Health Secrets*, Bradley J. Wilcox, MD, writes about the residents of Okinawa,[7] an island chain of Japan, where you'd find more one-hundred-year-olds than anywhere else in the world. Their secret—their attitudes, diet, and lifestyle.

The Okinawans have an 80 percent plant-rich diet, in addition to a healthy diet of soy foods and fish. Exercise; no smoking; maintaining a healthy low-fat diet, which in turn reduces weight gain; an active social lifestyle; as well as a spiritual and religious base belief concept have contributed to their longevity.

We learn from Wilcox that the modern-day Okinawan (the younger generation) are today more exposed to Western culture. They smoke and the diet has changed, so too has the lifestyle, and the consequences of these changes have resulted in changes in the general health of these Japanese people.

The older Okinawans, by observing spiritual and cosmic laws, were able to live in harmony with nature and in attunement with the cosmic vibrations—keys to their longevity. As the Okinawans remove themselves from their traditional way of life and healthful living, they begin to witness the adverse affects on their health and longevity.

H. Spencer Lewis, former imperator of the Rosicrucian Order for North and South America, outlines the simple periods of human life, which is, in effect, a study of the effect of spiritual and cosmic laws on human life on earth.

The human life[8] can be divided into periods of seven, and one can actually trace individual progress in all areas of life, including the physiological, psychological, and spiritual changes and manifestations that occur at key periods in the lives of us all.

This is important because we can learn from the Okinawans and from observing carefully the cycles of life how we may be able to remain in alignment with the natural law and cosmic vibrations, which is constantly emanating from the earth, and by moving in its rhythm, remain free from stress and be successful in our personal and business affairs.

After carefully examining the simple periods, studying the teachings of the cycles of life, and applying it judiciously, it is clear that the relationship between the physical body, (the lowest of the four lower bodies), and its corresponding element, earth, had to by necessity correspond. This relationship, when analyzed, intimates to us the lives we must lead if we are to survive this planetary journey, which is primarily a physical one.

The earth as a physical domain offers all the physical comforts and acumen needed for our physical development, but not only the physical but the mental, emotional, and spiritual as well since they should all develop in concert so as to create and maintain balance. This development begins at birth, with the environment playing a vital role in the stages of our development.

During the first three seven-year periods of life here on earth, we develop more and more as physical beings. While this will continue throughout our physical lives, the mental, psychic, and emotional development also comes into attunement with our cosmic consciousness.

At each seven-year period of our lives, ages one to seven and then fourteen through twenty-one and so on, we transcend each period, growing intellectually and spiritually till eventually we become primarily spiritual beings, which is what we were meant to be anyway.

Assuredly, for each and every one of us, although the journey's path might be different, the destination is the same. The physical being eventually departs (our physical strength eventually wanes), leaving mostly a spiritual being in its wake, and by the time this stage has been reached, we should have become self-masters through wisdom, knowledge, and understanding.

For those on the path of knowledge, this is the mastery of self which is what is to be sought and attained, the attainment of the highest spiritual self can only be achieved with diligence, perseverance, patience, faith, and fearlessness in alliance with cosmic and spiritual laws.

The question, then, is how does the physical body correspond to the fourth quadrant of matter, the earth? Proverbs 3:19-20 states "The Lord by wisdom founded the earth; by understanding He established the heavens; by His knowledge the depths were broken up, and clouds drop down the dew."

There are two laws under which all men on earth must abide: spiritual (God's law) and cosmic (universal nature's law). Both are unchanging, and it is only through wisdom, understanding, and knowledge we are sustained.

Both the physical body and the fourth quadrant of matter earth are physical in nature, each dependant on the other for its sustenance. The physical body cannot develop without the earth's sustenance, and the earth will decay if physical man fails to exercise correct judgment upon it.

We have learned through scientific study that our life form can only exist where there is water and the correct balance of nitrogen, oxygen, and other gases. The earth is the only planet providing the resources necessary for the existence of life as we know it, and for man's development and advancement, there is an interdependent relationship, for we cannot exist naturally without the earth.

The lowest form of existence is earthly, and man's lowest nature is the physical. The task is to develop the physical body so that it may transcend its base nature and, by so doing, reach its highest self, which is the etheric. This can only be achieved via this physical journey and by working through the experiences gathered as we make this journey.

Some have made the determination that life is too hard and have chosen (wrongfully) to cut their lives short. Others have made poor choices, believing that the easier or more convenient choices would satisfy them. That choice becomes their destiny, wrongly or rightly.

As earth's *protectors*, we must decide if a mother (Mother Earth) is worth protecting. The choices we make will determine our fate.

As *preservers*, we are obligated to maintain a safe and secure environment, not only for our purposes and for the future generations but also for the sake of the environment itself.

Preservationists philosophically believed it was important to save the environment for its own sake so that nature could be enjoyed in the future. The conservationists philosophy was that the environment should be saved and its natural resources used for production and be replenished for the benefit of all who live in the world communities.

John Muir, one of the founders of the preservationist movement, in 1892, through his Sierra Club, championed the cause to preserve the environment with his wilderness preservation movement and efforts to create national parks. The Sierra Club's mission was to convince others that the rain forests needed and were worthy of protection from companies bent on missions to destroy them.

Theodore Roosevelt, the twenty-sixth president of the United States, was one of the leaders of the scientific conservationists who wanted to save the environment for human purposes. The United States government, recognizing the importance of protecting the wilderness and the environment, in 1890, founded the first national park in the United States, the Yosemite National Park in Northern California. Today there are thousands of parks all across the United States.

There were others who felt just as strongly as John Muir and President Roosevelt did that we were a part of nature and not owners of it and it was our responsibility to preserve and conserve the environment so that it would remain an inhabitable place for us all.

Both the preservationist and conservationists viewpoints speak to the importance of the earth and its resources for life's continuance, and while the philosophical views may vary slightly, the goal remains the same: The earth is important, and as its keepers, we must share in the responsibility of its upkeep. Our physical growth and development, alongside our mental development, depends on it.

The earth contains all that we need for our physical journey here. In fact, even modern-day technology, through scientific probing, only recently has been able to tap into what was always available in the air, electromagnetic waves, which has yielded us all the modern communication technological devices now at our disposal, and there's more to come.

However, we must be cognizant of our role as procurer, protector, and preserver. As we deplete, borrow, and take out, we must replace, replenish, and repair, thus ensuring our continuance in meaningful ways for the abbreviated physical journey each of us must embark on.

CHAPTER 25

WATER
THE THIRD QUADRANT OF MATTER

I indeed baptize you with water unto repentance, but He who is coming after me is mightier than I whose sandals I am not worthy to carry, He will baptize you with the Holy Spirit and fire.

—Matthew 3:11[1]

Water (H2O), the third quadrant of matter, plays a significant role in the mastery of self and in its relationship to the emotional body. This body houses the power of desire and feelings, and like the ebb and flow of water, it can be gentle, soothing, and refreshing and yet at times volatile, violent, and overpowering.

Colorless, odorless, and tasteless, water equals life, and scarcity of it means, sooner or later, the nonexistence of life. It is the only natural substance found in the three states of matter—solids, liquids, and gases—each altered by temperature changes (see page 153, figure 1). Water can be described as the perfect meal. In fact, you can survive on just water alone for at least forty days; without water and just food, three to five days.

What are some of the other characteristics of this solvent. Well, it is perfectly symmetrical (round), and the molecules are so close together that it is described as sticky or clumpy. It contains one atom of oxygen and two atoms of hydrogen of opposite polarity on each side, and since opposites attract, the positive polarity of the hydrogen attracts the negative polarity of the oxygen, thereby causing the clumping or stickiness and hence the fluidity of water.

You only recognize that water is a series of separate molecules or droplets if you accidentally or purposefully place a plastic bottle once filled with water (leave a little at the bottom) on your desk or table (which I did) at room temperature and let it sit sealed or covered for a few days. Then watch as the little water at the bottom of the bottle begins to slowly evaporate, leaving in its wake thousands of beads or tiny droplets of water that almost resemble beads of sweat on the inside of that bottle.

Water cannot be made. However, you can make a multitude of beverages from this universal solvent. It is a universal solvent because it is able to dissolve most substances. In fact, no other liquid is able to do this better than water.

Another property of water worth-mentioning is its pH levels, particles of hydrogen or hydroxyl ions measurable from 0 to 14 on the scale. Low pH means the water is more acidic; high pH means water is more base or alkaline. Neutral or pure water is measured at pH 7, which means it is neither acidic nor alkaline.

More acidic water is a pH number lower than 7. Therefore, from 0 to 6, water is acidic or containing low pH levels, and from 8 to 14, water is more base or alkaline and is considered to have a high pH level. In either case, it is not worth drinking.

The reason this is important is because pollutants in water can seriously alter life on our planet. A one-point alteration from a pH 7 to a pH 6 means the water is ten times more acidic. A two-point alteration means it is twenty times more acidic or corrosive and so on and has more hydrogen ions. At high acidic levels (low pH), aquatic life becomes extinct and fish begins to die. Too corrosive and plant life becomes extinct. Eventually, the environment will become inhospitable for humans, and human life will also vanish.

At high pH levels (above pH 7), water tastes bitter and becomes infested with bacteria. Chlorine is often used for purposes of disinfecting water that contains deposits from pipes, for instance. These deposits could cause a rise in the pH level of the water to above eight or higher, creating the same problems as when pH levels are too low.

Water therefore and its relationship to life on earth is a study in how we balance the resources entrusted to us. The relationship between the emotional body, and water the third quadrant of matter, is a search for equilibrium to avoid the volatility of the emotional body's charge and thus maintain neutrality and keep us free from emotional stress.

Interestingly, the composition of water as a percentage of the earth's surface is approximately the same as its composition within the human body, about 70 percent for each.

Seventy percent of the earth is water, and 30 percent is land, of the human body, 70% is water; the rest is composed of bones, tissue, and so on. Water's composition in the same proportion on earth as in our physical bodies is not accidental, but by design, like the universe, we are geometrically perfectly aligned and created under spiritual and cosmic laws.

Water serves the same purpose for the earth as it does for the body, transporting nutrients through-out the entire system in a cyclictic motion. Water cycles the earth completely, and it is the same water in Japan, as it is in Russia and/or in the United States and elsewhere, and it is the same water that has been around since the beginning of time.

It is the only liquid that is above as it is below and resides in approximately the same amount. It is in everything we eat and drink. In fact, nothing that is made is without it, even though that thing may not be noticeably composed of it in its present form.

How does water, the third quadrant of matter, relate to the emotional body? Through the development of our conscience, intuition, and power, as well as through the various symbolisms of water.

The physical body's power is generated from the third quadrant of matter and manifests itself in the form of life and feelings. Earth's stresses, meaning its aridity and/or wetness, the dryness of its deserts and/or the density of its jungles of trees and forests, are directly linked to and affected by the power of water or lack thereof, just as the physical body's development and growth is affected by the power of the emotional body, which in effect is the amount of control we have or exercise over our feelings, passions, and consciousness.

The emotional body is the most volatile of the lower bodies, and its corresponding element, water, is just as volatile as the other elements. Water's power is observed by its affect on life, on the element of fire, and on its unstoppable destructive force.

Water's cycle in the earth is a complete continuum, no beginning or end, and throughout the cycle, it changes or can change state from liquid to solid to gas/vapor and back again continuously and instantaneously. This too parallels the emotional body and its charge, especially when it pertains to passion, changing from one emotional state to another—anger to love or hot to cold in almost the blink of an eye.

The Water Cycle

Important to keep in mind in its cycle is that there is no starting point of the water cycle[3], and according to the USGS (United States Geological Survey), evaporation (water rising into the atmosphere as vapor from the earth), sublimation (ice and snow melt but skip the water stage and becomes vapor from its solid state), and evapotranspiration (water evaporating into the atmosphere from plants and earth's soil) all causes condensation, which is the formation of clouds filled with water vapor that eventually causes precipitation, and these clouds then release the water as rain.

The rainwater then falls back onto earth and into the soil. Some stay there in ponds, lakes, reservoirs, and streams (our freshwater); some make its way into rivers and some into streams. These streams carry the water into the oceans.

Infiltration allows water to seep deep into the ground, into rocks underground. Some of the water remains on the surface of the earth or soil, making its way into various openings in the land and emerge as springs. The water keeps moving, most of it finding its way into oceans, and then once again, the process repeats itself over and over again.

Why is the water cycle important? It mirrors the cycle of water within the human body.

According to the USGS,[4] the human brain is composed of about seventy percent water; the lungs, 90 percent water; and blood, 83 percent water. Our body cells are full of water, and as in the cycle of water on earth, the water in the human body within the bloodstream transports the dissolved foods, enabling our bodies to utilize the nutrients, minerals, proteins, carbohydrates, and other metabolized chemicals in the food. This water also transports waste out of our bodies.

Water's power goes far beyond its obvious benefits. In the self-mastery classes, we discuss water, its healing effects, as well as its use in solving problems. Faith only benefits from the actions that reinforce it. Hence, faith without action is dead. Water is used symbolically as well as to reinforce an act of faith.

Signs or symbols (including spoken words) trigger certain responses within the brain and, when done repeatedly, with a fixed intent or belief, automatically actuates the brain. For example, when our bodies feel unclean, we believe that by taking a bath, we will become cleansed. At work is both a physical act (bathing) in combination with a psychological belief the action will lead to the desired feeling.

Any belief, when combined with a physical act, reinforces belief, especially if there is proof or results, even if the results are not directly related to that particular act.

Consider the use of holy water as a means of cleansing. The holy water is not necessarily holy because it was obtained from a religious store or dipped out of a chalice at a local church, nor is it holy simply because it came from a particular hole in the ground. For all practical purposes, it is like any other water.

Let us examine another example. What makes food kosher or holy? Is it not the same cheese and/or meat we all consume? So what sets the kosher or halal food apart from other cheeses and meats is its preparation. It is the power and meaning that a rabbi or an imam confers on the food that makes it kosher.

The holy water receives its power to heal from the power conferred on it and, of course, our belief. Material things and symbols become conferred with special qualities through the strong link of mind and brain.

When we engage in a concrete act or action, for example, using water to baptize a baby, the strength of that external action, along with the meaning of that action, gives the symbol or material its power. Therefore, the water used to baptize that infant becomes imbued with the power to cleanse both physically and spiritually, as well as to bless and protect, as in the words used during the baptism as the act is being carried out. The priest says, "I baptize you, [the name of the child or person], in the name of the Father, Son, and Holy Spirit."

Water has long been used for spiritual renewal or rebirth, as well as for physical and spiritual cleansing, thus giving it a symbolic and a concrete meaning. In various passages of the Bible, in Acts, Romans, Matthew, John, and others, being baptized is symbolically associated with one's renewal or rebirth.

When John the Baptist baptized Jesus, he did so with water; immediately thereafter, Jesus was baptized with the Holy Spirit. While John the Baptist's baptism of Jesus was mostly symbolic, the belief was that water baptism was the ultimate in the cleansing and renewal process for those wishing to be born again. The concrete act of John went beyond the symbiotic, and in that instance, John the Baptist's mission was completed by his act and Jesus's mission was birthed.

Jesus, in participating in the ritual, completed the prophecy and was baptized with the Holy Spirit, and from that moment on, was given the authority to baptize with the Holy Spirit. His coronation was instantaneous. In fact, nowhere in the Bible does it ever say that Jesus baptized anyone with water, although his disciples did. The concrete act of Jesus being immersed in the water used the strength of that external action and then invested that specific act with a meaning.

Water's connection to the emotional body therefore is not only due to its power but also its symbolic and concrete meaning to life itself—one of cleansing, renewal, revival, and rebirth.

In the self-mastery classes, students are instructed on the water technique, which is used to solve problems. To help solve a problem, you fill a glass with water, and just prior to going to sleep, drink half the glass of water at the same time silently affirming, "This is all I need to do to solve the problem [state the problem] I have." Go to bed and to sleep, and then in the morning, drink the remaining half glass of water, mentally repeating the same information again, "This is all I need to do to solve the problem [state the problem] I have."

The results of this seemingly simple exercise is that you will either awaken during the night or morning from a dream that will give you information for solving the problem or you will receive a flash of insight during the course of the day that would provide information for you to use in solving the problem. You should repeat this exercise as often as you feel it necessary to.

Dr. Mahmoud Ali's water therapy, which helps to correct diseases and ailments like constipation, diabetes, pulmonary TB, hypertension, and other dysfunctions, instructs patients to drink 1.5 liters or six glasses of water each and every day to help cleanse and rid the blood and body of toxins. These six glasses of water is equivalent to receiving blood transfusions daily. Not only does it rid the body of these toxins, it also enables you to lose weight naturally, even without exercise.

I have undertaken this exercise, and the results are phenomenal. You can indeed avoid doctor bills, tablets, medicines, and so on by just drinking water. By faithfully following this routine of six glasses of water first thing each morning and then waiting one hour before eating, according to some medical reports, in one day to four weeks, you will correct bodily ailments and diseases, from constipation and diabetes to cancer, pulmonary TB, and hypertension. Additionally, you will lose weight without exercising. What is more amazing is that the water does not allow you to lose more weight than you're supposed to.

The colon and intestines are activated and work more effectively to produce new fresh blood daily, easily excreting toxins from the body rather than from the blood. Additionally, there is also a difference in skin elasticity.

In an on-air interview conducted by Mike Adams[5] of Truth Publishing with Dr. Batmanghelidj, author of *Water for Health, for Healing, for Life*, Dr. B stated that during his stint in an Iranian prison, he stumbled on the healing properties of water. The following excerpt is taken directly from the interview. That interview[5] and other related information can be found on; http://www.naturalnews.com/Report_water_cure_1.html.

Mike: Welcome, everyone. This is Mike Adams with Truth Publishing, and today I'm very excited to be welcoming Dr. Batmanghelidj, author of *Water for Health, for Healing, for Life*. Welcome, Dr. Batmanghelidj.

Dr. B: Thank you very much for inviting me to be on the air with you and giving me the opportunity of sharing my thoughts on the future of medicine in this country.

Mike: I think there are many, many people who have read your books. People are intrigued by the idea that water can be a therapy, a healing substance for the human body. What is it about water? How did you first become aware of these healing properties of water?

Dr. B: Well, it's very bizarre. As you know, I'm a regular doctor, an MD. I had the honor and the privilege of being selected as one of the house doctors, and I had the extreme honor of being one of the last students of Sir Alexander Fleming, the discoverer of penicillin. I mention his name so that you know I was immersed in medical school and research. And some years later, I had to give two glasses of water to a person who was doubled up in abdominal pain from his disease because I had no other medication to give him at that moment. And he was in excruciating pain, and water performed miraculous relief for him. It gave him relief—within three minutes, his pain diminished, and within eight minutes it disappeared completely, whereas he was doubled up eight minutes before and he couldn't even walk. He completely recovered from that situation. And he started beaming from ear to ear, very happy, asked me what happens if the pain comes back? I said, "Well, drink more water." Then I decided to instruct him to drink two glasses of water every three hours. Which he did, and that was the end of his ulcer pains for the rest of the duration that he was with me.

Mike: And from that episode then, what happened next?

Dr. B: That woke me up because in medical school, I'd never heard that water could cure pain that kind of pain, in fact. And so I had the occasion to test water as a medication in subsequently over three thousand similar cases. And water proved every time to be an effective medication. I came away from that experience with the understanding that these people were all thirsty and that thirst in the body can manifest itself in the form of abdominal pain to the level that the person can even become semiconscious because that's the experience I had. And water picks them up every time. So when I came to America in 1982, I went to the University of Pennsylvania, where I was invited to continue my research and did research in the pain-relieving properties of water. I asked myself, why does the pharmaceutical industry insist on using antihistamines for this kind of pain medication? So I started researching the role of histamine in the body, and the answer was there—histamine is a neurotransmitter in charge of water regulation and the drought management programs of the body. When it manifests pain, in fact, it is indicating dehydration.

So the body does manifest dehydration in the form of pain. Now, depending on where dehydration is settled, you feel pain there. Very simple, and I presented this concept at the international conference as the guest lecturer of a conference on cancer, explaining that the human body manifests dehydration by producing pain, and pain is a sign of water shortage in the body, and water shortage is actually the background to most of the health problems in our society. Because if you look at what the pharmaceutical industry is doing, they're producing so many different antihistamines as medication. Antidepressant drugs are antihistamines; pain medication are antihistamines; other medications are directly and indirectly antihistamines. So that is when my work was published. The scientific secretariat of the Third Interscience Board Conference of Inflammation invited me to make this presentation on histamine at their conference in 1989, in Monte Carlo. And I did that, and so it became a regular understanding that histamine is a water regulator in the body. But unfortunately, this information is not reaching the public through the medical community because it's not a moneymaker.

So that's when I began to consider writing for the public, so that the public could become aware of the problem directly without the interference of a doctor, and that's how I have generated all my medical information for the public. Of course, I have published extensively for the scientific community, but no one is picking up. In fact, the NIH, the Office of Alternative Medicine, had its first conference when the office was created, and I was asked to make my presentation, but when the proceedings of the conference came out, my presentation was censored after the proceedings. So there is a movement afoot within the NIH group of people to keep a closed lid on my information so that it doesn't get out because obviously they are more in favor of the drug industry because it is now obvious that they are getting paid by them.

Mike: I think it is, first of all. That is an amazing account of what has been happening, and I think it is fair to say too that the pharmaceutical industry and organized medicine, in general, really doesn't want to promote anything that is free or near-free to the average patient. Sunlight is available at no charge; water is available at nearly no charge—would you agree that their thinking is if people can cure their diseases and achieve a high state of health on their own with these free substances, then that diminishes their profits and their importance?

Dr. B: Absolutely. That's why I've created an organization now called National Association for Honesty in Medicine. Because I think it's totally dishonest, in fact, criminal, to treat a person who is just thirsty and give them toxic medication so that he gets sick and dies earlier than normal.

From the excerpt, we learn a little more about the healing power of water, in addition to the suppression of certain natural (holistic) scientific discoveries associated with many of natures' gifts, including water and the sun.

The Awakening Project's teaching section discusses how water senses emotion[6]. Alpha Lo, in consultation with Karen McChrystal, MA, discussed Masaru Emoto's discoveries, linking water to emotions and how water responds to how we think and feel.

In summarizing Emoto's four-step approach, our emotions and thoughts are energy. We can send and receive electrical impulses, which are similar to electrical current. These pulsations are contained throughout our bodies—in our brains, nervous system, heart, auras, etc. How these electrical currents behave is determined by our emotional states, our thoughts, and levels of consciousness.

I have stated or overstated in previous chapters that the emotional body, like the other three lower bodies, contains its own emotional charge and is quite volatile, and since these lower bodies interrelate, the currents or electrical impulses in the different areas and systems of the body also correlate and thus affect each other.

According to Masaru Emoto, the heart current, which contains the strongest electrical pulsation or current (made up of ions and electrons) emits an electromagnetic field. For the purpose of clarification, radio signals, TV signals, and cell phone signals are all transmitted via electromagnetic (electricity and magnetism) fields of current or waves. For a transmitted message to be received, what is required is power (electricity) symbols (music, language, or a code such as the Morse code) and a transmission reception system (radio, TV, cell or telephone, human being, etc).

Electromagnetic waves are invisible electronic impulses, which are quite similar to light. In fact, electricity, light, magnetism, and heat are characteristics of the same electromagnetic spectrum and radiate in space at the speed of light. This discovery of the electromagnetic wave gave birth to wireless transmission and the reception of radio waves and, subsequently, wireless communication. Incidentally, the human body has the very same characteristics as electromagnetic energy.

In Emoto's experiment[7], the ions and the electrons in the heart current, when it comes into contact with an atom, causes an increase in energy, which is released in the form of photons. These photons then form the electromagnetic field the heart pacemaker cells emit. The cells' charges can change from negative to positive as the heart's current is carried. Therefore, negative emotional feelings such as anger, sadness, and/or guilt, Emoto states, cause incoherent emissions of the photons, whereas emotional feelings of love, peace, and bliss cause the photons emitted to be coherent with each other.

The third step is the electromagnetic field pattern formed based on the emotion, which can cause either constructive or destructive interference, depending on whether it is a positive or negative emotion or emotional state. The final step, Emoto states, is how the electromagnetic field interacts with water. Water in this case has now become the transmitter.

In this phase, the electromagnetic energy in the water, which is attracted to coherent light, which is strongest at points of constructive interference, will attract the water, which will then migrate to those places where there is a geometrically patterned electromagnetic field.

In the resulting images,[8] the water and the light (as Emoto states and shows) become quantumly entangled at those areas of constructive interference, forming frozen, beautiful geometric patterns when we are in emotionally positive, peaceful, blissful states and incoherent patterns when we are not.

Water exposed to words "Thank you"
Credit: http://www.intelligentinfiity.org/watersenses.html

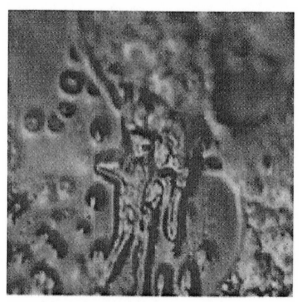

Water exposed to words *"You make me sick"*
Credit: http://www.intelligentinfiity.org/watersenses.html

A separate study published by James King, November 13, 2008, http://www.
asuwebdevil.com, reveals how water scarcity affects human emotions.

Amber Wuitich, assistant professor in the School of Human and Social
Change, and Kathleen Ragsdale, assistant professor in the Department of
Sociology, Anthropology, and Social Work, Mississippi State University,
discovered in their collaborated study that in a Bolivian squatter settlement,
water shortages[9] were linked to emotional distress.

If water can be affected emotionally by us, it is quite reasonable to conclude
also that water can and does affect us emotionally as well, and taking this to its
logical conclusion, we therefore can control water and the way it behaves, and
its behavior will strongly depend on our emotional thrust or our desires.

There being a strong link between the emotional body and the third
quadrant of matter (water) is doubtless, and how clearly we understand and
are able to utilize this association could impact and determine not only our
health positively or negatively but also our spiritual well-being.

Matthew14:25, says, "Now in the fourth watch of the night Jesus went to
them walking on the sea."[10] The fourth watch is 3:00 a.m. to 6:00 a.m. Verses
26 to 33 tells the rest of the story of how fearful Jesus's disciples were. They
thought they were seeing a ghost because, obviously, Jesus had defied the laws
of nature and science by walking on water. Peter was told to come out to him
walking on the water. He began to, but the moment he began to doubt, he
began to sink.

In Matthew 8:26, he said to them, "Why are you fearful, O you of little
faith? Then he arose and rebuked the winds and the sea, and there was a great
calm."[11]

The point of these passages are to show the correlation between emotion,
faith, water, and even air and our ability to control how we are affected by
the third quadrant of matter, as well as the second quadrant of matter—air or
wind—and how it can affect us based on our belief.

The self-mastery lessons provided here is in understanding the power of
the mind and our relationship to this power and how we utilize it. In the
beginning of this chapter on water, I quoted Matthew 3:11, where John the
Baptist baptized Jesus with water, and immediately thereafter, Jesus was
baptized with the Holy Spirit (fire).

There is a correlation between these two quadrants of matter: water,
with its power of emotion and feeling, and fire with its cleansing power. The
combined power of compassion and healing with water, along with the power
to forgive, cleanse, make anew, or reborn is demonstrated through the usage
of the first and third quadrants of matter and in the sequence of the event as
documented in Matthew 3:11.

Clearly there is a correlation between the elements, which hopefully, all can begin to clearly see. In this specific instance, we see how through our faith and belief, and positive thoughts and thinking, water can effect changes in our lives and enable us to utilize its power to help, heal, and change the very essence and energy of our environment and of those around us.

CHAPTER 26

AIR
THE SECOND QUADRANT OF MATTER

And you he made alive, who were dead in trespasses and sins, in which you once walked according to the course of this world, according to the prince of the power of the air, the spirit who now works in the sons of disobedience.
—Ephesians 2:1-2[1]

Air is the second quadrant of matter and relates to the mental body. Air is responsible for intellect, memory, judgment, and the power to differentiate or reason. The mental body, created in the true image of God, is the immortal spirit. Understanding the relationship between the mental body and air in self-mastery is synonymous to understanding the relationship of the immortal spirit (our intellect) to our Christ self or to God since the mental body is intended to be the vehicle for the mind of God.

While the lower mental body remains the vehicle for the carnal mind, (i.e., our earthly intellect or intelligence), the higher mental body is synonymous with our Christ consciousness (spiritual wisdom or intellect).

If each of us live, managing to avoid life's land mines, allowing us to the threescore and ten years allotted and beyond, we would eventually evolve from physical beings to complete spiritual, intellectual beings, for long after our physical strength has wained, our intellect will remain and our spirit will live on, and we should have grown to a greater spiritual understanding of our relationship to God and to the universe.

As humans, we often tend to believe in that which our senses can discern and dismiss that which is not visible. It is so with air as well. We only seem to become acutely aware of its existence when we are either without it (i.e., it is in a composition that causes us discomfort), or it is extremely odorous and has already caused great harm.

If we examine existence, for example, we see a person or thing within our field of vision or discern it aurally. We then believe it exists because of these tangibles. However, if removed or if that person or thing cannot be perceived by our senses, we will conclude that that thing or person as nonexistent.

Air is everywhere and in all things, yet it is invisible. Although we cannot see it, we can measure its effect in its rapid currents, sometimes referred to as wind, hurricane, or tornado. We can also hear its effects through that howling, seemingly distressed sound it generates as it blows. These intangibles, which we cannot necessarily catch in a bottle, nevertheless, convinces us of its existence.

The air we breathe in the United States is the same air (for the most part) inhaled in China, Japan, Australia, Egypt, and wherever one may travel to or choose to exist on earth because air envelopes the earth. This invisible gaseous substance is composed of approximately 78 percent nitrogen,[2] 21 percent oxygen, and a mixture of argon, carbon dioxide, and other gases in smaller compositions.

Humans and others within the animal kingdom breathe in oxygen and breathe out carbon dioxide. Plants also absorb oxygen from the air around them and breathe out carbon dioxide; additionally, plants, through a process of photosynthesis, synthesize sunlight and carbon dioxide to create other complex substances.

The fact is without oxygen, life on earth is nonexistent, and because it is a gas, we are able to harness oxygen and utilize it for emergency and nonemergency respiratory situations when the need for oxygen is necessary.

The release of pollutants and other destructive chemicals into the atmosphere has altered the composition of the air quality we normally breathe in. Additionally, deforestation has imperiled our planet in its ability to regulate and cleanse the atmosphere of some of the dangerous emittances we breathe in that cause the debilitating diseases prevalent in our world today.

Trees and plants, natural air cleansers, are rapidly becoming extinct as the natural barriers that protect us from air-borne diseases and pollutants.

According to a study conducted by NASA and ALCA (Associated Landscape Contractors of America) on household plants, it was discovered that plants[3] like the bamboo palm, Chinese evergreen, English ivy, and the peace lily are excellent in varying degrees in removing air pollutants like benzene, trichloroethylene, and formaldehyde and help promote indoor air purification.

Benzene is a solvent contained in items like inks, oils, paint, gasoline, and plastic, as well as in many detergents, pharmaceuticals, and dyes—items we use daily and oftentimes place food items in, on, or in proximity to.

Formaldehyde is found in pressed wood products, such as your desk, vanity drawers and tables. Urea formaldehyde foam insulation is used in virtually all homes to seal cracks and keep drafts out. It is used extensively in trailer homes. Consumer products like your grocery bags, waxed paper, facial tissue, and paper towels are all treated with urea formaldehyde resins and numerous common household cleaning products also contain this chemical.

Trichloroethylene, a commercial product, is found in varnishes, lacquers, paints, and adhesives, among other items common to many households.

In a research conducted by NASA and ALCA, twelve plants were tested. The following were determined to be great for purifying about 1,800 square feet of indoor air space of the three pollutants mentioned[3]. They were ranked as the top twelve in order of their effectiveness.

Bamboo palm
Chinese evergreen
English Ivy
Fiscus
Gerbera daisy
Dracaena "Janet Craig"
Dracaena "Marginata"
Corn cane
Mother-in-law's tongue
Peace lily
Pot mum, chrysanthemum
Dracaena Warneckei

These plants purify the indoor air by filtering out the toxins, pollutants, and carbon dioxide we exhale and replaces them with oxygen, and while most house plants may be able to do this, some are more effective than others in filtering the toxins. Care, however, must be exercised since some of these plants are poisonous or can cause severe irritations.

The English lily, for example, contains sap that can cause poisoning in animals and humans. If the berries of the English ivy are ingested, coma and even death can occur.

While philodendrons are determined to be among the best house plants for removing formaldehyde from the air, it is nevertheless a poisonous plant because of the oxalates it contains; therefore, excellent substitutes would be the aloe vera, spider plants, or golden pothos, provided that the toxin (formaldehyde) is at lower concentrations.

Chrysanthemum, peace lily, as well as the gerbera daisy are notable for the removal of the toxin benzene. Incidentally, these plants are not only great for air purification, but also excellent for interior decorating. (For the complete results, you can access http://www.humseeds.com or visit http://www.blankees.com/house/plants.)

This information is significant in understanding the mental body's need for clarity in utilizing its capacity to think and reason soundly. An environment free of pollutants promotes attentiveness, mental alacrity, and the ability to think clearly.

A recent study conducted in 2008 by the National University of Singapore concluded that room air temperature affects the physiological, mental alertness as well as the perceptions of its occupants. There are other studies showing in varying degrees that temperature, color, and light affects the mood as well as the physiological disposition of individuals.

The Chinese have been for years studying energy as it relates to our health and environment, including space relationship (indoor space). This energy is referred to as chi, the vital life force energy of the universe contained in every living thing. Disruptions in the flow of this chi or energy create imbalances or disease through its blockages.

Part of this energy are the electromagnetic fields of energy all around us that science and technology have been able to tap into and utilize for technological devices, such as the cell phone and other forms of wireless communication and communication devices.

Self-healing techniques practiced at the now extinct Chi Lel Qigong medicineless hospital center demonstrated how chi practitioners were able to heal themselves naturally of all types of incurable diseases like cancer, diabetes, heart disease, lupus, and paralysis. Once you go beyond scientific measurements to the chi level deep inside the cell to where the energy resides, each of us can communicate with our chi level using our minds, and through this means, we can heal ourselves.

Feng shui[4] is the ancient Chinese art of balancing the energies of any space, thus assuring the health of its inhabitants. *Feng* means "wind" and *shui* means "water," and this art is based on the principle that all things have energy and thus are alive, with all of us having a connection to everything, especially to nature; thus, we are able to utilize these resources to do anything and everything, including self-healing.

Feng shui is important at this juncture because of its intrinsic relationship to the second quadrant of matter, air, and therefore the intellect or mental body. Additionally, its five elements comprise of three quadrants of matter—water, fire, and earth, plus wood and metal, with color (which is light) as an expression of these five elements.

The corresponding colors for each element are green or brown for wood, red or orange for fire, blue for water, yellow or brown for earth, and white or gray for metal.

The placement of items within a space and colors utilized within those spaces will either harmonize those areas (good feng shui, bringing peace, happiness, and prosperity) or provide disturbing currents of energy flow (bad feng shui or disharmony).

We therefore see the importance of the quadrants of matter working together as a system to provide balance to our lives. Disharmony prevails when environmental hazards and toxins are allowed to pollute the environment. The need for feng shui, reiki, and chi becomes so much more important because of the diseases and the illnesses caused by man to man's environment.

According to the EPA (Environmental Protection Agency), toxic air pollutants can cause, among other diseases, cancer and birth defects, and most of the toxins we inhale are man-made, emitted from transportation vehicles like cars, trucks, and buses, as well as from stationery sources, such as refineries and factories.

Volcanic eruptions and forest fires can also emit air toxins, so even though some of us may appear to have the seemingly good fortune of living thousands of miles from volcanic eruptions, we are just as unsafe from harmful pollutants as those living side by side to these eruptions.

Toxins enter our bodies by being ingested through the mouth (either drinking or eating), through skin contact (touching), or through the nostrils (inhaled). Studies conducted by the EPA and other organizations concluded that toxic air deposits contribute to reproductive failure, birth defects, and diseases in animals, humans, wildlife, and in general, to the environment.

Ginny Walden's[5] story in the Web story *The Power of Chi Lel, The Mind Body Connection* points clearly to the power of self-healing and positive thinking, as well as how far behind Western medicine is in its use of Eastern methods of natural healing. Ginny Walden healed herself of advanced stage 3 breast cancer using Chi Lel after months of chemotherapy, negative programming, and surgery. By merely changing the way she thought, remaining positive and exercising faith, Ms. Walden was able to tap into the mind/body connection, utilizing the power of the mind to completely and irreversibly return her cells to normality.

While we do know that toxins do have harmful effects on the physical body, it is still not known to what extent these toxins affect the mind's development or the mental aspect of the human. What we do understand is that it is our knowledge, understanding, and wisdom and how we choose to apply that knowledge to our lives that allows us to transcend the mistakes made, learn from our mistakes, and create a better world for ourselves and everyone around us.

Thousands of Ginnys are living examples of this power that resides deep within us, awaiting exploration at the urging of our belief and faith.

Equally important and insightful in the development and mastery of self to create wellness is a more dynamic understanding of the inner workings and complexities of the mind at its various levels. In this regard, the second lower body (the mental body), will interchangeably be stated as the mental and/or mind, which in effect refers to one and the same.

There are many grades or levels of the mind or mental body. That complex mechanism we refer to as the brain, which controls the human functions like intelligence, thought, memory, and emotion, is a far more complex mechanism than science has given it credit for, and the physical mind, even at its pinnacle, is really not as discerning as we may think. Therefore, to understand some of these complexities of the mental body requires the mind to be dissected into its various grades or levels, and these grades or levels to be illuminated.

Sri Aurobindo, in his doctrine on the aspects of mind, divides the mind into seven grades or levels[6], beginning with the **physical mind** or the mental physical mind.

This mind is limited by the physical view and feelings of things, and seldom does it go beyond the outward. It is guided by experiences or external knowledge, so there is no divine aspiration or uplifting spiritual deliverance the individual undergoes. Therefore, to arrive at the conception and knowledge of a divine existence requires the individual to exceed the evidence of the senses of the physical mind.

Because the physical mind's primary influence is the senses, if there are physiological or psychological deficiencies or perceptual inaccuracies, the resulting information perceived, analyzed, and acted upon will be based on inaccuracies. One's reasoning cannot rise above the premise on which it is based; therefore, if the premise contains perceptual inaccuracies, then the results will follow. It is therefore unwise to base important decisions solely on the musings of the mental physical mind.

The **vital mind** acts as a mediator between man's imaginative emotions and desires, and the real emotions and desires. The vital mind's function therefore is not thinking or reasoning. It is not inquisitive in the sense that it wants to perceive or find the value of things, but rather it is formulating or imagining what can be done (in the future). The vital mind therefore fantasizes and generally awaits the will to help make whatever that person wants to happen occur.

Actions based upon the vital mind's influence do not always allow individuals to accurately separate truth from fiction or reality from the ideal; thus, individuals may sometimes act impulsively, being driven by emotional desires and not rational, logical, clear thinking. In this instance, the will is driven by the impulse. The vital mind will mediate according to the will's desire. The subsequent actions will therefore be in accordance with the desires of the will regardless of its consequences.

It is imperative that individuals strive for high ideals in the imagination of things desired while being able to recognize what can realistically be achieved at that given moment. This is training and preparation for the vital mind to be a great mediator.

The next grade or level is the **mental mind**, which is also referred to as the **thinking mind**. The thinking mind is described by Aurobindo as seated just below the spiritual mind and has three divisions or parts: (1) thinking mind, (2) dynamic mind, and (3) externalizing mind.

The thinking mind or mind proper, concerns itself with ideas and knowledge. It is the intellect that formulates its ideas from analysis and reasoning, whereas the dynamic mind creates and puts forth the mental forms for the realization of the idea or ideas. In other words, the dynamic mind plants the seeds and the externalizing mind brings the idea to life in terms of its expression in whatever form required for the idea to be fully manifested, be it through speech, creative artwork, music, and so on, and without regard for its correctness.

The thinking mind is therefore rational and analytical and carefully plans appropriate actions or responses based on the particular situation. Responses are generally, though not always, based on moral judgments.

The next level is the **higher mind**, which is the first level of the spiritual mind, beyond the rational mind and above the level of what Aurobindo describes as the pure thinking mind. The higher mind is the inner awakening—the discovery of your inner being or soul—with unlimited potential, no longer limited by the mental, vital, or physical existence. This awakening can extend into a consciousness of the cosmic mind and into a oneness with universal matter. There is no longer a wall between our external and subliminal self.

Once this inner awakening occurs, the inner self is now capable of ascending beyond the present mental level into an even higher spiritual level. We begin to see our connection to all things and all others.

According to Aurobindo, the higher mind is the first step out of human intelligence and into a spiritual clarity that is capable of spontaneous inherent knowledge, "a luminous thought mind, a mind of spirit-born conceptual knowledge."

The next ascended level of the mental body is the **illumined mind**, which is in effect a mind of spiritual light. The illumined mind is above the higher mind; thus, the illumined mind is likened unto an inward visible light that envelopes the thought process. A spiritual manifestation of divine reality, which Aurobindo describes as "a fiery ardor of realization and a rapturous ecstasy of knowledge."

The illumined mind works by vision and not primarily by thought (which is how the higher mind would work). Thought, however, is a slower process because thought requires significant sounds or other devices to give ideas exactitude and an expressive body. The illumined mind receives visions.

Consciousness proceeded by sight possesses greater power for knowledge than the consciousness of a thinker. Similarly, perceptual power of the mind's eye or inner sight is more powerful and direct than the perceptual power of thought.

Because of how insight is received, the illumined mind, according to Aurobindo, has a greater consciousness because of its "truth-sight and truth-light power."[7] The thought-mind is illumined with a direct inner vision and inspiration, springing forth spiritual sight into the heart and spiritual light and energy into the feelings and emotions. Its knowing is through the illumined mind's truth-sight, truth-light intuitive power.

The next ascended mental/mind body is the **overmind**, the highest level of mental consciousness one can achieve without transcending the mental system or being incomprehensible to all, except those who have also transcended this system, which are a minute few. In the overmind of the mental body resides the region of the "Great Gods" (the ascended masters). An ascended master is one who has mastered time and space and in the process gained the mastery of self in the four lower bodies and the four quadrants of matter, in the chakras and the balanced *threefold flame*," (power, wisdom, and love),[8] "transmuted at least 51 percent of his Karma and fulfilled his divine plan."—through Christ and the putting on of that mind which was in Christ Jesus"—"let this mind be in you which was also in Christ Jesus" (Philippians 2:5)."

Ascended masters therefore inhabit the spirit planes or God's kingdom (God's consciousness) and oftentimes teach unascended souls residing on the etheric plane or the kingdom of heaven.

Other writings refer to the Great Gods as the powers that oversee the workings of this world. There is multiplicity of the mind, not the mind as we know it, but according to Aurobindo, the overmind permeates the entire lower hemisphere of knowledge and ignorance, linking it with the greater truth-consciousness, yet shielding the greater truth from us and, instead, intervening with an infinite set of possibilities with the aim of allowing us to continuously seek the spiritual law of our existence as an obstacle and passageway of possibilities.

Remember that there is only one source of truth that we must continually seek.

The overmind has the capacity to separate and yet combine the powers and aspects of all comprehensions. Then, there is the **supermind**, which is a divine or absolute consciousness. Yogi Sri Aurobindo's description of supermind is "it is a mind totally beyond mind and mental activity, it does not transcend up, but draws down, creating a transformed, supramental, glorified, perfect, divinised body, free of all illness and imperfection and in divine harmony, thus eventually bringing about a collective evolutionary transformation."[9]

The supermind is therefore a new existence of truth-consciousness. There is no need to seek or search for truth. The supermind lives in truth; its form and expression are truth. This is its very nature.

One of the most powerful possessions and one of the five gifts we possess is the mind. While the attainment of the overmind or supermind level of consciousness is indeed a powerful revelation, the truth is still a continued journey until we have completely and absolutely surrendered to God's will. The truth is revealed only to those who truly seek it, and that journey could be tedious yet fulfilling.

In studying these various grades or levels of the mind, we are able to observe the complexity of the mental body, the growth of our consciousness, and the insignificance of our earthly/physical intellect in comparison to the level we can achieve spiritually within the mental body. Isaiah 55:8-9 says, "For my thoughts are not your thoughts, nor, are your ways My ways says the Lord. For as the heavens are higher than the earth, so are My ways higher than your ways and My thoughts than your thoughts."[10]

This is our challenge as we sojourn to self-mastery and to the achievement of our highest spiritual self, the place where God's consciousness resides. This quest's fulfillment can only be revealed to those who are ardent seekers of the truth and truly desire to be like unto him.

God's superior wisdom and unfathomed greatness cannot be measured or equaled, and nothing can challenge his might. Lucifer tried; God allowed him to exist, but because no darkness can be where there is light, he was cast out of heaven along with one-third of his angels.

God's purpose in each of us is manifested through the threefold Christ flame (power, wisdom, and love), which is in the center of the heart of all of God's children. This spark of life is ignited and burns brighter and brighter as we manifest our Christ self and move further and further away from the nonreflective abyss of darkness, Lucifer.

We can begin to recognize our forward progress to the I AM THAT I AM, which is God in us and in the universe, by our steps toward that light and away from darkness and by our manifestation of the threefold flame of *power*, *wisdom*, and *love*.

First, power, synonymous to most with control, is the ability to lead and/or to guide others, with those individuals willingly giving up control or their power in order to be guided, yielding their power willingly. The actions and even the ability to think independently appear to be abrogated to that individual in power.

It is one thing to acquire or be given power willingly. However, seizing power by controlling the will of someone, in effect, stripping them of their will to choose by employing the use of various forms of mind control, is in opposition to the will of God. Power barren of choice is an abuse of power and does not allow the Christ self to be made manifest.

Governments and nations during times of war, and even in times of peace, have used torture, mind control, brain washing, electric shock, and numerous inhumane methods to obtain information or compliance from those they may have temporary power over. The end, they seem to claim, justifies the means. The benefits are never permanent.

Once power is not freely granted by a majority of those who wish to be led, then power is not truly vested in that leader, government, or nation exercising power and is not an expression of godliness.

What role then does free will play in the exploration of self-mastery and in this discussion of the relationship between the second quadrant of matter, air, the mental body, and power? It is in the *power of the mind*.

The abusers of power recognize that to control the will of man is to have power over him. Power over man is power over will, and so in order to control man's will, that person's mind must be controlled, and so power abusers have utilized various methods, including some of the methods described above, as well as money, wealth, and position, in order to gain and then maintain control or power over the minds of others, a clear hindrance to self-mastery.

Power should then be always exercised in accordance with God's will, utilizing compassion and constraint and in balanced accordance with the other two aspects of the threefold flame, wisdom and love. Thus, true power recognizes and adheres to our Christ self and therefore demonstrates both compassion and constraint in its exercise.

Wisdom

> And to man He said, Behold, the fear of the Lord, **that is wisdom,**
> And to depart from evil is understanding.[11] (Job 28:28)

God gives wisdom, and he is the only source through which it can be attained. No one else can give it, and while self-mastery may be attained through efforts put forth by the individual, becoming wise in the use of our increasing mental faculties is given only by God, and that we must ask for.

> For the Lord gives wisdom. From his mouth comes forth knowledge
> and understanding.[12] (Proverbs 2:6)

Almost every passage of every book of the Bible that talks about wisdom indicates that it comes from God; the wise seek it.

How important is wisdom? Again, many passages of the Bible speaks about its importance: "Happy is the man who finds wisdom, and the man who gains understanding"[13] (Proverbs 3;13). "Wisdom is better than strength . . . . Wisdom is better than weapons of war"[14] (Ecclesiastes 9:16-18). Therefore, to fear the Lord is to be wise since he is the source of all wisdom, and as he giveth, so can he take away as well. "The Lord by wisdom, founded the earth"[15] (Proverbs 2:19).

Scientist have many lofty theories regarding how the earth came into being, yet none is wiser than he. And regardless of the theories of how it came to be, it is clear who brought it into being, yet those who claim to be wise still theorize about the existence of God.

Man in his limited understanding of wisdom defines it as experience plus knowledge plus the ability to apply them practically or critically. This means then that the lack of either experience or knowledge indicates or suggests a lack of wisdom or that individual is unwise and lacks the ability to apply prudence to a given situation.

Man left to his own devices would seldom make decisions wisely. His decisions would more than likely be based on a current need, attention, and/or desire. This would then be prioritized and acted on. Even if those decisions seem logical or reasonable, we must examine the premise upon which those decisions rest, and man is notorious for making decisions one dimensionally, oftentimes hoping on luck for its correctness.

Decisions should not only be based on that which is visible or tangible (our senses), but must also take into consideration science and spiritual and cosmic laws. Therefore, wise decisions are those that take into consideration all of God's laws.

Decisions believed to be rightly made cannot rise above the premise on which those decisions are based, and if the premise does not consider all possibilities, then that decision would never be sound. We must therefore ask for wisdom so that we will get understanding and knowledge to choose wisely every time, but it requires an understanding of all of God's laws—spiritual and universal/cosmic—and the affect of these laws on our daily decisions.

Returning to the worldly definition of wisdom which is experience, in combination with knowledge and the ability to act based on these two combinations, lacks true depth of wisdom and indeed is merely carnal or worldly wisdom. Spiritual truths are not of human wisdom but revealed by God[16] (1 Corinthians 2:10); therefore, to understand things that are spiritual requires us to be spiritual or to acquire that spiritual realization.

Mastering self through wisdom therefore requires a transcendence of human or physical intellect, knowledge, and experience.

Love

> You shall love the Lord your God with all your heart, with all your soul, and with all your mind, this is the first and great commandment. And the second is like it: You shall love your neighbor as yourself. On these two commandments hang all the Law and the Prophets. (Matthew 22:37-40)

So then what is love? It is not so easily defined, even though it is mentioned often and spoken of even more often, but always seems to be in a state of nascency.

Words such as affection, affectionate devotion, attachment to, passion, and desire are all used in describing feelings referred to as love between individuals, and these are all emotional, positive feelings of belonging and sharing.

The spiritual definition of love centers around obedience to God and to his commandments or laws. Real love as described in the book of Matthew involves the heart, soul, and mind.

The chapter entitled "The Impedance to Self-Mastery" in this book discusses how information is processed in man's nature. This is worth reiterating at this juncture in order to fully understand Matthew's words, "Love God with all your heart, soul and mind." Restated, the body is the first tier of man's nature, the soul is the second tier and resides in the psyche or mind of man, and the third tier is the spirit, the core of man, within the heart-house of man.

Information enters the gateway of the first tier, the body, to be processed within the soul. Spiritual love can only be processed spiritually; and worldly or carnal love, only carnally. At the level of the soul, a decision is made whether the information, in this case, *love for God*, is conducive to the lifestyle of that individual. If acceptable, the information is transferred to the spirit to be processed for manifestation. If unacceptable, it is discarded.

The soul is the living potential of God, and this potential becomes fulfilled when the soul is rejoined to the spirit (the heart of man), allowing man to achieve his higher self. It is then and only then can the potential of God be realized in man. Therefore, *loving God with all your soul* means loving with the measured expression of God's capacity to show love.

The spirit, which resides in the heart-house or heart of man, is able to receive information directly from the creator (God). However, to communicate with the spirit of man, man's spirit must also be holy just as God's spirit is holy. Man's intelligence resides within the heart, and all final decisions are made within the heart or within the spirit of man.

Also, within the heart is housed the threefold flame of power, wisdom, and love.[17] As previously stated in the chapter, the blue plume is spiritual power and relates to faith, goodwill, and divine intent. The yellow plume is divine wisdom and relates to knowledge, which is the expansion of intelligence as it relates to godliness, and the pink plume is divine *love*. It is the life crown housing qualities of mercy, compassion, justice, and creativity, as well as God's happiness.

When the heart is in tune to the teachings of God, the higher self and sense faculties are developed.

Therefore, to *love God with all your heart* means that this love must be in divine ordinance with a balance of divine power and wisdom. Love God with all your mind. The soul resides within the mind of man, and this mind being referred to is the spiritual mind of man, the higher mind or overmind, where God is.

Therefore, true love is the capacity to realize God's potential first in one's self, and then as Matthew 22:37-40 continues to state, "Love your neighbor as yourself," to realize God's potential in everyone else.

After having taken a closer look at the mental body and its relationship to air, we begin to understand why science is still a long way off in determining the full capacity of the human mind.

And while we have continued to make great strides in our effort to live more enriched lives, man still remains basically selfish and exploitative, thus debilitating and, in some cases, retarding the strides made to find cures for many of the self-made illnesses created that are slowly and irreversibly destroying the planet.

CHAPTER 27

FIRE
THE FIRST QUADRANT OF MATTER

Moreover, you led them by day with a cloudy pillar. And by night with a pillar of fire. To give them light on the road which they should travel.

—Nehemiah 9:12[1]

The first quadrant of matter is fire, corresponding to the etheric body (the memory body) and envelope of the soul holding the blueprint of the divine plan.[2]

The element *fire* represents energy, passion, and might or strength. Within the heart, there's the spirit, and in order for an act to be completed, it requires will. Your fire is your will.

Physical fire is a flammable, combustible vapor that contains chemicals (gases) that mixes with oxygen in the air around it. The flame we see is energy-changing electrons and released energy-changing protons. When charged or excited (through the application of heat or electrical charge), the atoms within this vapor begin to excite the electrons that then moves to higher states or levels of energy. These levels of energy correspond to a specific wavelength of light that corresponds to a specific color.

The blue color we witness in a flame is the hottest, having the greatest energy, and is usually at the center of the flame. The red portion of the flame is the least hot, having a lower temperature or less energy and is further away from the center. The yellow-and-orange flame are all colors of light being emitted by the excited electrons and represents varying degrees of energy with its corresponding light.

The two most important aspects of the first quadrant of matter, fire, to be examined as it relates to the etheric body are energy and light.

Etheric comes from the word ether, the upper regions of the sky, beyond the clouds; or ethereal, light, airy, and intangible.

According to M. L. and E. C. Prophet, in *Saint Germain on Alchemy for the Adept in the Aquarian Age*, the etheric frequency and the etheric plane of consciousness is the repository of the fiery blueprint of the entire physical universe. The etheric plane is the highest plane in the dimension of matter; this is where higher evolved souls reside or abide between embodiments or reincarnations.

Everything emits energy, and energy, in turn, is emitted in colors of light, referred to as auras. In humans, these colors are in constant flux, meaning they seem to change intermittently from one color to the next or blend into more than one color, depending on mood, emotion, and physical stability or instability (ease or disease). In objects, the energy or aura is more static.

We know there are electromagnetic fields around all objects, although for the most part, these fields are invisible to the naked eye. Like electricity, we observe or feel the effect of the current or electromagnetic pulsation, even though we cannot actually see the current itself.

The best way to discuss energy is to observe it through its colors and in relationship to the human body's energy centers or chakras (wheels). The chakras can be likened unto a spiraling funnel or cone, dispersing energy throughout the body.

As in the discussion of fire, the flame produced by the burning fire emits colors, and the colors represent the energy within that flame or the measurable temperature of various parts of the flame.

Similarly, each of us have seven energy centers that allow the flow of light in, out, and from one part of our cells to another. Each of these centers corresponds to a particular radiance of light or energy that emits a specific color and controls the balance of health within that area and subsequently within our entire bodies.

The colors that comprise white light are ROYGBIV—red, orange, yellow, green, blue, indigo, and violet. Each color contains a certain wavelength value that corresponds to a certain degree of energy. The *color red* has symbolic, psychological, religious, metaphysical, and astronomical meaning, as do all the other colors.

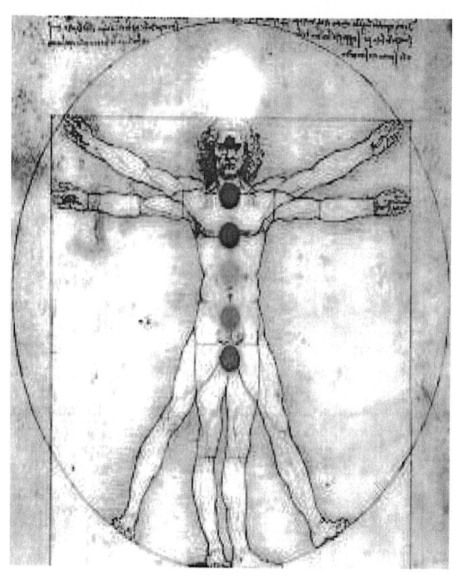

Chakras and corresponding colors (figure 2C)[3]
Photo credit: *http://www.crystalinks.com/chakras.html*[4]

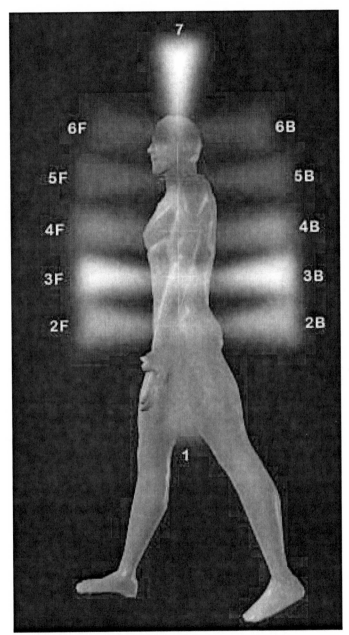

Chakras and corresponding colors (figure 2D)
Photo credit: *http://www.crystalinks.com/chakras.html*

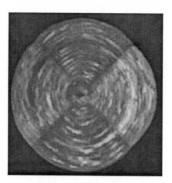

Root chakra

The red color consists of the longest wavelength of light, and because the rod cells in the human eye is insensitive to red light, red was adopted and used in night vision and nighttime low-lighting situations. Symbolically, the color red (though not an absolute color) is often associated with the emotions of aggression, anger, courage, hate, and passion.

Red is also associated with danger, guilt, energy, fire, and hell. As an activist, someone involved in community work, the color red connects or connotates them with honor, sacrifice, and leadership, while politically, with communism and socialism. Morally, red connotes sex (due to its association with passion), and for the religious community, red became associated with sin, perhaps due to its connotation with hell (fire). And socially, to warn or draw attention to violence and negativity, red is often used.

Metaphysically, red is the first *chakra* (the Sanskrit word for *wheel*), located at the base of the spine and signifying survival and stillness. It is also associated with the earth and the human being's grounding in the physical world. There is therefore a definite connection between this color and the fourth quadrant of matter, earth, which is associated with the physical body.

This root chakra[5] contains primary cells said to have all of the knowledge of creation, providing us humans with the innate ability to reproduce (create new life) since time began. The root chakra provides vitality to the adrenals, kidneys, spinal column, colon, legs, and bones and overall vitality to the physical body.

While red fruits and vegetables are important for nourishing this area of the body, avoidance of red meats and dairy products are essential for maintaining vibrancy in this chakra.

Failure to maintain balance in this root chakra devoids the organs mentioned of light. Tension develops and cells begin to die, leading to diseases like prostate cancer, cysts, urinary track disorders, sexual dysfunctions, as well as blockages, causing constipation and other malfeasances.

The root chakra provides vital lessons for the physical, spiritual growth, and self-mastery of the following: instinct, survival, and self-preservation, which are all part of the resident energy force.

The element of this chakra is earth, the fourth quadrant of matter; thus, mastery of the physical body, stability, patience, aspiring toward being healthy, increasing courage, and improving the four selves—self-concept, self-esteem, self-awareness, and self-disclosure—oftentimes become lifelong ambitions, drives, and goals.

Overindulgence must be avoided since there is a tendency for individuals to become self-centered and insecure, gravitating toward being overly concerned with physical survival, which in turn can lead to negative qualities such as greed, anger, and violence.

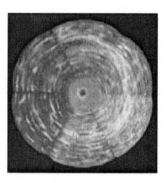

Spleen chakra

Next to red, orange has the next longest light wavelength, and in the visible spectrum, it is seen between the red and yellow spectrums of light. This color was named after the fruit and, metaphysically, is responsible for balance and sexual as well as reproductive functions. This chakra is located just beneath the navel (see figure 2C).

This second chakra is known as the spleen chakra[6] or sometimes referred to as the sacral plexus—*sacral* from *sacrum*, which is the triangular bone that is part of the spinal column forming the back of the pelvis. The spleen assists in helping the body maintain proper blood condition, including filtration and purification of the blood. The element is water, the third quadrant of matter, which is connected to the emotional body.

Bone diseases or imbalances in this area are usually related to emotional upheavals and would often manifest itself in areas such as the kidneys, chest area, and bladder. The color orange connects to this energy center.

The spleen chakra area is also responsible for digestion and sexual potency as well as for maintaining balance within the body's immunity system and thus its strong connection to water, liquids, and internal cleansing. Failure to maintain balance within this energy center can have adverse effects on the ovaries, testicles, prostrate, genitals, womb, bladder, and spleen. Orange fruits and vegetables and lots of liquids help to maintain and preserve balance and prevent diseases within this energy center.

I make it a practice to drink six glasses of water each morning (1.5 liters) and then wait forty-five minutes to an hour before consuming any type of food. This practice helps to assist in the transfusion and cleansing of the blood each day.

When diseased, the spleen can become enlarged and hard, quite the opposite of its characteristic soft, fleshy appearance.

Emotional balance, desire, and pleasure comes from within this energy center as well as sexual pleasure, movement, change, or the assimilation of new ideas. Working harmoniously with family and others assist in promoting those qualities that provide continuous positive energy for the spleen chakra's function.

Exercise care not to overindulge in sex or food since these qualities may lead to blockages within this area, causing sexual difficulties, jealousy, and possessive desires—all negative energy.

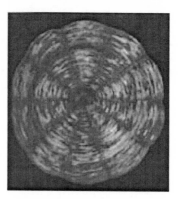

Solar plexus chakra

Yellow light or color is connected to the third chakra. Its energy center is the solar plexus[7]. This color of light stimulates both the long and medium wavelengths of light and is the color between green and orange within the light spectrum.

Yellow has numerous symbolic meanings. Psychologically, the color is associated with cheerfulness and thus is used extensively in products made specifically for children, such as toys and clothing, along with red, blue, and green. These colors generate energy in children and adults alike.

Metaphysically, yellow is the color of intellect and mental clarity and therefore is associated to the second quadrant of matter, air, which is connected to the mental body.

There is a strong association of yellow with this planet's main energy source and the sun's rays. You almost immediately think of heat, energy, and *fire* (the first quadrant of matter), an element connected to this chakra and associated with the etheric body.

The solar plexus happens to be the center or central area of the human body. *Solar* pertains to the sun, and *plexus* is the network or central area of nerves or vessels within the body. It is the seat of emotions and hence the feelings of butterflies in the stomach area when nervous or anxious. This chakra not only vitalizes the nervous system, but it also assists in digestive processes.

Cells within this energy center can become void of light due to emotional upheavals that would generally take the form of either anger or victimization. This may result in blockages affecting the pancreas, adrenals, stomach, liver, muscles, and gallbladder.

Additionally, because of the solar plexus's network of nerves, stomach aches, cramps, ulcers, and other ailments in this area could be quite debilitating and can easily and quickly lead to degeneration of other energy centers, causing cells to die in those areas as continued stress occurs. Yellow fruits and vegetables, as well as starches, are important to the maintenance of nutritional balance within this area of the body.

The feelings of immortality, personal power, and authority derive from positive energies becoming centered in the spleen chakra. The will, self-control, and mastery of desire are also part of this center's radiant energy, and so is humor and laughter.

Care must be exercised regarding the negative energies this center could attract—hate, fear, anger, too much emphasis on power, and seeking after power or recognition, or being overly ambitious; thus, biting off more than one can chew, these tendencies can lead to blockages and eventually the loss of energy, light, and cells within this center, causing imbalances and diseases.

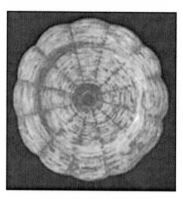

Heart chakra

The color green has the fourth longest wavelength in the light spectrum. A subtractive color created out of a mixture of yellow and blue, green light's perception is one of energy. Green, however, is a cool color. This means that unlike red and orange, green does not evoke passion and/or excitement, but rather it can calm, soothe, and comfort.

Symbolically, the color is closely associated to nature and things of nature; it is therefore connected to the physical body and the earth, the fourth quadrant of matter.

Green is the traditional color of Islam and is used symbolically in religious ceremonies and celebrations.

Metaphysically in Hinduism, green represents the heart chakra, the fourth chakra. Its frequency is linked to healing and alchemy. Healers and those connected with the medical field often emit the color green in their aura.

The heart chakra's function[8] is to anchor the life force from the higher self, energize the blood and physical body with the life force, and provide a continuous circulation of blood. Minor blockages of cells to light in the heart chakra can cause severe complications to the health and livelihood of an individual.

The heart chakra is connected to the second quadrant of matter, air, which is associated with the mental body and responsible for intellect. When the heart chakra radiates positive energy centered on divine unconditional love, forgiveness, compassion, understanding, and oneness with spiritual and cosmic law, there is balance and peace in the life of the individual, and the achievement of self-mastery is not only possible but also apparent.

Acceptance, peace and contentment, honesty or openness, and harmony are qualities that would manifest themselves when there is balance within the heart chakra. On the other hand, imbalance can and will affect the heart, the thymus gland (the ductless gland behind the breastbone in children not yet in puberty), and the circulatory system. Once the circulatory system is affected, the arms, hands, as well as the lungs will begin to degenerate.

Green fruits and vegetables are extremely important in maintaining a disease-free body. A steady and staple diet of natural green foods harmonizes the physical human body with nature, a recommendation most nutritionists also offer.

Care must be exercised to avoid negative qualities such as the repression of love and emotional instabilities. These will cause imbalance in this energy center and will most certainly lead to circulation and heart problems.

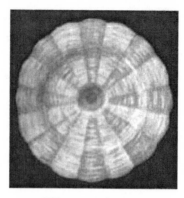

Throat chakra

The fifth chakra is the throat chakra,[9] associated with communication and creativity and the color *blue*.

The color blue's wavelength is the fifth longest in the spectrum. In color communication, blue is considered to be soothing and calming and can produce that effect.

In feng shui, colors create balance once used correctly. Energy in feng shui is described as yin and yang, opposites yet two of the same. Like matter and energy, one cannot exist without the other. Yin energy is calming or inert; yang energy is excitable.

Blue color according to Feng Shui has yin energy. It is calm and soothing and reflects love because of its healing and relaxing energy. Like green, blue is part of nature; however, it represents, in this case, the sky and sea, creating a feeling of peace and trust.

Feng shui associates blue with adventure and exploration; darker blues are associated with intellect and wisdom. "Blues" music is called "the blues" because of its tonality—sad, longing, melancholy, and prodding.

In metaphysics, blue represents truth, serenity, and harmony. Its calming effect can lower body temperature. The electrical energy we emit is blue, and we clearly recognize this when we see that blue electrical spark, during static electricity emittance. Not only is blue the color of electricity, but it is also the fastest moving frequency in the physical.

The throat produces sounds in the form of vibrations, and through this sound (which is the voice), we get rhythm, and this vibration and rhythm could be in the form of either music or words (language), and these are all characteristics of, as well as the functions of, the fifth chakra.

Energy is released through sound. The louder the sound, characteristically, the more energy is released. This sound energy can also be translated into wavelengths with its corresponding light frequencies.

We energize through words, creating actions. We therefore must be mindful of the words or energy we exude since we can transmit positive as well as negative energy.

Truth and speaking the truth allows for the flow of creativity, which comes from the mind and impacts the world with positive energy. It is through the art of communication that we connect with others, unite, and expand our world.

In the world of rhythm, we use the throat chakra to become in tuned with the vibrations around us, and with a healed and healthy fifth chakra, one's words are kind, clear, and truthful. "For by your words you will be justified and by your words you will be condemned" (Matthew 12:37).[10]

We take lightly the power of the spoken word, but spirituality has taught us that it is from the word that life began and everything became energized, and from that word came forth the light, which is every man and in every man. "In the beginning was the Word, and the Word was with God and the Word was God" (John 1:1).[11]

To really understand the power of this verse, you *must* study it, break it down, dissect it, parse it, and then its substantive meaning will awaken in you and flood your understanding with its brilliant light.

The mastery of self requires an understanding of not so much the physical world (although it is helpful) but beyond the physical—an understanding (even if it's just working knowledge) of spiritual and cosmic laws and man's connection to it and to all things within the universe. "And the word became flesh and dwelt among us, and we beheld His glory, the glory as of the only begotten of the Father, full of grace and truth" (John 1:14).[12]

I do not profess to be a doctor of divinity, with a profound propensity for dissecting gospels and passages from the Bible. Therefore, I ask questions from those who possess a keener understanding of these things. I then pursue its truths, asking for wisdom, knowledge, and understanding, and so I am made more aware of the deeper meanings of these things.

It is there for all men. We, however, must ask truthfully and purposefully and it will be given sometimes in the form of inspiration to create and produce things even outside of one's so-called earthly knowledge and understanding. All inspirations for good derives from one source; for some, it is in the power of speech or language; for others in the form of music or song. The power lies within the fifth chakra energy center.

The throat chakra controls and affects the thyroid, hypothalamus glands, parathyroid glands, as well as the mouth and the throat. The thyroid affects the rate at which all tissues metabolize. It regulates the volume of oxygen the tissues consume and the amount of heat they produce. In other words, the thyroid gland is the energizer that stimulates the tissue cells to the necessary level of activity so that it can perform its metabolic work.

Dysfunction occurs in the thyroid when there is excessive or insufficient production of thyroid hormone. This could invariably lead to imbalance in these areas, causing thyroid diseases like thyroid cancer, tumors, and other complications. A balanced amount of light must enter these cells.

Blue and purple fruits and vegetables are excellent for nourishing the throat chakra and for maintaining balance in this area. Foods such as purple grapes, blue berries, purple lettuce, and eggplant are all excellent support for the throat area.

Many have been inspired by some of the past and present great spiritual and political leaders and motivational speakers who were able to inspire, help create, and cause change in United States and around the world through the power of their spoken words. Some have done so through books and writings; and others, through creative writing of plays and other art forms.

The qualitative lessons of the throat chakra must include wisdom, loyalty, honesty, kindness, gentleness, and reliability in addition to truth, knowledge, and the strive toward peace, which means, there must be mindfulness of how information is communicated and how knowledge is used and to avoid ignorance if this energy center is to be maintained in a healthful state and if self-mastery is to be achieved.

The phrase "Sticks and stones can break my bones, but words could never hurt me," is a fallacy. Wars do not begin with bullets, but rather they begin with words, whether in written form or spoken, which is more immediate, words if chosen unwisely can escalate into physical force.

"The pen is mightier than the sword" is more representative of the power of words.

The sixth chakra is located between the eyes on the brow[13] or forehead. This area is also referred to as the third eye and is represented by the color purple or indigo (sometimes also referred to as dark blue).

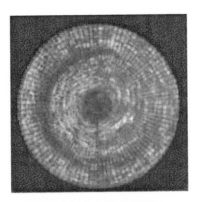

BROW CHAKRA

The third eye or all-seeing eye is associated with clairvoyance, psychic abilities, dreaming, as well as the imagination and has its relationship to the physical eye at the base of the brain. Its element is light.

Images viewed with the physical eye are projected onto the pineal gland (pine-shaped), the eyelike conical gland at the base of the brain. A small replica of the image is then projected onto the third eye or brow chakra.

The pineal gland, which produces melatonin, affects the human's body clock; hence, it affects sleep/wake and other bodily functions. I often speak to my classes about getting rid of their alarm clocks permanently and setting their internal time clocks to awaken at any time they wish. Programming this activity is quite simple, and many are already doing this without being quite aware that they are indeed programming.

For instance, if you wish to awaken at 6:00 a.m., while in bed, just prior to going to sleep the night before, picture or imagine a clock, set the clock to the time you want to wake up in the morning—in this case, it is 6:00 a.m. While seeing the time in your mind's eye (the all-seeing eye), tell yourself, *This is the time I want to awaken* [mention the time], *and this is the time I will awaken* [again mention the time]. You will awaken at the time you wish. It is that simple.

Some of my students mention having success at this exercise the first time they attempt it; others are not so successful the first time around, while others say they've been doing it for years, though not consciously aware of what is at work.

What I suggest for those who may not have achieved success the first time around is keep on doing it. You eventually will.

Resetting the body clock is like reprogramming the mind to weed out bad habits formed and ingrained over time. Some people need more programming and effort than others. Along with exercise, you must also pay attention to your belief system and attitude. The more you believe in your ability to do and the more serious you regard what it is you're attempting to do, the greater will your success be.

I do not sleep with or awaken to an alarm clock, and I get up at my appointed time, regardless of the hour I went to sleep the night before. Along with affecting sleep/wake, the pineal gland also assist in making your imagination real. In order to create anything, we must first imagine it or visualize it; if that thing cannot be visualized, you will not be able to create it, unless of course you are copying or replicating from an image that is before you, and in that case, you are not really creating.

We create the visible from the invisible, and no tangible object created was not first imagined by its creator; thus, that imagined object, though not yet tangible, is real to its creator. All that creator did was find a way to materialize that imagined creation.

We have numerous examples, all glaringly obvious especially in technological advancements, of how real imagination is: cell phones and computer technology.

The color dark blue, indigo, or purple is the color between red and blue. This color has long been used to denote royalty, since it was worn by the noble or royalty (kings and members of his court). This is the color of the brow chakra.

Metaphysically, purple or violet represents light, which is the element of the third eye or all-seeing eye. Purple is an excellent color for healing, especially when using crystals. In fact, purple quartz crystals assist with emotional problems, rheumatism, epilepsy, and in the reduction of pain. Sapphire and other blue crystals are also useful when performing healing that involves the bones and/or deep tissue work.

As previously mentioned, the brow chakra's center energizes the central nervous system and man's ability to create, visualize, perform psychically, imagine, and project.

Maintaining balance and flow in this energy center is vital to the functioning of the pituitary and pineal glands, the left eye, nose, and ears. Blockages in the cells can impede hearing, create problems with balance, cause sinus issues, as well as problems with the physical vision, especially in the left eye.

Foods such as purple grapes and lettuce, eggplant, as well as other purple and/or blue fruits and vegetables help to nourish and neutralize this energy center, creating balance and eliminating disease.

For all, but especially children, it is important that images viewed are positive. Television shows and movies containing extreme violence and other negative content (which can create negative impressions and influences) should be carefully monitored or avoided altogether. While children should be allowed to use their imagination, it should be done constructively, and this can only happen if the images and the impressions formed based on what children are allowed to view are positive.

Between ages fourteen to twenty-one, the intuition begins to develop at an accelerated pace and spiritual law begins to take hold if that child was exposed to spirituality. If not, then his or her spiritual progress would be greatly impeded. While there may be a sense of right and wrong, this concept would be based more on the environment and societal standards, rather than on a deeper sense of self-awareness.

If this energy center is not fed positive spiritual light, concepts of the soul and its function in self-mastery would be limited to the physical senses as an awareness of self. Insight that is based primarily on experience develops at an accelerated pace when combined with an understanding of how spiritual and cosmic forces works collectively to produce insight, especially when experience is lacking or limited.

Imagination, which is instinctively part of the way the mind creates, processes, and works out situations, is generally based on how the self has been developed. Self-concept and self-esteem allow for positive constructive imagination; positive self-awareness allow for the release of positive thinking, especially during moments of restlessness.

Vital lessons that need to be developed within the brow chakra's energy center include perception that goes beyond duality and seeing with the physical eye; a sound mind, which means good concentration and the ability to focus; and peace of mind, which means controlling the imagination and having an awareness that worrying about that which you have no control over is useless, and yet, understanding that God is always in control. Wisdom beyond carnal knowledge and earthly intellect (spiritual insight), both in words and deeds, is a gift given to those who ask, a vital lesson indeed to be developed within the brow chakra.

When the pineal gland is activated, that individual appears to possess supernatural power and is able to see beyond the physical into a higher consciousness state and thus the brow chakra's association to the ethereal or etheric body.

Devotion, which is a sense of loyalty, trust, and dependability, characterized by honesty and trustworthiness, is another lesson to be honed.

Care must be exercised that cynicism and fear are not programmed into the consciousness and subconsciousness. These are negative qualities that can easily translate into mistrust of people, disloyalty, and a detachment bordering on calculated coldness, mistrust, and meanness. Other negative and harmful effects can be blockages that release negative energy in the form of tension.

Tension and other negative energies is generally localized in weakened areas or energy centers. In the case of the brow chakra, negative qualities and/or energy in this center will manifest itself in the head or eye area in the form of severe headaches, such as migraines and even blockages of blood vessels and blood flow to the brain, which can lead to or cause brain aneurysm and/or a stroke.

Constant bad dreams is also a sign that the brow chakra energy center need to be balanced and that more attention ought to be directed toward the positive qualities and/or lessons this chakra provides for self-mastery.

Going back to the flame, the hottest part of the flame is the blue wavelength or light. The violet or dark blue light is positively charged with divine freedom and thus helps to burn off Karma from other lifetimes.

In meditational problem-solving exercises as practiced by several schools, including the Silva Mind Control, students are taught to visualize problems surrounded by a blue light or mirror. Once the problem has been focused on and studied carefully, they are then asked to visually change the color of the light or mirror to white and place within this light the solution, and there on after, each time the problem is thought about, it is viewed as the solution framed in white.

This is, in effect, another practical way of Karmatic dissolution of current issues that do not have to follow you through lifetimes.

Life is real. However, most of our material pursuits in life are but illusions. They are unreal and very temporary. What is real is the alchemy of the soul—the refining of the spiritual self to its highest consciousness and to the achievement of the "I AM THAT I AM."

In the drive toward mastery of self, how do we begin to recognize that material and earthly pursuits are illusions? When we begin to see them for what they are—temporary trappings.

Like the day, all these material pursuits are fleeting and are soon gone, and like the day soon past, we must begin again the next day, assuming that there will be a next day.

The illusion is the appearance that what we need is always one step ahead of us, and we somehow must acquire more of the same or of other things for our so-called earthly happiness. It is indeed an illusion, for it is never enough.

Take for example monetary wealth. While it is believed for those without that it brings happiness, the many stories and examples of the wealthy should clearly indicate that this is very untrue. Comfort is not happiness, for comfort is also temporary, as we're constantly shifting position, and like the earth, it is a huge continuous circle with no beginning and no end.

Those with wealth know and realize that at any moment, it can all be gone, and further, once it is acquired, standards change—lifestyle, living accommodations, friends, pursuits, attitudes, and furthermore, the wealth itself becomes a distraction that requires constant effort and attention to maintain and keep up the illusion of appearances.

Does this then mean that we ought to give up our pursuits of earthly achievements? If it is selfless, no. However, we ought to begin to process our roles differently, with an understanding, wisdom, and knowledge of what is important. Is it people or things? Is it what you can get or what you can give? what is it that you prioritize? Pursuit should be the light.

Crown chakra

The seventh chakra is the crown chakra,[14] which connects you, the individual, with the higher consciousness states or higher realms of thought.

The crown chakra is pure consciousness. This is your spiritual connection or understanding, and it controls all the other chakras. The usage and mastery of this energy center provide bliss, the peace that passeth all understanding, the knowing, and the spiritual awakening.

The color associated with this chakra is violet; however, white light is also shown in some photographs of the crown chakra, white light being the color frequency or octave above purple and is representative of pure conscious energy.

Violet light is the shortest wavelength of light at the visible end of the spectrum, with the highest frequency of vibrational speed and containing the most energy. Because this light is not visible to the human eye, it cannot be utilized by most people.

The violet light appears purple because of the red long wavelength light it also contains. In fact, when red and blue are mixed, the resulting color is violet.

In feng shui, violet can be beneficial in the treatment of nervous and emotional disturbances, arthritis, acute cases of consumption, and insomnia. Known as the color of the spirit, violet enhances spiritual power and creativity.

Due to its short wavelength, technology has been able to utilize ultraviolet light to help eradicate microorganisms in the environment and in foods, acting as an effective sanitizer.

In the beginning of this discussion of the first quadrant of matter, it was stated that the two most important aspects of our discussion on fire as it relates to the etheric body would be light and energy. Ultraviolet light rays provides us with an excellent example of the light's emittance of energy and the effect it can have on the human being, as well as on the planet. It is the ultraviolet waves emitted by the sun that often produces the sun burn we experience.

The relationship between the crown chakra (controls the other chakras), the pituitary gland associated with this chakra (the master gland that controls other endocrine glands), and violet light (associated with the crown chakra) is not incidental—it is divine.

The pineal and pituitary glands, as well as the cerebral cortex, the central nervous system (CNS), and the right eye are controlled by the crown chakra. In fact, in some studies, it is suggested that the pituitary and pineal glands should be switched in regards to the sixth and seventh chakras because of the functions of each. However, the pituitary gland is the master controller of almost all endocrine glands in the body.

This bean-shaped organ, located in the base of the brain, secretes hormones that controls and promotes growth and water balance in the body. Undersecretion and/or oversecretion of hormone can lead to abnormalities in individuals, such as dwarfism (severe undergrowth), acromicria (enlargement of the body), Simmonds' disease (premature aging), and Frohlic's syndrome (obesity, dwarfism, and retarded sexual development).

The crown chakra's energy center is associated with thought and will, and both thought and will are developed, honed, and maintained from our experiences, which in turn rests on the development of our four selves—self-concept, self-esteem, self-disclosure, and self awareness.

Our will is God's will when we are inspired to do that which characterizes God, as in the fruit of the spirit, which include the provision of love, joy, peace, long-suffering, providing kindness, goodness, faithfulness, gentleness, and in our exercise of self-control.

Because we are tempted to do good as to do evil, our inspirations, characterized through tendencies, impulses, and urges will be tempered through obedience to God, to spiritual and cosmic laws. Self-mastery techniques teach us how to utilize the resources at our disposal and employ our fire (the will) positively.

The crown chakra has the ability to connect with the divine, both living or dead, as well as with human or nonhuman spiritual helpers, it possesses the most intense electrochemical power, allowing us to reach far beyond the physical plane. Its qualitative lessons are in the unification of the higher self with the human personality, providing oneness with the infinite and perception beyond time and space, in addition to pure consciousness.

Care must be exercised that negative qualities, such as confusion, depression, lack of inspiration, alienation, and hesitation, not permeate the crown chakra, as these qualities could often lead to personality and mental disorders.

To continuously energize this center, purple fruits and vegetables are necessary. Also fasting, in combination with prayer, should be part of the routine of an individual attempting to perfect self-mastery.

Light is indeed energy, and the quality or color of its emittance determines the amount of energy radiated. Red, green, and blue light waves in measured quantities will produce the white light we see, even though yellow, violet, orange, and dark blue are also colors of the spectrum.

We as human beings are energies, and we therefore radiate light. Our radiance (spiritual light) is determined by our levels of spiritual energy, which is determined by how well we have mastered self. What colors and light waves do you radiate? In light waves, shorter rays equals higher energy.

In Buddhism and Hinduism, white is the highest spiritual transformation. It is self-mastery, pure consciousness, light, and manifestation. In the Bible, no gospel or book has ever mentioned anyone as ever having seen God, what has been mentioned in several writings in reference to the face of God is "a bright light" or fire (as in the Holy Spirit) or "brilliant radiance" or a light so brilliant or bright that it could not be looked upon, for God is pure consciousness and spiritual energy can only be experienced in its essence or characteristic, which is radiant spiritual light.

How does the first quadrant of matter correspond to the etheric body? It is through energy and light, spiritual force, and awakening. The color of the light wave determines its level of energy or wavelength, and the color emitted determines the spiritual, emotional, physical, and etheric energy.

> I indeed baptize you with water . . . . He will baptize you with the Holy Spirit and Fire.[15] (Matthew 3:11)

> Then there appeared to them divided tongues, as of fire and sat upon each of them. And they were all filled with the Holy Spirit."[16] (Acts 2:3)

In various books of the Bible, God, in communicating, did so through fire, a symbolic representation of his power, might, spiritual force, and energy.

The source of energy and light for our planet is the sun. It is indeed the face of God—always there, omnipresent, omniscience, and omnipotent each and every day—and though millions of miles away, we feel its presence.

GLIMPSE THE FACE OF GOD

Is it not the same sun
That shines on everyone?
And where does it go at night?
It awaits the day
Behind the night light,
watching and waiting
observing transactions
Under moonlit or blackened skies,
anticipating, without reacting,
in silent observation,
encourages the day
and bids the night to be gone
and in its brilliant glow,
exposes hidden deeds
for all the world to know.
Yet, never utters a word,
it's purpose, not to tell,
but with its light to show,
that which we must be mindful of,
and that which we ought to know.
And still, with exceeding love
and resplendent, radiant energy divine
faithfully, silently
its light never ceases to shine.
Yes, its love exceeds all mortal plans
each day it breaks the sod,
and as we dare gaze up towards the sun,
We glimpse the face of God.

Trevor Fraser, August 10, 2009

CHAPTER 28

BODY CONNECTION

The Four Selves

There is an interconnective relationship to all things and everything in the universe. When this synchronicity becomes imbalanced, there is dysfunctionality. This interconnectivity forms an interdependency of separate parts, and these separate parts combine to function as a system.

A system is a combination of parts working interdependently to form a whole, and so is self-mastery. The combination of parts in self-mastery involves the four selves, four lower bodies, and the four elements and hence my reference to this method of self-mastery as Body Connection or the 4-4-4 connection to self-mastery, *not unalike interconnective boxes.*

444 Interconnections
Artwork Concept by T.L. Fraser
Artwork Design by Kristin Metzler

As one examines the 4-4-4 Interconnection (boxes), and follow the pathway of straight lines, you clearly witness how the connections of each quadrant evolve in connection to the others, such as for example, the physical body to earth and earth to self disclosure, or the mental body to air and air to self concept, etc, while still having its connection or interdependency to each other as well.

Let's reiterate the four selves once again: self-concept, self-esteem, self-awareness, and self-disclosure. Each seem to be independent of the other but are not.

If we take self-awareness and place it at the top left of a box and then on the right side clockwise place self-concept; lower right, self-esteem; and lower left, self-disclosure, we get four ends or connective points within a square box, producing a continuous connection of traceable lines with no fixed beginning or end. Let's examine how each one of these points, though seemingly separate, form interdependent and interlocking lines so as to create a complete square or, in this case, a heightened and more developed self.

In *self-awareness*, the more aware of self we are, the more able we are to control our actions and behavior. Awareness of self translates into knowing self, and this can only happen by first developing and then becoming aware of our self-concept.

Self-concept is the mental image or idea we have about who we are—our intelligence, abilities, skills, personality, and so on—and these characteristics develop not in a vacuum but in tandem with the experiences we face, overcome, and succumb to.

We become more and more aware of our characteristics, both positive and negative, based on our experiences, both positive and negative, and other's help to color our self-concept with the various tones that eventually filter through. We therefore must allow data to filter through instead of us filtering out that which does not support our current perspective. Aligning oneself with individuals who would provide the most positive tones to the development of our self-concept is also paramount.

The self-esteem measures the self-concept. It represents the degree to which we feel positive or negative about our self-concept. Our self-esteem is therefore inextricably linked to our self-concept just as our self-concept is linked to and affects our self-esteem. One supports the other.

In order to raise self-esteem, we must engage in activities that raise the self-concept, and the better we feel about ourselves (the degree of positivity or highness of self-concept), the better is our self-esteem.

An example I've used in my lectures is an individual declaring, "I'm a darn good driver" (self-concept), and another saying, "I'm the best driver on this planet" (self-esteem). Self-esteem is measurable, although too much of it can possibly make that individual sound cocky or arrogant, but remaining humble and keeping things in perspective as one begins to master various aspects of self-concept allows for a well-developed self-esteem.

Self-disclosure, the fourth point on the square of the four selves, is revealing or expressing personal biographical data, ideas, and feelings about oneself. Usually these revelations are verbal, but not always, since communication is both verbal and nonverbal.

The revelation of personal information in self-disclosure often will occur based on the revealer, who the information is being revealed to, and what the actual information being revealed is.

Self-disclosure is primarily based on trust and confidence on the part of the discloser—trust that the revelation would be treated discretely if so desired and hope that trust will be developed or strengthened with the receiver and, above all, confidence and trust in self.

The discloser also must have a feeling of confidence that the revelation (while it may be embarrassing) would not be diminishing to his or her character but would instead bolster their image.

Self-disclosure gets to the point of being disclosed data only after travelling the path of awareness of and then confidence and courage in the acceptance of self (or in the ability to change) enough to then reveal it to others, whatever it is. These four selves build on each other; they do not and cannot exist independent of each other. Where one ends the other begins.

The interdependency of the four selves working as a system therefore rests on the positive development of self that we refer to as our self-concept. The more positive our self-concept, the higher our self-esteem; the higher our self-esteem, the more recognizable are our abilities to do and become, and we are not afraid to express our thoughts and ideas. We are also less critical of self and more aware of our likes, dislikes, triggers, reactions, and deeper responses, in other words, the more acute our self-awareness will be.

So you see how this all work together. The more aware of self we are, the less critical and more accepting of others we become. Differences are no longer a means of polarization but rather unique qualities that bonds us together. Once we become more acutely aware of self, we are able to articulate our personal ideas, needs, and desires better. We become much better at sharing.

When these four selves are working together uniformly and interdependently as a system, we refer to that individual as being balanced and connected, as being whole.

Similarly, the four lower bodies function interdependently not as four separate bodies but one body with each of the four bodies forming overlays of each other, with each body having a distinct function.

The four lower bodies are the physical, emotional, mental, and etheric bodies. Their interconnection appears like layers of energy vibrating away from the center of the earthly body. Each of the lower bodies is joined by an auralike sphere of energy vibrating at a different octave and emitting a different color (see figure 1, page 54).

The innermost field is the physical body, the vessel that takes us from one point to another on the face of the earth; hence, it is called the vehicle for the earth's journey. We do not have human attributes without the physical body, and once we possess a physical body, we most likely will have human attributes.

At various phases, periods, or cycles of our lives, more emphasis is placed on the development of one of the four lower bodies than at or during other periods. For example, in ages one to seven, there is a strong emphasis on the discovery and development of physical attributes and a child becomes extremely excited at his or her ability to perform certain physical feats. While at age twenty-one, more emphasis is on the psychic development of the individual, therefore the physical, for instance, takes a backseat. Without the physical body, it is impossible to develop the other bodies.

The next layer of the four lower bodies is the emotional body (the feeling body). Its development as previously stated is dependent on and should be in tandem with the development of the physical body.

The feeling body has more to do with the heart than with cognition, so there's always a struggle between the mental and physical bodies to rein in the emotional body; we thus find the emotional body to be very volatile and the most misused of the four lower bodies.

The mental body forms the next layer of energy and is referred to as the intellect or the vessel for the mind of God. This body is the central clearing house, the computer where every action and reaction gets processed and stored, so no activity carried out by the physical body occurs without being filtered and processed within the mental body, and this body's connection to the emotional allows for the appropriate response that the physical body acts in accordance with.

Clarity within the mental body and its alignment to higher qualities in spirit, truth, and godliness help to direct the decisions of the mental body, the emotional response, and the resulting physical action. Elevating the mind to its potential spiritual qualities and godliness is what makes it the vessel for the mind of God.

The etheric body is the memory body—the Christ consciousness in us. It is the highest of the four lower bodies and is the link between the lower bodies and the higher aspirations to be Christlike in spirit and in truth.

Mastery of the four lower bodies is unachievable without achieving our Christ consciousness, and our Christ consciousness is not the same consciousness as in the mastery of the four selves. The latter relates to the physical journey or the soul's journey and perfecting that walk so that we can begin the spiritual journey in perfection of the four lower bodies.

We all are provided blueprints of our journey or of the divine plan; however, we choose to walk along different paths, but that journey's end remains the same for all—the unification of soul and spirit in the "I AM THAT I AM" Christ consciousness.

Thus, we witness the necessity of and connection to all that we experience, as well as the importance of each of these four lower bodies in moving us forward and upward and eventually returning us to the perfection from which we all came.

The four elements—earth, water, air, and fire—are dependent on each other for the existence of life on the planet and the continuance of spiritual development to the Christ consciousness and to the "I AM THAT I AM" presence.

Each element is related and connected to one of the four lower bodies and ultimately affect how that lower body is developed, as well as how the interdependent other bodies and selves are developed and mastered.

Again, each of the lower bodies relate to a quadrant of matter. The physical body, the lowest of the four lower bodies, for example, has an interdependence and connection to the fourth quadrant of matter, earth, the solid state of matter.

The earth exists for a reason, and so does every form on the face of it. Everything possessing life is nourished by the earth and nourishes the earth whether or not it is realized, and when that purpose and life's journey of that life form comes to an end, to the earth the physical form returns, once more as dust, to nurture the earth and to begin and continue the cycle again, over and over.

We as humans arrive on the face of the earth with a blueprint (map) of our journey. We are provided with, upon our arrival, all the physical necessities for the journey, depending on the blueprint of what is required of us on this journey. In our bodies, our bones, teeth, cells, and tissues are all manifestations of the earth—its rigidity, stability, and permanence.

We are taught how to travel, some being better than others. However, regardless of how well we are instructed or how well we retain the lessons taught or experienced, through free will and the freedom of choice, based on those teachings and experiences, we choose.

Within the earth's physical space, there exists the other quadrants of matter—water, air, and fire—with each connected to one of the lower bodies. The earth does not exist in balance without the three other elements—air, water, and fire—and if the earth does not exist without them, neither does life on earth.

In fact, science has determined that the existence of life anywhere in the universe is determined by the existence of these elements and/or their compositions in certain quantities. Therefore, it stands to reason that depletion of these elements would create an imbalance and thus produce an adverse effect on the earth and therefore on life, and as we so witness, as these resources become tarnished, the air more polluted, the waterways more stagnated, and more fires raging, producing more toxins in the air, quality of life on earth becomes depleted and, as we have witnessed over the years, diminished.

There is that indelible connection between the four major elements or quadrants of matter, not only as each relate to the four lower bodies but as each relate to the other and to our existence.

Visualize the earth as the mother and water as the nourishment the mother needs to rid herself of toxins, to replenish, to refresh, and as a means of food. Water is the source that carries the vital nutrients via its oceans, rivers, streams and ponds, gathering in its wake these nutrients from rocks, soil, other compositions, and compounds upon the face of the earth as well as underneath.

Therefore, without $H2O$, the third quadrant of matter, the mother slowly begins to die, her body becoming cracked, parched, dry, and dehydrated, eventually Mother Earth becomes malnourished and crumbles like the dust she's composed of. As the mother dies, so does all her children and all life forms within her bosom, each withering away.

Water thus characterizes change and is necessary for the survival of all things. In fact, 70-75 percent of the human body is water. It is our blood (liquid), lymph, and other fluids that carry and brings energy and waste between our cells and from one area of our body to another, regulating our body temperature, fighting diseases, and helping to stabilize our physical bodies.

The mother (earth) also requires air, the second quadrant of matter, whose function is to distribute nutrients that cannot otherwise be distributed via waterways. Through the air, these nutrients are blown and if there are toxins in the air, it too is carried to places far and wide upon the face of mother earth.

Just as important as water is to life on earth, so too is air, which allows life forms to breathe and not suffocate. The air we breathe contains oxygen, nitrogen, hydrogen, helium, argon, neon, and carbon dioxide, with oxygen and nitrogen in larger compositions of approximately 21 percent and 78 percent, respectively.

In pure forms or states, the two major gases would cause or create health risks for most life forms on earth. Therefore, the mix or dependency of one on the other creates a balance—again the interdependency of gases, elements, and all life forms on each other.

Air, both mobile and dynamic, is thus the gaseous form of matter. It assists water in its evaporation and condensation, transporting water in the form of steam and vapor around the globe to places both temperate and frigid. It is part of nature law's attempt to maintain balance and order within the universe.

Without air, the steam from water, could not be carried, and condensation and evaporation would not occur; thus, it would not rain, and without rain, Mother Earth would not be able to provide for her children, as we are dependent on water for crops (which we live on for food) to grow—simplified, but true facts, as again we witness interconnections.

Greenhouse gases and carbon dioxide emissions create imbalances within the water and air compositions. All imbalances eventually create disease, and diseases create more imbalances; thus, equilibrium is no longer equal but rather unequal and uneasy living for all life forms.

Many scientific articles over the years have discussed the significant relationship between air and water. In fact, one such article out of *Soil Science*, published as far back as 1953 by N. Collis-George, School of Agriculture, Cambridge, England, in their volume 76 article, number 4, entitled "Relationship Between Air and Water Permeabilities in Porous Media,"[1] examined the relationship between these two quadrants of matter and their effect on soil based on the movement of the two working in tandem. The article suggests a significance in permeability within the soil far greater when the two, air and water, are combined than when present singly.

While there is a certain amount of oxygen in water at all times, oxygen is constantly entering and leaving water. The amount of oxygen entering is determined by the amount already in the water. Oxygen always seem to find it's correct balance in water. Thus, there's always diffusion whenever it gets to the point of saturation. Again we witness natural law at work, creating balance or equilibrium and a connection equally vital for this to occur.

The sun is our source of energy. Additionally, it is a source of vitamins, nutrients, and nourishment. There must be a balance struck between sunlight (heat) and the other elements for life to perpetuate.

While the sun provides a natural source of energy or heat, fire provides transformation and a combustible source of energy. We mankind create fire out of a need to process and transform elements rapidly. Fire, the transformation of all things, and the first quadrant of matter, has the power to transform solids into liquids, gas, and back again. In other words, fire possesses the power to transform the state of any substance.

Within the human body, fire is represented by our energy, and it is our energy that binds the atoms together. In fact, it is the energy in all matter and in all things that creates the illusion of solidity.

We are dependent on fire for food. Fire transforms food into energy, and this energy converts food into stored energy (fat) and muscle. For fire to be produced, oxygen must be present along with carbon dioxide. In fact, without oxygen, fire does not exist since it needs or requires oxygen to breathe or to create combustion and thus the interconnection or interdependency between air and fire.

To accomplish, we must be energized physically and mentally. Desire is fire burning within, driving us steadfastly to accomplish and complete tasks before us. The greater the desire, the greater the energy we engineer toward the fulfillment of that particular goal.

Light is also a source of energy. In fact, light emits energy in various degrees; thus, a healthy body emits and absorbs sufficient light to regenerate the cells. The regeneration creates more energy, and this pushes us further and harder to accomplish and hence light's synonymity with life.

There is truly an interconnection and interdependency between and in all things animate and inanimate. Nature and cosmic law allows this relationship to unfold seamlessly and in perfect balance. Human life forms often create the imbalances we observe and then nature has to constantly and continuously correct and create equilibrium.

On March 10th, 2011, Japan was rocked by a devastating earthquake which then caused a tsunami, the resulting waves of more than 30 feet claimed many lives, washed away towns, villages and devastated cities.

Why is this significant?, the effect was felt not only in the residing areas around Japan, but thousands of miles away in the United States, along the west coast. California felt the shock wave of this event directly in the form of floods and tsunami warnings in Hawaii. If you believed prior, that we are not connected in every way to all energies abound, and what happens in one area, community, country or nation, does not affect us in other parts of the globe, reconsider it, we must become more conscious.

Consider this event another awakening as to how deeply we are indeed connected to each other. None can escape the effects of cosmic and spiritual law.

We must begin to recognize that mastery of self begins with selflessly understanding our relationship to all things and everyone around us. This is the key to harmonious living. Just examine what our greed, selfishness, and ingratitude has caused. Each of us must thus do our part, for we are masters of our destiny and not victims of fate; hence, if one of us succeed, know that we all can, but if one of us fail, we all have.

AFTERWORD

To some, self-mastery may seem to be just too complicated, too tiresome, and lonely a journey, filled with too many ups and downs. Well, you've just described life itself.

At some point in your life, in those quiet reflective moments, you ought to (if you don't) pause and then ask yourself, "Who am I really and what is my purpose in this life?" The problem is that most often than not, we don't think hard and long enough or wait for answers—too busy pursuing the next project, the next dollar, and the next moment.

If you are serious about wanting answers about self-improvement and self-mastery or merely about the betterment of your life, then do it now. Ask yourself this question, "Who Am I Really?" and then attempt to answer it immediately in twenty-five words or less (write it down), and remember, you're not your name or even the biographical data we can all observe. Search deeper.

You must also ask yourself, "Am I doing what I love most at this juncture in my life?" If the answer is "No, not really," ask "Why not, and what do I need to do to get there?" Formulate a clear procedure and timetable to get you there. If your answer is yes, then find out how you can make what you do more meaningful and fulfilling for others to experience as well. In other words, find ways to touch others meaningfully with what you do.

You may have heard this question asked. You may have been asked it or have asked it yourself: "What do I want to be when I grow up?" Sometimes it is a serious question; other times it's laced with sarcasm, yet there are times it is used as a humorous punch line. Be it as it may, if you retrospectively attempt to seriously answer this question, you'll find that it may answer questions about your self-mastery you've never really thought about.

Here are some lessons I have learned from attempting to answer these questions.

I never thought of teaching as a career or even a job. I was interested in music. I played the piano, wrote songs, and dreamt songs that to this day, I still have a ton of them hummed into tape recorders. In fact, I was so enthralled with music and the arts that I planned college around music, deciding that since I don't want all my eggs in one basket, I will major in communications, the closest art form to music I felt I could do in college instead of majoring in music.

Teaching came about after I received a phone call from a friend that a college was looking for someone to teach communications. I thought to myself, *Why not, I'm not that busy anyway.* The fact is I wanted to produce shows, write plays and poetry, write and play music, sing, dabble in the arts, be on stage, and perform before an audience, and not necessarily music performances, and it did not matter the size of that audience. In fact, I loved humor and even thought of myself as a comedian. I even auditioned as a stand-up comedian, but thought better of it after that audition did not go very well.

Teaching college? Nothing that I did prior pushed me in this direction. As events unfolded, I took on the teaching assignment and realized that I could do all that I wanted to as an artist, teaching.

I could be on stage (the classroom) two to three times a week, perform before a captive audience (the students), practice some of my one-liners, and in fact, use anecdotes as I impart the lessons and get paid for it, and each week, for fifteen weeks, I get to do it again and again, performing before a new audience every three to four months, year after year.

I was hooked. The teaching phase grew on me. You can have fun doing it and learning. I was having fun, and if I was having fun doing it in my unique style, I knew the students were having fun learning as well because it wasn't really teaching to me—it was performing, bringing my best material and having the audience leave, sometimes mesmerized, wanting to return again for another engagement. Most of them expressed how much they enjoyed and looked forward to my classes. I'm quite sure some did not; they never told me. They just didn't show up for classes—their loss.

Teaching gave me the opportunity to perform but in a different arena, and the money, while it was important, was never the first or even the second most important thing.

I have reiterated this time and time again to my students: "Do not start a business, create a device, begin a service, take an assignment or job for the money or because you believe you can become wealthy, and while you may eventually, you'll never be truly satisfied and/or happy."

Do what you do because you love it in spite of its immediate financial remuneration or rewards. If you do it well, others will recognize it and compensate you for it, but more than that, you'll continue to do it well and derive a lot of satisfaction from it along the way. If it's a service you are providing, the more people desiring that service, the more important the service will become and the more in demand you'll be. The end result is that you will become successful, and if you measure that according to material gains, then I suppose that means material wealth. Albeit, the problem with material wealth is it is never enough and thus can take you down paths you may wish you had never ventured.

Honestly ask and truthfully answer the questions, "Who am I really?" and "Am I doing what I love most at this juncture?" Then examine your four selves: self-concept, self-esteem, self-disclosure, and self awareness. Especially work on self-concept. If it's not so good, work on making it good. If it's good, work on making it better. If it's better, work on mastering it as well as mastering the other selves.

The pursuit of material wealth is an illusion. The acquisition of wealth for the sake of wealth is an exercise in greed, avarice, and self-indulgence, which does absolutely nothing in the transformation of the spirit or in the enrichment of the soul, and self-mastery requires constant transformation. Self-mastery lies in the pursuit of things within, not in pursuit of the illusions without. Once we seek, we will find, and once we find, we must share. It is part of our blueprint, from ordinary to extraordinary and from a metallic base state of being to gold.

Please don't misunderstand me. There is nothing wrong with wealth you've earned through the positive services you've rendered and/or provided toward the enrichment of the lives of others. Control it. Never let the accumulation of wealth control you.

We are connected to all things and to everything around us. We absorb all energies just as our energy is absorbed by all. That's the body connection. Know this, for it is true: Stay connected positively and grow.

If you're where you wish to be in life at this very moment—truly positive—accepting who you are and what you are without criticism, then you are on the right path to truly mastering self. Once there, you must find ways to make life more meaningful to and for others. Your transformation is never complete without this.

You have not truly mastered self until you have through your efforts, allowed all things and everyone connected to you to journey toward self-mastery as well. This is what I truly hoped to accomplish through these pages.

I hope the lessons in this book and the experiences I have shared are worthy contributions toward the understanding of your body connection, transformation, and self-mastery.

It is not a journey's end but a glorious beginning.

NOTES

Chapter 1

1. Bureau of Justice Statistics, September 30, 2006, *Organized Crime Digest* pg 13.

Chapter 2

1. Astral plane...pg 17: Saint Germain on Alchemy: For the Adept in the Aquarian Age.
2. Astral body...pg 18: Saint Germain on Alchemy:
3. Astral projection, pg 18: Saint Germain on Alchemy:
4. Alpha region, pg 18: Workbook, Mind Control, basic lecture series.

Chapter 3

1. Mt. 6:33 "Seek ye first the kingdom . . ." pg 23.
2. "I AM THAT I AM," pg 25; *Saint Germain on Alchemy: For the Adept in the Aquarian Age.*
3. Poem, pg 25: *Saint Germain on Alchemy: For the Adept in the Aquarian Age.*

Chapter 4

1. Proverbs 4:23, "Keep your heart . . ." pg 27.
2. Corinthians 1:8, "Spiritual truths are not . . ." pg 27.
3. 1 Thessalonians 5:23; Hebrews 4:12, pg 27. Five gateways: eye, smell, hearing, taste, and touch. Threefold nature of man: carnal, 1 Corinthians 3:1-3; natural, 1 Corinthians 2:14; and spiritual, 1 Corinthians 2:1.

4. 1 Corinthians 1:1-3, man in his carnal state, page 28.
5. Plane of relativity, page 29: *Saint Germain on Alchemy: For the Adept in the Aquarian Age.*
6. Plane of Absolute, page 29: *Saint Germain on Alchemy: For the Adept in the Aquarian Age.*
7. Divine ego, page 29.
8. Threefold spiritual flame, page 29: *Saint Germain on Alchemy: For the Adept in the Aquarian Age.*

Chapter 5

1. Influence on perception, page 32: Inter-Act, 12th ed.; Making Connections, 7th ed.; Human Communications, 11th ed.
2. Matthew 18:3-4, "Become as little children . . ." pg 33.
3. Matthew 7:5, "Hyprocrite . . ." pg 34.

Chapter 6

1. Ecclesiastes 3:1, "To everything there is a season . . ." pg 38.
2. Four lower bodies, pg 39: *Saint Germain on Alchemy: For the Adept in the Aquarian Age.*
3. Three higher bodies, pg 39: *Saint Germain on Alchemy: For the Adept in the Aquarian Age.*
4. Leviticus 11:1-47, reference on foods to consume, pg 41.
5. John 1:4, "Life and the life was the light of men . . ." pg 42.
6. Chakras, pg 42: http://www.Crystalinks.com.
7. Silva Mind Control, pg 43: Workbook, Mind Control, basic lecture.

Chapter 7

1. Mental Body, pg 46: *Saint Germain on Alchemy, For the Adept in the Aquarian Age.*
2. Romans 7:14, "The law is spiritual . . ." pg 47.
3. Beta, Alpha, Theta, Delta, pg 47: Workbook, Mind Control, basic lecture series.

Chapter 8

1. Empathic Responsiveness, pg 50; Human Communications, 11th ed.
2. Perspective Taking, pg 50; Human Communications, 11th ed.

Chapter 9

1. Color of the etheric body, pg 53; http://www.Kheper.net.
2. Divine plan, pg 55; *Saint Germain on Alchemy: For the Adept in the Aquarian Age.*

Chapter 10

1. Galatians 5: 22-23; "But the fruit of the spirit . . ." pg 57
2. I AM THAT I AM, pg 58: *Saint Germain on Alchemy: For the Adept in the Aquarian Age.*
3. 1 Peter 5:7, The indispensables; "But also for this very reason . . ." pg 58.

Chapter 11

1. Cosmic law—pg60; Self Mastery & Fate with the Cycles of Life

Chapter 12

1. Family system—pg 64; Inter-Act, 12th Edition
2. Self Concept formation—pg 65; Inter-Act, 12th Edition
3. Behavior modeling—pg 65; Inter-Act, 12th Edition
4. Family rules & goals—pg 67; Inter-Act, 12th Edition
5. 4th Period of seven years—pg68; Self Mastery & Fate
6. 5th Period of seven years—pg68; Self Mastery & Fate

Chapter 13

1. 814 elected officials under the age of 35—pg 70; Columbia News Service
2. Age 35-42. Period six—pg 70; Self Mastery & Fate with the Cycles of Life
3. 7th Period—pg71; Self Mastery & Fate
4. The average age of an elected official—pg 72; Columbia News Service
5. 8th Period—pg 72; Self Mastery & Fate
6. Next cycle of 7 years, age 56 to 63—pg 73; Self Mastery & Fate
7. Early settlers used the Bible—pg 73; Saint Germain on Alchemy
8. "No people can be bound to acknowledge . . ." pg 73, George Washington's final address.

2. The experience of *flow*, pg 90; *Saint Germain on Alchemy: For the Adept in the Aquarian Age*.
3. Good programming consists of four principles, pg 90; Workbook, Mind Control, basic lecture series.
4. Luke 6:45; Matthew 12:35; "A good man out of the good . . ." pg 91.
5. Proverbs 4:23, "For out of it springs the issues of life" pg 91.
6. Experiences are then stored in the form of impressions, pg 92; Self-Mastery and Fate with the Cycles of Life.
7. Mental House Cleaning, pg 93; Workbook, Mind Control, basic lecture series.
8. "If you would only learn to listen . . ." pg 93; *Saint Germain on Alchemy: For the Adept in the Aquarian Age*.

Chapter 18

1. Listening, pg 94; *Inter-Act*, 12th ed.; *Making Connections*, 7th ed.; *Human Communications*, 11th ed.
2. Appreciative Listening, pg 95; Inter-Act, 12th ed.; Making Connections, 7th ed.; Human Communications, 11th ed.
3. Empathic Listening, pg 95; Inter-Act, 12th ed.; Making Connections, 7th ed.; Human Communications, 11th ed.
4. Discriminative Listening, pg 95; Inter-Act, 12th ed.; Making Connections, 7th ed.; Human Communications, 11th ed.
5. Analytical Listening, pg 96; Inter-Act, 12th ed.; Making Connections, 7th ed.; Human Communications, 11th ed.
6. Overcoming poor listening habits, pg 97; Human Communications.
7. Loci and peg systems, pg 98; Workbook, Mind Control, basic lecture series.
8. Be an active listener, pg 99; Inter-Act, 12th ed.; Human Communications, 11th ed.
9. I will have superior concentration, pg 101; Workbook, Mind Control, basic lecture series.
10. Remembering, pg 101; Human Communications, 11th ed.
11. Loci system, pg 102; Online Memory Improvement Course.
12. Peg system, pg 102; Online Memory Improvement Course.
13. Evaluating, pg 103; Human Communications, 11th ed.
14. Objectives of effective listening, pg 104; Human Communications, 11th ed.

Chapter 19

1. Matthew 7:3, "And why do you look at the spic . . ." pg 106.
2. Self-Concept, pg 107; Inter-Act, 12th ed.; Making Connections, 7th ed.; Human Communications, 11th ed.
3. False consensus effect, pg 108; Making Connections, 7th ed.
4. Hierarchy of Self-Concept, pg 108; Making Connections, 7th ed.
5. Collectivist cultures, pg 109; Making Connections, 7th ed; Human Communications, 11th ed.
6. Acculturation, pg 109; Human Communications, 11th ed.
7. Gender, a cultural variable, pg 109; Human Communications, 11th ed.
8. Mixing of three elements, pg 110; *Saint Germain on Alchemy: For the Adept in the Aquarian Age.*
9. Masculine Polarity . . . synthesis, pg 110; *Saint Germain on Alchemy: For the Adept in the Aquarian Age.*
10. Hindu tradition, pg 111; *Saint Germain on Alchemy: For the Adept in the Aquarian Age.*
11. Androgynous men and women, pg 111; Gender Differences in Communication.
12. Five guidelines to improving, pg 111; Making Connections, Intro to the Study of Communication.
13. "My increasing mental . . ." pg 113; Workbook, Mind Control, basic lecture series.
14. "Every day in every way," pg 113; Workbook, Mind Control, basic lecture series.

Chapter 20

1. Personal self-esteem, pg 115; Inter-Act, 12th ed; Making Connections, 7th ed; Human Communications, 11th ed.
2. Factors do affect . . ., pg 115; Inter-Act, 12th ed.; Making Connections, 7th ed.; Human Communications, 11 ed.
3. Self-Fulfilling Prophecies, pg 116; Making Connections, 7th ed.
4. Drastic changes in our social . . ., pg 117; Inter-Act, 12th ed.; Human Communications, 11th ed.

Chapter 21

1. Talking to yourself, pg 123; Workbook, Mind Control, basic lecture series.
2. Self-awareness . . . open self, pg 123; Introduction to Group Dynamics.
3. Consider our subconscious a storehouse, pg 129; Dreams and What They Mean
4. Self-dialogue; listen; blind reduction; observe different selves; pg 130; Human Communications, 11th ed.

Chapter 22

1. Self-disclosure, pg 131; Human Communications, 11th ed.
2. Primary factors influencing self-disclosure, pg 131; Human Communications, 11th ed.
3. Affiliation; competence and self-esteem; gender, pg 132; Human Communications, 11th ed.
4. Qualifying factor influencing disclosure, pg 134; Human Communications, 11th ed.
5. Guidelines for self-disclosure, pg 136; Human Communications, 11th ed.
6. Responding to self-disclosure, pg 138; Human Communications, 11th ed.
7. Four major advantages of describing . . ., pg 143; Inter-Act, 12th ed.

Chapter 23

1. Culture is . . .,—pg 145; Inter-Act, 12th ed.; Making Connections, 7th ed.; Human Communications, 11th ed.
2. High and low context, pg 147; Inter-Act, 12th ed.; Making Connections, 7th ed; Human Communications, 11th ed.
3. High and low power distance, pg 148; Inter-Act, 12th ed.
4. Masculine and feminine, pg 149; Inter-Act, 12th ed.

Chapter 24

1. Proverbs 3:19-20, "The Lord by wisdom founded . . ."; pg 152.
2. Four elements, pg 153; Cooper, Adrian; Our Ultimate Reality.

3. Quadrants of matter, pg 153; *Saint Germain on Alchemy: For the Adept in the Aquarian Age.*
4. Some observed effect, pg 154; Environmental Protection Agency (EPA).
5. Greenhouse gases, pg 155; Environmental Protection Agency (EPA).
6. One hundred ninety-five countries in the world, pg 157; Rosenberg, Matt; About.com.
7. Residents of Okinawa, pg 160; World's Greatest Treasury of Health Secrets.
8. Human Life, pg 160; Self-Mastery and Fate with the Cycles of Life.

Chapter 25

1. Matthew 3:11, "I indeed baptize you with water . . ." pg 164.
2. Seventy percent of the earth is water, pg 165; NASA, Weighing Earth's Water from Space.
3. Water cycle, pg 166; United States Geological Survey.
4. "The human brain is . . ." pg 167; Water Science for Schools.
5. Interview Mike Adams, pg 169; with Dr. Batmanghelid.
6. Water senses emotion, pg 172; Alpha Lo in communication with Karen McChrystal.
7. Emoto's experiment, pg 172; Messages in Water.
8. Images of water exposed to words "Thank you"; image of water exposed to words "You make me sick," pg 173; Dr. Masaru Emoto.
9. Water shortages were linked to emotional distress, pg 175; vol. 67; issue 12, December 2008; pgs 2116-2125.
10. Matthew 14:25, "Now in the fifth watch . . ."; pg 175.
11. Matthew 8:26; "Why are ye fearful . . ." pg 175.

Chapter 26

1. Ephesians 2:1-2, "And you he made alive . . ."; pg 177.
2. Air composition, pg 178; CRC Handbook of Chemistry and Physics.
3. Plants like the bamboo, pg 179; Plants for indoor air pollution abatement.
4. Feng shui, pg 180; http://www.whatisfengshui.net.
5. Ginny Walden's Story, pg 181; The Power of Chi-lel.
6. Sri Aurobindo, aspects of mind, pg 182; The Doctrines of Minds.
7. Truth sight-truth light power, pg 184; Sri Aurobindo's Illumined Mind.
8. Threefold flame, pg 184; *Saint Germain on Alchemy: For the Adept in the Aquarian Age.*

9. Supermind . . . it is a mind totally beyond, pg 185; Sri Aurobindo's Supermind.

10. Isaiah 55:8-9, "For my thoughts . . ." pg 185.

11. Job 28:28, "And to man he said, 'Behold . . . '"; pg 186.

12. Proverbs 2:6, "For the Lord gives wisdom . . ."; pg 186.

13. Proverbs 3:13, "Happy is the man who finds . . ."; pg 187.

14. Ecclesiastes 9:16-18, "Wisdom is better than strength"; pg 187.

15. Proverbs 2:19, "The Lord by wisdom . . ."; pg 187.

16. 1 Corinthians 2:10, Spiritual truths are not of human . . .; pg 187.

17. Power, Wisdom, and Love, pg 188; *Saint Germain on Alchemy: For the Adept in the Aquarian Age*.

Chapter 27

1. Nehemiah 9:12, "Moreover, you led them by day . . ."; pg 190.

2. The first quadrant, pg 190; *Saint Germain on Alchemy: For the Adept in the Aquarian Age*.

3. Figure 2C, photo credit, pg 192; http://www.crystalinks.com/chakras.html.

4. Figure 2D, photo credit, pg 193; http://www.crystalinks.com/chakras.html.

5. Root chakra, pg 194; http://www.crystalinks.com/chakras.html.

6. Spleen chakra, pg 196; http://www.crystalinks.com/chakras.html.

7. Solar plexus, pg 198; http://www.crystalinks.com/chakras.html.

8. Heart chakra, pg 200; http://www.crystalinks.com/chakras.html.

9. Throat chakra, pg 202; http://www.crystalinks.com/chakras.html.

10. Matthew 12:37, "For by your words . . ."; pg 203.

11. John 1:1, "In the beginning was the word . . ."; pg 203.

12. John 1:1-14, "And the word became flesh . . ."; pg 203.

13. Brow chakra, pg 204; http://www.crystalinks.com/chakras.html.

14. Crown chakra, pg 210; http://www.crystalinks.com/chakras.html.

15. Matthew 3:11, "I indeed baptize you with water . . ."; pg 212.

16. Acts 2:3, "The there appeared to them . . ."; pg 212.

Chapter 28

1. Relationship between air and water, pg 220; "Relationship Between Air and Water Permeabilities in Porous Media," Soil Science.

BIBLIOGRAPHY AND SUGGESTED READINGS

Bureau of Justice Statistics, September 30, 2006, *Organized Crime Digest*

Prophet, Mark L.; Prophet, Elizabeth Clare, Bk 2, Saint Germain on Alchemy, For the Adept in the Aquarian age; Summit University Press, 1986 http://findarticles.com/p/articles/mi_qa4441/is_200609/ai_n17194955/?tag=content;col1

Verderber, K.S; Verderber, R.F; Berryman-Fink, C; Inter-Act, 12th ed., Pub. Oxford Press, 2010; ISBM: 978-0-19-537891-7

Seiler, W.J; Beall, M.L; Communicating, Making Connections, 7th ed; Pub. Pearsons Education Inc. 2008

Devito, J.A; Human Communications, 11th ed. Pearson Education Inc., 2009; ISBN: 13-978-0-205-52259-0 http://www.crystalinks.com/chakras; 2005; accessed 2007; Crystal, Ellie

Silva, Jose; Workbook "Mind Control" Basic Lecture Series MC101 CR-MC 202 GSI-MC 303 ESP—MC 404 AESP, Silva Mind Control International Inc., Laredo TX 78040 http://www.kheper.net, Bennett, Steve, Storm, Karma; 'transformation-evolution-metamorphosis'; Kheper version 1 "Nature of Realities"; 1998-2000; version 2 "The (First) Integral Paradigm" 2004-2006; version 3 "Gnostic Metaphysics, Transformation, Sentientism" 2009; accessed 2007

Brennan, Barbara; "Hands of Light," Pub. Pleiades Books, 1987; Pub. Bantam, 1988; ISBN 0553345397

Spencer, Lewis, H; Self-Mastery and Fate"; Roscrucian Library ISBN 0912057459y

Celock, John; "Young Elected Officials Take the Country by Storm"; Columbia News Service, April 5, 2004; http://www.jrn.columbia.edu/student work/ CNS/2004-04-05/537.asp

George Washington's Farewell Address (To the People of the United States); Pub. Independent Chronicle, September 26, 1796; http://www.earlyamerica. com/earlyamerica/milestones/farewell/; accessed 2007

Burbank Masonic Lodge No. 406, Masonic Presidents of the United States, of the fifty six signers; accessed 6/13/2007; http://www.calodges.org; http:// www.usa citylink.com/usa/declaration.html

Wilmshurst, W. L. "The Meaning of Masonry," 1996-2010; Pietre-Stones Review of Freemasonry; accessed, 2007; Modified 6/30/2005. Pub. Crown Publishers, Inc., June 1980; Edition Published by Gramercy Books, Division of Random House Value Publishing; ISBN 9780517337941

Howard, Robert; United States Presidents and the Illuminati (Masonic Power Structure); http://www.theforbidddenknowledge.com/revelation2.shtml http://ivarfjeld.wordpress.com; Pope's Ring King of the Fisherman, Catholic Encyclopedia (1913)

Hefner, Alan G., the MYSTICA, (online encyclopedia of the occult, mysticism, magic, paranormal and more, 1997-2010; http://www.themystica..:om/mystica/ articles/a/astral.body.html; accessed 2007, last modified June 24, 2010

Singer, Jerome; Switzer, Ellen; "Mind Play"; Pub. Prentice Hall Int'l Inc. A Spectrum Book, 1980; ISBN 0-13-553369-8; 0-13-583351-5 pbk

Muure, Prof. Dr. Jaap ; University of Amsterdam, Department of Psychology, Roetersstraat 15, 1018 WB Amsterdam, the Netherlands; Online Improvement Course; memory.uva.nl/memimprovement/eng/; accessed 2010; last update 2008

Vanfossen, Dr. Beth; Gender Differences In Communication; National Center for Curriculum Transformation Resources on Women (NCCTRW); Institute for Teaching and Research on Women; http://pages.towson.edu/ncctrw/default.htm

Seiler, W.J; Beal, M.L; Making Connections, 6th ed.; Pub. Pearson Education Inc., 2004; Trienholm, Sara; Introduction to the Study of Communications, 6th ed.; Pub. Allyn & Bacon, 2005

Luft, Joseph; Introduction to Group Dynamics, 3rd ed.; Pub. Mayfield Publishing Co. 2004; The Pfeiffer Handbook of Structured Experiences; Intact Teams and Workgroups; Pub. John Wiley & Sons, 2004

Wippler, Gonzalez-Migene; Dreams and What They Mean; 1998; Pub. Llewelyn Worldwide Ltd; ISBN 0-87542-288-8

Cooper, Adrian; Our Ultimate Reality; Pub. Ultimate Reality Publishing; November 10, 2007; ISBN 10: 0979910609; 13: 978-0979910609

Environmental Protection Agency (EPA); http://www.epa.gov/climate change/ accessed 2007; updated 6/15/2010

Rosenberg, Matt; Geography, http://www.about.com, accessed 2008; November 2005

Mosquin, T; Rowe, S.J; April/June 2004; Bio Diversity, vol. 5, no. 1; http://www.ecospherics.net/pages/earth manifesto.htnl

Msqaa, Ed; Mother Earth Spirituality: Pub, June 26, 2006; Emerson, Gary M; 1/25/2005; by Inayat 2012

Wilcox, Bradley; World's Greatest Treasury of Health Secrets; Pub. Bottom Line Pub., 2006; ISBN 0-88723395-3

NASA Earth Observatory. Weighing Earth's Water from Space; Ward, Alan; 12/23/2003; http://www.earth observatory.nasa.org http://www.usgs.gov; accessed 2007; last update 4/27/2010

USGS, Water Science for Schools; The water in you; accessed 2010; updated 4/27/2010 http://www.naturalnews.com/Report_water_cure_1html; accessed 2009; Adams, Mike, interview with Dr. Batmanghelidj; Truth Publishing/water cure.com http://www.omaep.com/prevfondamentale/prevfondcdrhtm; Omega Institute; Prenatan Education

Reiko, Dewey; Messages in Water; The spirit of Ma'at interviews Dr. Masaru Emoto; http://www.enwaterment.com; accessed 2010

http://www.enwaterment.com/vibration.pdf; Image of water exposed to words "Thank you"; Image of water exposed to words "You make me sick"; Pub. http://www.WellnessGoods.com. Photo credit http://www.WellnessGoods.com; accessed 2008; updated 2010

Wutich, Amber; Ragsdale, Kathleen; Cultural Anthropology, University of Florida; Water shortages were linked to emotional distress; vol. 67; issue 12, December 2008; pgs 2116-2125; http://www.sciencedirect.com/science

Lide, David R.; CRC Handbook of Chemistry and Physics, 1997 Edition; Skorucak, Anton; http://www.physlink.com; created 1995; accessed 2010

Wolverton, B.C.; John son M.S, Anne; Bunds, K; Interior Landscape Plants for Indoor Air Poll on Abatement Final Report, September 15, 1989; Sverdrop, Technology Inc; NASA, John C Stennis Space Center, Science & Technology Lab; Stennis Space Center, MS; http://www.blankees.com/house/plants http://www.whatisFengshui.net; 2007-2008; accessed 2010 http://www.chimachine4u.com; 2002-2009; accessed 2009; Chi Machine International; The Power of Chi Lel; The Mind Body Connection—Ginny's Story

Aurobindo, Sri; Mind of Light; The Doctrines of Minds (Esoteric Psychology); Pub. Lotus Press 1971; Sri Aurbindo Ashram 1953, 2003; http://www.kheper.net

N. Collis George School of Agriculture, Cambridge England; vol. 76; no. 4; October 1953; "Relationship Between Air and Water Permeabilities in Porous Media"; European Journal of Soil Science; http://www3.interscience.wiley.com; 1999-2010; accessed 2010

INDEX

U

ultraviolet light rays, 210
unknown self, 123-24
USGS (United States Geological
Survey), 166-67, 239

V

vigilance, 44, 48, 52

W

Walden, Ginny, 181, 234
Power of Chi Lel, The, 181, 240
warming effect, 154. *See also* greenhouse
gases; pollutants; pollution
Washington, George, 73, 229-30, 238
water, 164-66
water cycle, 166
Water for Health, for Healing, for Life
(Batmanghelidj), 169
wavelength, 190-91, 194, 196, 200, 202,
208, 210, 212. *See also* colors

white light, 36, 53, 83, 113, 191, 210,
212. *See also* colors
Wilcox, Bradley J., 160
*World's Greatest Treasury of Health
Secrets, The,* 160
Wilmshurst, W. L.
Meaning of Masonry, The, 74
wisdom, 48, 110, 186-88
withdrawal effects, 46
*World's Greatest Treasury of Health Secrets,
The* (Wilcox), 160
Wright brothers, 36
Wuitich, Amber, 175

Y

yearly life cycles, 61
yellow plume, 29-30, 189. *See also* wisdom
Yosemite National Park, 162

CPSIA information can be obtained at www.ICGtesting.com
Printed in the USA
LVOW11s1423080914

403031LV00001B/178/P